WEBSTER'S
NEW
CROSSWORD PUZZLE
DICTIONARY

COMPACT EDITION

© Geddes & Grosset Ltd., New Lanark, Scotland 1990

Published by Russell, Geddes & Grosset, Windsor Court,
New York, N.Y. U.S.A.

Printed in the U.S.A.

This book is not published by the original publishers of
Webster's Dictionary or by their successors.

ad	he	ox
ae	ho	
ah		
an		pa
as	if	pe
at	in	pi
am	is	
ax	it	
	id	Ra
		re
be		
bi	la	
by	lo	so
do	ma	ta
	me	ti
	mu	to
eh		
el		
em	né	up
en	no	us
ex	nu	Ur
fa	of	we
	oh	wu
	om	
go	on	
	os	xi
	or	
ha	Og	
hi	op	ye

ace	dry	god
ado	dub	goo
age	dug	got
apt	dun	goy
arc	dye	gum
arm		gun
ash		gut
ate	ear	guy
auk	eat	gym
awe	ebb	gyp
	eel	
	e'en	
bad	e'er	had
bag	ego	hag
ban	eke	ham
bar	elf	hap
bat	emu	has
bed	eon	hat
beg	era	hay
bet	ere	hem
bid	err	her
big	ewe	hew
bit	eye	hey
boa		hid
bob		hip
bog	fad	his
boy	fag	hit
bra	fan	hob
bud	far	hod
bug	fat	hoe
bum	fed	hog
bus	few	hop
buy	fey	hot
	fez	how
	fib	hub
cad	fin	hue
can	fir	hug
cap	fit	hum
con	fix	hut
cot	flu	
coy	fly	
cry	fob	ice
cue	foe	icy
cup	fog	ill
cur	fop	inn
cut	fry	ion
	fur	irk
		ivy
dab		
dam	gab	
dan	gad	jab
dew	gag	jag
did	gap	jam
die	gas	jar
dig	gat	jet
dim	gel	Jew
din	gem	jib
dip	get	jig
dog	gin	job
don	gnu	jog
dot	gob	jot

jug	nag	pit
jut	nap	ply
	nay	pod
	née	poi
keg	nee	pop
ken	net	pot
key	new	pox
kid	nil	pry
kin	nip	pug
kip	nit	pun
kit	nod	pup
	Noh	pus
	nor	put
lab	not	put
lad	now	
lag	nth	
lam	nub	qua
lap	nun	
law	nut	
lax		rag
lay		raj
lea	oaf	ram
led	oak	ran
lee	oar	rap
leg	oat	rat
lei	obi	raw
Leo	odd	ray
let	ode	red
lid	off	rev
lie	ohm	rib
lie	oil	rid
lip	old	rig
lit	one	rim
lob	ore	rip
log	our	rob
lop	out	roc
lot	ova	rod
low	ova	roe
lox	owe	rot
lug	owl	row
		rub
		rue
mad		rug
man	pad	rum
map	pal	run
mar	pan	rut
mat	pap	rye
men	par	
met	pat	
mew	paw	
mix	pay	sac
moa	pea	sad
mob	peg	sag
mom	pen	sap
mop	pep	sat
mow	per	saw
mud	pet	say
mug	pew	sea
mum	pie	see
	pig	set
	pin	sew
nab	pip	sex

sex	thy	war
she	tic	was
shy	tie	wax
sic	tin	way
sin	tip	web
sip	toe	wed
sir	tog	wen
sit	ton	wet
ski	too	who
sky	top	why
sly	tor	wig
sob	tot	win
sod	tow	wit
son	toy	woe
son	try	wok
sop	tub	won
sot	tug	woo
sou	tun	wow
sow	two	wry
spy		
sty		
sub	urn	yak
sue	use	yam
sum	Ute	yap
sun		yaw
sup		yea
		yen
	vat	yes
	vet	yet
tab	vex	yew
tag	via	yin
tan	vie	yip
tap	vim	yon
tar	viz	you
tat	vow	
tax		
tea		zap
tee	wad	Zen
ten	wag	zip
the	wan	zoo

abbé	awed	boar
abed	AWOL	boat
abet	awol	bode
able	awry	bode
ably	axes	body
abut	axes	Boer
ache	axis	bogy
acid	axle	bola
acme		bold
acne		bolo
acre	babe	bolt
aeon	baby	bomb
aery	back	bone
afar	bade	Bonn
agar	bail	bony
aged	bait	boor
agog	bake	bore
ague	bald	bore
ahoy	bale	born
AIDS	Bali	both
airy	balk	bout
ajar	balm	bowl
akin	bane	brad
alas	bare	brag
alga	base	bran
alit	bask	brat
ally	bass	bred
alms	bate	brew
aloe	bath	Brie
also	baud	brig
alto	bawd	brim
alum	bawl	brow
amen	bear	brut
amid	beat	buck
amok	beau	bulb
anal	beef	bull
anew	beep	buoy
ankh	beer	burn
anna	beet	burp
anon	bend	burr
ante	bent	bury
anus	best	bush
anus	best	busy
apex	beta	butt
apse	bevy	buzz
aqua	bias	byte
Arab	bide	
area	bier	
aria	bike	café
arid	bile	cage
army	bind	cagy
arty	bite	cake
ashy	blab	calf
Asia	bled	calm
atom	blew	came
aunt	blob	cane
aura	bloc	care
aver	blot	case
avid	blow	cask
avow	blue	cast
away	blur	caul

cave	cosy	dewy
cavy	cote	dhow
ceca	coup	dial
cede	cowl	dice
cell	cozy	died
cent	crab	diet
chap	crag	dike
char	cram	dine
chat	craw	dire
chef	Cree	disc
chew	crew	disk
chez	crib	diva
chic	crop	dive
chin	crow	dodo
chip	crux	does
chit	Cuba	doge
chop	cube	dole
chow	cued	dolt
cite	cull	dome
city	cult	Doña
clad	curb	done
clam	curd	doom
clan	cure	door
clap	curé	dope
claw	curl	dory
clay	curt	dose
clef	cusp	dost
clew	cuss	dote
clip	cute	doth
clod	cyst	dour
clog	czar	dove
clot		dove
cloy		down
club	Dada	doze
clue	dais	drab
coal	damn	drag
coat	dank	draw
coax	dare	dreg
coca	dark	drew
cock	data	drip
code	date	drop
coed	daub	drub
coif	dawn	drug
coil	daze	drum
coin	D-day	dual
coke	dead	dude
cola	deaf	duel
cold	deal	duet
colt	dean	dull
coma	dear	duly
comb	debt	dumb
come	deed	dune
cone	deem	dupe
cony	deep	dusk
cool	deer	duty
coon	deft	dyed
cope	defy	dyer
Copt	deli	dyke
copy	demo	
core	deny	
corn	dewy	each

earl
earn
ease
east
easy
ebon
echo
ecru
Edam
eddy
edge
edgy
edit
eely
egis
Eire
eked
élan
else
emir
emit
Emmy
enow
envy
epic
ergo
Erie
erne
Eros
Erse
espy
etch
even
evil
ewer
exam
exit
expo
eyed
Ezra

face
fact
fade
fain
fair
fake
fall
fame
fang
fare
faro
fate
faun
fawn
faze
fear
feat
feed
feel

feet
fell
felt
fern
feta
fête
feud
fiat
fief
fife
file
find
fine
fink
Finn
fire
firm
fizz
flag
flap
flat
flax
flea
fled
flee
flew
flip
flit
floe
flog
flop
flow
flub
flue
foal
foam
foci
fogy
föhn
folk
foot
fore
fort
foul
four
fowl
foxy
free
fret
frog
fuel
full
fume
fund
furl
fury
fuse
fuss
fuzz

Gael
gaff
gaga
gain
gait
gala
gale
gall
game
gamy
gaol
gape
Gaul
gave
gawk
gaze
gear
geld
gelt
gene
gent
gibe
gild
gill
gilt
gird
girl
gist
give
glad
glee
glib
glob
glow
glue
glum
glut
G-man
G-men
gnat
gnaw
goad
goal
goat
goes
go-go
gold
golf
gone
good
goof
gook
gore
gory
gout
gown
grab
gram
gray
grew
grid

grim	hole	jeer
grin	holy	jerk
grip	hone	jibe
grit	hood	jink
grog	hoof	jinx
grow	hook	jive
grub	hoop	Joel
guff	hoot	john
gulf	hope	join
gull	horn	joke
guru	hose	jolt
	host	Jove
	hove	jowl
hail	howl	judo
hair	huff	juju
hake	huge	July
hale	hula	jump
half	hull	June
hall	hump	Jung
halo	hung	junk
halt	hunt	Juno
hang	hurl	jury
hare	hurt	just
hark	hymn	jute
hate	hype	
hath		
haul		kale
have	iamb	kayo
hawk	ibex	keel
haze	ibid	keen
hazy	ibis	keep
head	iced	kelp
heal	icon	keno
heap	idea	kepi
hear	ides	kept
heat	idle	khan
heck	idly	kill
heed	idol	kiln
heel	ikon	kilo
heir	imam	kilt
held	Inca	kind
helm	inch	king
herb	inky	kink
herd	into	kiss
here	iota	kite
hero	Iowa	kith
hers	Iran	kiwi
hewn	Iraq	Klee
hick	iris	knee
hide	iron	knew
hi-fi	isle	knit
high	itch	knob
hike	item	knot
hind		know
hire		kohl
hiss	jade	kola
hive	jail	kook
hoax	jamb	kris
hobo	Java	
hoed	jazz	
hold	Jeep	lace

lack	lire	Mars
lacy	lisp	mask
lade	list	mate
lady	live	matt
laid	load	maul
lain	loaf	maze
lair	loam	mazy
lake	loan	mead
lama	lobe	meal
lamb	loci	mean
lame	lock	meat
lamé	lode	meek
lane	loge	meet
Laos	logo	melt
Lapp	logy	memo
lash	loin	mend
lass	loll	menu
late	lone	mere
lath	look	mesa
laud	loom	mess
lava	loop	mete
lawn	loot	mica
laze	lope	mice
lazy	lore	mien
lead	lory	mike
leaf	lose	mild
leak	loss	milk
lean	lost	mill
leap	loth	mime
leek	loud	mind
leer	lour	mine
left	lout	mini
leis	love	minx
lend	luau	mire
lens	luck	Miró
Lent	lull	miry
lent	lure	miss
less	lurk	mist
lest	lush	mitt
levy	lust	moan
lewd	lute	moat
liar	lynx	mock
lice	lyre	mode
lick		mold
lied		mole
lien	mace	moll
lieu	Mach	molt
life	made	monk
like	magi	mono
lily	maid	mood
Lima	maim	moon
limb	main	moor
lime	make	moot
limn	male	mope
limp	Mali	more
limy	mall	more
line	malt	moss
link	mama	most
lint	mane	most
lion	Manx	mote
lira	many	moue

move	obey	peal
mown	oboe	pear
much	odor	peat
muck	ogle	peck
muff	ogre	peek
mull	Ohio	peel
muon	oily	peep
murk	okra	peer
muse	Oman	pelf
mush	omen	perk
musk	omit	pert
muss	once	Peru
mute	only	peso
mutt	onto	phew
myna	onus	pica
myth	onyx	pick
	ooze	pier
	oozy	pike
nail	opal	pile
name	open	pill
nape	opus	pine
nave	oral	pink
navy	orgy	pint
Nazi	Oslo	pipe
neap	ouch	pity
near	ours	pity
neat	oust	pixy
neck	ouzo	plan
need	oval	plat
neer	oven	play
neon	over	plea
nerd	Ovid	pleb
Nero	ovum	pled
news	owed	plod
newt	oxen	plop
next	oyez	plot
nice		plow
nick		ploy
nigh	pace	plug
nine	pact	plum
Noah	page	plus
node	paid	pock
noel	paid	poem
noes	pail	poet
none	pain	poke
non-U	pair	poky
nook	pale	pole
noon	pall	poll
nose	palm	polo
nosh	pane	pony
nosy	pang	pooh
note	papa	poop
noun	pare	poor
nova	park	Pope
nude	pass	pore
nuke	past	pork
null	pâté	pose
numb	pate	post
	pave	posy
	pawn	pouf
oath	peak	pour

pout	redo	sack
pray	reed	safe
prey	reef	saga
prig	reek	sage
prim	reel	sago
prod	rein	said
prom	rely	sail
prop	rend	sake
prow	rice	sale
puce	rich	salt
puck	rick	same
puff	ride	sane
puke	rife	sang
pull	rift	sank
pulp	rile	sari
puma	rind	sash
pump	ring	sate
punk	riot	save
puny	rise	sawn
pupa	risk	scab
pure	rite	scan
purl	road	scar
purr	roam	scat
push	roan	Scot
puss	roar	scow
putt	robe	scud
pyre	rock	scum
	rode	scut
	rode	seal
quad	rôle	seam
quay	role	sear
quid	roll	seat
quip	Rome	sect
quit	rood	seed
quiz	roof	seek
	rook	seem
	room	seen
race	root	seep
rack	rope	seer
racy	ropy	self
raga	rose	sell
rage	rosé	send
raid	rosy	sent
rail	rota	Serb
rain	rote	serf
rake	roué	sewn
rand	rout	sexy
rang	rove	shad
rape	ruby	shag
rapt	ruck	shah
rare	rude	sham
rash	rued	shed
rasp	ruff	shin
rate	ruin	ship
rave	rule	shod
raze	rune	shoe
read	rung	shoo
real	runt	shop
ream	ruse	shot
reap	rush	show
rear	rusk	shun

shut	sofa	swig
sick	soft	swim
sigh	soil	swop
sign	sold	swum
Sikh	sole	sync
silk	solo	
sill	some	
silo	soon	tack
silt	soot	taco
sing	sore	tact
sink	soul	tail
sire	soup	take
site	sour	talc
Siva	sown	tale
size	span	talk
skew	spar	tall
skid	spat	tame
skim	spat	tang
skin	spay	tape
skip	sped	taro
skit	spew	tart
skua	spin	task
slab	spit	taut
slag	spot	taxi
slam	spry	teak
slap	spun	teal
slat	spur	team
Slav	stab	tear
slay	stag	teat
sled	star	teed
slew	stay	teem
slid	stem	tell
slim	sten	tern
slip	step	text
slit	stet	Thai
slob	stew	than
sloe	stir	that
slog	stop	thaw
slop	stow	thee
slot	stub	then
slow	stud	they
slug	stun	thin
slum	stye	this
slur	such	thou
slut	suck	thud
smog	sued	thug
smug	suer	thus
smut	suet	tick
snag	Suez	tide
snap	suit	tidy
snip	sulk	tied
snob	sung	tier
snot	sunk	tiff
snow	sure	tile
snub	surf	till
snug	swab	tilt
soak	swam	time
soap	swan	tine
soar	swap	tint
sock	swat	tiny
soda	sway	tire

toad	Urdu	wast
to-do	urge	wave
toed	used	wavy
tofu	user	waxy
toga	Utah	weak
toil		weal
told		wean
tole	vain	wear
toll	vale	weed
tomb	vane	week
tome	vary	weep
tone	vase	weft
took	veal	weir
tool	Veda	weld
toot	veer	well
tope	veil	wend
tore	vein	went
torn	veld	wept
tort	vent	were
toss	verb	wert
tote	very	west
tour	veto	what
tout	vial	when
town	vice	whet
trap	vied	whew
tray	vier	whey
tree	view	whim
trek	vile	whip
trim	viol	whir
trio	visa	whit
trip	vise	whiz
trod	viva	whoa
trot	void	whom
true	vole	wick
tsar	volt	wide
tuba	vote	wife
tube		wild
tuck		wile
tuft	wade	will
tuna	wadi	wilt
tune	waft	wily
turf	wage	wimp
Turk	waif	wind
turn	wail	wine
tusk	wait	wipe
tutu	wake	wire
twig	wale	wiry
twin	walk	wise
twit	wall	wisp
tyke	wand	woad
type	wane	woke
tyro	want	wolf
tzar	ward	womb
	ware	wont
	warm	wood
ugly	warn	woof
undo	warp	wool
unit	wart	word
unto	wary	wore
upon	wash	work
Ural	wasp	worm

worn
wove
wrap
wren
writ

Xmas
xray
X-ray

yang
yank
yarn
yawl

yawn
yeah
year
yell
yelp
yeti
yoga
yogi
yoke
yolk
yore
your
yowl
yo-yo
yuan
yule

zany
zeal
zebu
zero
zest
Zeus
zinc
zing
Zion
zone
zoom
zoos
Zulu

aback	ALGOL	April
abaft	Algol	apron
abase	alias	aptly
abate	alibi	arbor
abbey	alien	arced
abbot	align	ardor
abhor	alike	arena
abide	alive	argot
abode	allay	argue
A-bomb	alley	Arian
abort	allot	Aries
about	allow	arise
above	alloy	armed
abuse	aloft	armor
abyss	aloha	aroma
ached	alone	arose
acorn	along	arras
acrid	aloof	array
actor	aloud	arrow
acute	alpha	arson
adage	altar	Aryan
adapt	alter	ascot
adder	amass	ashen
addle	amaze	ashes
adept	amber	Asian
ad hoc	amble	aside
adieu	amend	askew
adios	amigo	aspen
adlib	amiss	aspic
adman	amity	assay
admen	amnia	asset
admin	among	aster
admit	amour	astir
adobe	ample	atlas
adopt	amply	atoll
adore	amuck	atone
adorn	amuse	atria
adult	Andes	attar
aerie	angel	attic
affix	anger	audio
afoot	angle	audit
after	angry	aught
again	angst	augur
agape	anion	aural
agate	anise	avail
agave	ankle	avast
agent	annex	avert
agile	annoy	avoid
aging	annul	await
agony	anode	awake
agree	antic	award
ahead	anvil	aware
aimed	aorta	awash
aioli	apace	awful
aisle	apart	awing
alarm	aphid	awoke
album	aphis	axial
alder	apish	axiom
alert	appal	Aztec
Aleut	apple	azure
algae	apply	

babel	belie	boggy
bacon	belle	bogus
badge	belly	bolas
badly	below	bombe
bagel	beret	boned
baggy	berry	bongo
baize	berth	bonny
baked	beryl	bonus
baker	beset	booby
baled	betel	boost
balky	bevel	booth
balmy	bhang	booty
balsa	Bible	booze
banal	bided	boozy
bandy	bidet	borax
banjo	bight	bored
banns	bigot	borer
Bantu	bijou	boric
barge	biker	borne
baron	bilge	borne
basal	bimbo	bosom
based	binge	bossy
bases	bingo	bosun
bases	biped	botch
basic	birch	bough
basil	bison	bound
basin	bitch	bound
basis	bitty	bowel
Basle	black	bower
basso	blade	bowie
baste	blame	boxer
batch	bland	brace
bated	blank	braid
bathe	blare	brain
batik	blasé	brake
baton	blast	brand
batty	blaze	brass
bawdy	bleak	brave
bayou	bleat	bravo
beach	bleed	brawl
beady	bleep	brawn
beard	blend	braze
beast	bless	bread
beaus	blest	break
beaux	blind	bream
bebop	blink	breed
bedim	bliss	breve
beech	blitz	briar
beefy	block	bribe
befit	blond	brick
befog	blood	bride
began	bloom	brief
begat	blown	brier
beget	blowy	brine
begin	blurb	bring
begot	blurt	brink
begun	blush	briny
beige	board	brisk
being	boast	broil
belay	boded	broke
belch	bogey	brood

brook	candy	chose
broom	caned	chunk
broth	canny	churn
brown	canoe	chute
bruin	canon	cider
bruit	canto	cigar
brush	caper	cilia
brusk	capon	cinch
brute	carat	circa
buddy	cared	cited
budge	caret	civet
buggy	cargo	civet
bugle	carol	civic
build	carom	civil
built	carry	claim
bulge	carve	clamp
bulgy	cased	clang
bulky	caste	clank
bully	catch	clash
bumpy	cater	clasp
bunch	catty	class
bunco	caulk	clean
bunny	cause	clear
burin	caved	cleat
burly	cavil	cleft
burnt	cease	clerk
burro	cedar	click
bursa	ceded	cliff
burst	cello	climb
busby	chafe	clime
buses	chaff	cling
bushy	chain	clink
butch	chalk	cloak
butte	chaos	clock
butyl	charm	clone
buxom	chary	close
buyer	chase	cloth
bylaw	chasm	cloud
byway	cheap	clout
	cheat	clove
	check	clown
cabal	cheek	cluck
cabby	cheep	clump
cabin	chess	clung
cable	chewy	coach
cacao	chide	coast
cache	chief	coati
cacti	child	COBOL
caddy	Chile	cobol
cadet	chili	cobra
cadge	chill	cocky
cadre	chime	cocoa
caged	china	coded
cagey	China	codex
Cajun	chink	colic
caked	chirp	colon
calve	chive	color
calyx	chivy	comet
camel	choke	comic
cameo	chord	comma
canal	chore	conch

coney	cruel	delay
conga	cruet	delft
conic	crumb	Delhi
co-opt	crush	delta
coped	crust	delve
copra	crypt	demon
copse	cubed	demur
coral	cubic	denim
cored	cuing	dense
corgi	cumin	depot
corny	Cupid	depth
corps	cured	derby
couch	curio	deter
cough	curly	deuce
count	curly	devil
coupé	curry	Dhaka
cover	curse	diary
covet	curve	diced
covey	cushy	dicey
cower	cycle	dicta
cowry	cylic	digit
coyly	cynic	dimly
coypu	Czech	dinar
cozen		dined
crane		diner
crash	dacha	dingy
crass	daddy	dirge
crate	daffy	dirty
crave	dairy	dishy
crawl	dairy	ditch
craze	daisy	ditto
crazy	Dakar	ditty
creak	dally	divan
cream	dance	dived
credo	dandy	divot
creed	Dante	divvy
creek	dared	Dixie
creel	dated	dizzy
creep	datum	dodge
crêpe	davit	dogma
crept	dazed	doily
cress	dealt	doing
crest	death	Dolby
crick	debar	dolce
cried	debit	doled
crier	debug	dolly
cries	debut	domed
crime	decal	Donna
crimp	decay	donor
crisp	decor	donut
croak	decoy	doped
crock	decry	dopey
crone	defer	Doric
crony	Defoe	dosed
crook	Degas	doted
croon	de-ice	doubt
cross	deify	dough
croup	deign	douse
crowd	deism	dowdy
crown	deist	dowel
crude	deity	dower

downy
dowry
dowse
doyen
dozed
dozen
draft
drain
drake
drama
drank
drape
drawl
drawn
dread
dream
dress
dried
drier
drift
drily
drink
drive
droll
drone
drool
droop
dross
drove
drove
druid
drunk
drupe
dryad
dryer
dryly
ducal
ducat
duchy
ducky
dully
dulse
dummy
dumpy
dunce
duped
duple
durst
dusky
dusty
dwarf
dwell
dwelt
dying

eager
eagle
early
earth
eased

easel
eaten
eaves
ebony
éclat
edema
edged
edict
edify
educe
eerie
egret
Egypt
eider
eight
eject
eking
eland
elate
elbow
elder
elect
elegy
elfin
elide
elite
elope
elude
elver
elves
embed
ember
emcee
emend
emery
emote
empty
enact
endow
endue
enema
enemy
enjoy
ennui
enrol
ensue
enter
entry
envoi
envoy
epoch
epoxy
equal
equip
erase
erect
ergot
erica
erode
error
erupt

essay
ester
ether
ethic
ethos
ethyl
etude
evade
evert
evict
evoke
exact
exalt
excel
exert
exile
exist
expel
extol
extra
exude
exult
eying
eyrie

fable
faced
facet
faddy
faded
fagot
faint
fairy
faked
faker
fakir
false
famed
fancy
farad
farce
fared
fatal
fated
fatty
fault
fauna
favor
fazed
feast
fecal
feces
feign
feint
felon
femur
fence
feral
ferry
fetal

fetch	focus	gable
fêted	foehn	Gabon
fetid	fogey	gaffe
fetus	foggy	gaily
fever	foist	gamin
fiber	folio	gamma
fichu	folly	gamut
field	fondu	gaped
fiend	foray	gappy
fiery	force	gases
fifty	forge	gassy
fight	forgo	gaudy
filch	forte	gauge
filed	forte	gaunt
filet	forth	gauze
filly	forty	gauzy
filmy	forum	gavel
filth	found	gawky
final	found	gayly
finch	fount	gazed
finer	foyer	gecko
finis	frail	geese
fiord	frame	gelid
fired	franc	genie
first	frank	genii
fishy	fraud	Genoa
fitly	freak	genre
fixed	freer	genus
fixer	fresh	geode
fizzy	Freud	Ghana
fjord	friar	ghost
fiail	fried	ghoul
flair	fries	giant
flake	frill	giddy
flaky	frizz	gipsy
flame	frock	girth
flank	front	given
flare	frost	glacé
flask	froth	glade
fleet	frown	glare
flier	froze	glary
flies	fruit	glass
fling	frump	glaze
flirt	fryer	gleam
float	fudge	glean
flood	fugue	glide
floor	fully	gloat
flora	fumed	globe
floss	fungi	gloom
flout	funky	glory
flown	funny	gloss
fluff	furor	glove
fluid	furry	glued
fluke	fused	gluey
fluky	fussy	gnarl
flung	fusty	gnash
flute	futon	gnome
flyby	fuzzy	godly
flyer		gofer
foamy		going
focal	gabby	golem

golly	guile	henna
gonad	guilt	heron
goner	guise	hertz
gooey	gulag	hewed
goofy	gully	hiked
goose	gumbo	hiker
gored	gummy	hilly
gorge	gunny	Hindi
gorse	guppy	Hindu
Gouda	gushy	hinge
gouge	gusto	hippy
gourd	gusty	hired
gouty	gutsy	hitch
goyin	gypsy	hived
grace		hoard
grade		hoary
graft	habit	hobby
grail	Hades	hoist
grain	hadn't	hokum
grand	Hague	holed
grape	hairy	holer
graph	haled	holey
grass	hallo	holly
grate	halva	homey
grave	halve	honed
gravy	handy	honey
graze	Hanoi	honky
great	happy	honor
grebe	hardy	hooch
greed	hared	hooey
Greek	harem	hoofs
green	harpy	hooky
greet	harry	hoped
grief	harsh	horde
Grieg	Hasid	horny
grill	hasn't	horse
grime	haste	horsy
Grimm	hasty	hosed
grimy	hatch	hotel
grind	hated	hotly
gripe	haunt	hound
grist	haven	houri
groan	havoc	house
groin	Haydn	hovel
groom	hazed	hover
grope	hazel	howdy
gross	H-bomb	huffy
group	heady	hullo
grove	heard	human
growl	heart	humid
grown	heath	humor
gruel	heave	humpy
gruff	heavy	humus
grunt	hedge	hunch
guano	hefty	hurry
guard	heist	husky
guava	helix	hussy
guess	hello	hutch
guest	he-man	hyena
guide	he-men	hymen
guild	hence	hyped

Ibsen	jelly	knock
icier	jenny	knoll
icily	jerky	knout
icily	Jesus	known
icing	jetty	knurl
ideal	jewel	koala
idiom	Jewry	kooky
idiot	jiffy	kopek
idled	jihad	Koran
idler	jimmy	Korea
idyll	jived	kraal
igloo	joint	krona
Iliad	joist	krone
image	joked	kudos
imago	joker	
imbed	jolly	
imbue	jolty	label
impel	Jonah	labor
imply	joule	laced
inane	joust	laded
inapt	Judas	laden
incur	judge	ladle
index	juice	lager
India	juicy	Lagos
inept	julep	laity
inert	jumbo	lamed
infer	jumpy	lance
ingle	junky	lanky
ingot	junta	La Paz
inlaw	juror	lapel
inlay		lapin
inlet		lapse
inner	kabob	larch
input	Kabul	large
inset	Kafka	largo
inter	kapok	larva
Inuit	kaput	laser
inure	karat	lasso
ionic	karma	latch
Iraqi	kayak	later
irate	kebab	latex
Irish	kedge	lathe
irony	Kenya	Latin
Islam	ketch	laugh
islet	keyed	layer
issue	khaki	lazed
Italy	Khmer	leach
itchy	kinky	leafy
ivied	kiosk	leaky
ivies	Kiowa	leant
ivory	kited	leapt
	kitty	learn
	klutz	lease
jabot	knack	leash
jaded	knave	least
Jaffa	knead	least
Japan	kneed	leave
jaunt	kneel	ledge
jazzy	knell	leech
jeans	knelt	leery
Jello	knife	lefty

legal	lorry	manly
leggy	loser	manna
leggy	lotus	manor
lemma	louse	manse
lemon	louse	Maori
lemur	lousy	maple
Lenin	loved	march
leper	lover	marry
letup	lower	marsh
levee	lower	Masai
level	lowly	mason
lever	loyal	match
liana	lucid	mated
libel	lucky	matte
Libya	lucre	matzo
licit	Luger	mauve
liege	lumen	maven
light	lumpy	mavin
liked	lunar	maxim
liken	lunch	maybe
lilac	lunge	mayor
limbo	lupin	mazed
limed	lupus	mealy
limey	lurch	meant
limit	lured	meaty
lined	lurid	mecca
linen	lusty	medal
liner	lying	media
lingo	lying	media
linty	lymph	medic
lippy	lynch	melee
lisle	Lyons	melon
Liszt	lyric	mercy
liter		merge
lithe		merit
lived	macaw	merry
liven	maced	meson
liver	macho	messy
lives	madam	metal
livid	madly	meted
llama	Mafia	meter
llano	magic	metre
loamy	magma	metro
loath	magus	mezzo
lobar	Maine	Miami
lobby	maize	miaow
lobed	major	Micah
local	maker	micro
locus	Malay	Midas
lodge	Malta	middy
loess	malty	midge
lofty	mamba	midst
logic	mambo	Milan
Loire	mamma	milch
loner	mammy	miler
loony	Manet	milky
loopy	mange	mimed
loose	mango	mimer
loped	mangy	mimic
loper	mania	mince
Lorca	manic	mined

miner	muggy	nomad
mingy	mulch	nonce
minim	mulct	noose
minor	mummy	Norse
minus	munch	nosed
mired	mural	notch
mirth	murky	noted
misdo	mused	novel
miser	mushy	nudge
misty	music	nuked
miter	musky	nurse
mitre	mussy	nutty
mixed	musty	nutty
mixer	muted	nylon
mocha	Muzak	nymph
modal	muzzy	
model	myrrh	
modem		oaken
mogul		oakum
moiré	nabob	oases
moist	nacre	oasis
molar	nadir	obese
moldy	Nahum	occur
momma	naiad	ocean
monad	naive	ocher
Monet	naked	octet
money	named	odium
month	nanny	offal
mooch	nasal	offer
moody	nasty	often
moose	natal	ogled
moped	natty	ogler
moped	naval	ohmic
moral	navel	okapi
moray	nawab	olden
mores	needy	older
moron	negro	olive
Moses	Nehru	omega
mosey	neigh	onion
mossy	Nepal	onset
motel	nerve	oomph
motet	nervy	oozed
motif	never	opera
motor	newel	opine
motto	newly	opium
mound	newsy	optic
mount	nexus	orate
mourn	niche	orbit
mouse	niece	order
mousy	nifty	organ
mouth	Niger	oriel
moved	night	Orion
mover	ninny	Osaka
movie	ninth	Oscar
mowed	nippy	osier
mower	Nisei	other
moxie	noble	otter
mucky	nobly	ought
mucus	nodal	Ouija
muddy	noise	ounce
mufti	noisy	ousel

outdo	penal	plied
outer	pence	Pliny
outré	penis	pluck
ouzel	penny	plumb
ovary	penon	plume
ovate	peony	plump
overt	peppy	plush
ovoid	Pepys	Pluto
owing	perch	poach
owner	peril	poesy
oxide	perky	point
ozone	Perón	poise
	per se	poked
	pesky	poker
paced	petal	polar
pacer	peter	poled
paddy	petty	polio
padre	pewit	polka
paean	phase	polyp
pagan	phial	poppa
paged	phone	poppy
paint	phony	porch
paled	photo	pored
palsy	piano	porno
panda	picky	posed
panel	piece	poser
panic	piety	posit
pansy	pigmy	posse
panty	piker	potty
papal	pilaf	pouch
papau	pilau	pouff
papaw	piled	pound
paper	pilot	power
parch	pinch	prank
pared	pined	prate
Paris	piney	prawn
parka	pinky	preen
parry	pinto	press
parse	pious	price
party	piped	prick
pasha	piper	pride
passé	pique	pried
pasta	piste	prime
paste	pitch	prior
pasty	pithy	prism
patch	piton	privy
patio	pivot	prize
patsy	pixie	probe
patty	pizza	proem
pause	place	prone
paved	plaid	prong
payee	plain	proof
payer	plait	prose
peace	plane	prosy
peach	plant	proud
pearl	plate	prove
peaty	Plato	Provo
pecan	plaza	prowl
pedal	plead	proxy
peeve	pleat	prude
pekoe	plebe	prune

pshaw	radar	retch
psych	radii	revel
pubic	radio	revue
pudgy	radon	rheum
puffy	raged	Rhine
puked	rainy	Rhône
pulpy	rainy	rhyme
pulse	raise	rider
punch	rajah	ridge
Punic	raked	rifle
pupae	rally	right
pupil	ranch	rigid
puppy	randy	rigor
puree	range	riled
purge	rangy	rinse
purse	rapid	ripen
pushy	rarer	risen
pussy	raspy	riser
putty	Rasta	risky
pygmy	rated	ritzy
pylon	ratio	rival
Pyrex	ratty	riven
	raved	river
	ravel	rivet
Qatar	Ravel	roach
quack	raven	roast
quaff	rayon	robed
quail	razed	robin
quake	razor	robot
qualm	reach	rocky
quart	react	rodeo
quash	ready	Rodin
quasi	realm	rogue
queen	rearm	Roman
queer	rebel	Romeo
quell	rebel	rondo
query	rebut	roomy
quest	recap	roost
queue	recur	roped
quick	redid	ropey
quiet	reedy	rosin
quill	refer	rotor
quilt	refit	Rouen
quint	regal	rouge
quire	Reich	rough
quirk	reign	round
quite	Reims	rouse
Quito	relax	roust
quits	relay	route
quoit	relic	roved
quota	remit	rover
quote	renal	rowan
quoth	renew	rowdy
Quran	repay	rower
Qur'an	repel	royal
	reply	ruble
	repot	ruche
rabbi	reran	ruddy
rabid	rerun	rugby
raced	reset	ruing
racer	resin	ruled

ruler	scene	shark
rumba	scent	sharp
rummy	sci-fi	shave
rumor	scion	shawl
runic	scoff	sheaf
runny	scold	shear
runty	scone	sheen
rupee	scoop	sheep
rural	scoot	sheer
rusty	scope	sheet
rutty	score	sheik
	scorn	shelf
	scour	shell
saber	scout	shied
sable	scowl	shift
sabot	scrag	shine
sacra	scram	shiny
sadly	scrap	shirk
safer	scree	shirt
sahib	screw	Shiva
saint	scrub	shlep
salad	scuba	shoal
sally	scuff	shone
salon	scull	shook
salsa	scurf	shoot
salty	seamy	shore
salve	sedan	shorn
salvo	sedge	short
samba	seedy	shout
Samoa	seepy	shove
sandy	seine	shown
sappy	seize	showy
saran	semen	shred
sassy	senor	shrew
Satan	sense	shrub
sated	Seoul	shrug
satin	sepal	shunt
satyr	sepia	shush
sauce	sepoy	shyly
saucy	serge	sibyl
Saudi	serum	sided
sauna	serve	sidle
saute	set-to	siege
saved	seven	sieve
saver	sever	sight
savor	sewed	silky
savvy	sewer	silly
sawed	shack	silos
Saxon	shade	silty
say-so	shady	Sinai
scads	shaft	since
scald	shake	sinew
scale	shaky	singe
scalp	shale	sinus
scaly	shall	Sioux
scamp	shame	sired
scant	shank	siren
scare	shan't	sisal
scarf	shape	sissy
scarp	shard	sitar
scary	share	sited

sit-in	snare	spiky
Sitka	snarl	spill
sixth	sneak	spilt
sixty	sneer	spiny
sized	snick	spire
skate	snide	spite
skein	sniff	splat
skied	snipe	splay
skier	snook	split
skies	snoop	Spode
skiff	snore	spoil
skill	snort	spoke
skimp	snout	spoof
skirt	snowy	spook
skoal	snuff	spool
skulk	soapy	spoon
skull	sober	spoor
skunk	Sodom	spore
slack	Sofia	sport
slain	softy	spout
slake	soggy	sprat
slang	solar	spray
slant	soled	spree
slate	sol-fa	sprig
slave	solid	spume
sleek	solve	spurn
sleep	sonar	spurt
sleet	sonic	squad
slept	sonny	squat
slice	sooty	squaw
slick	soppy	squib
slide	sorry	squid
slime	sough	stack
slimy	sound	staff
sling	soupy	stage
slink	souse	stagy
sloop	south	staid
slope	sowed	stain
sloth	space	stair
slump	spade	stake
slung	Spain	stale
slunk	spare	stalk
slush	spark	stall
slyly	spasm	stand
smack	spate	stank
small	spawn	stare
smart	speak	state
smear	spear	stave
smell	speck	stead
smelt	speed	steak
smile	spell	steal
smirk	spelt	steam
smite	spend	steed
smock	spent	steel
smoke	sperm	steep
smoky	spice	steer
smote	spicy	stein
snafu	spied	stern
snail	spiel	stick
snake	spies	sties
snaky	spike	stiff

stile	swear	teddy
still	sweat	teens
sting	Swede	teeny
stink	sweep	teeth
stoat	sweet	telex
stock	swell	tempi
stoic	swept	tempo
stoke	swift	tempt
stole	swill	tench
stone	swine	tenet
stony	swing	tenon
stood	swipe	tenor
stool	swirl	tense
stoop	swish	tenth
store	Swiss	tepee
stork	swoon	tepid
story	swoop	terry
stoup	sword	terse
stout	swore	testy
stove	sworn	Texan
strap	swung	Texas
straw	sylph	thane
stray	synch	thank
strew	synod	theft
stria	Syria	their
strip	syrup	theme
strop		there
strum		therm
strut		these
stuck	tabby	thick
study	table	thief
stuff	taboo	thigh
stump	tabor	thine
stung	tacit	thing
stunk	tacky	think
stunt	tacos	third
style	taffy	thong
styli	taint	thorn
suave	taken	those
Sudan	taker	three
sudsy	talky	threw
suede	tally	throb
sugar	talon	throe
suing	tamed	throw
suite	Tamil	thrum
sulky	tango	thumb
sully	tangy	thyme
sumac	taped	tiara
sunny	taper	Tiber
sunup	tapir	Tibet
super	tardy	tibia
surer	tarot	tidal
surge	tarry	tiger
surly	tarry	tight
sushi	taste	tilde
swain	tasty	tiled
swami	tatty	timed
swamp	taunt	timer
swank	tawny	timid
sward	teach	tinge
swarm	teary	tinny
	tease	

tipsy	trill	umber
tired	tripe	umbra
Tirol	trite	umiak
titan	troll	unbar
Titan	troop	uncap
tithe	troth	uncle
title	trout	under
tizzy	trove	undid
toady	truce	undue
toast	truck	unfit
today	truer	unify
toddy	truly	union
Tokay	trump	unite
token	trunk	unity
Tokyo	truss	unlit
toled	trust	untie
tonal	truth	until
Tonga	tryst	unzip
tonic	tubal	upped
tonne	tubby	upper
tooth	tubed	upset
topaz	tuber	urban
toped	Tudor	urged
topee	tulip	urine
toper	tulle	usage
topic	tumid	usher
toque	tummy	using
Torah	tumor	usual
torch	tuned	usurp
torso	tuner	usury
torte	tunic	utter
total	Tunis	U-turn
toted	tunny	uvula
totem	tuque	
touch	turbo	
tough	Turin	vague
towel	turps	valet
tower	tutor	valid
toxic	twain	valor
toxin	twang	value
trace	tweak	valve
track	tweed	vaned
tract	tweet	vapid
trade	twerp	vapor
trail	twice	vault
train	twill	vaunt
trait	twine	vegan
trash	twirl	veiny
trawl	twirp	veldt
tread	twist	velum
treat	twixt	venal
trend	tying	venom
tress	typed	venue
triad	Tyrol	Venus
trial		verge
tribe		verse
trice	U-boat	verso
trick	udder	verve
tried	ulcer	vetch
trier	ultra	vexed
tries	umbel	viand

vicar	wedge	wooly
video	weedy	woozy
vigil	weeny	wordy
vigor	weepy	world
viler	weigh	wormy
villa	weigh	worry
vinyl	weird	worse
viola	Welsh	worse
viper	wench	worst
viral	wetly	worst
vireo	whack	worth
Virgo	whale	would
virus	wharf	wound
visit	wheal	woven
visor	wheat	wrack
vista	wheel	wrath
vital	whelk	wreak
vivid	whelm	wreck
vixen	whelp	wrest
vizor	where	wrier
vocal	which	wring
vodka	whiff	wrist
vogue	while	write
voice	whine	wrong
voile	whirl	wrote
vomit	whirr	wrung
voted	whisk	wryly
voter	whist	
vouch	white	
vowel	whizz	xebec
V-sign	whole	xenon
vulva	whoop	Xerox
vying	whore	Xhosa
	whorl	xylem
	whose	
wacky	widen	
waded	wider	yacht
wader	widow	yahoo
wafer	width	yearn
waged	wield	yeast
wager	wimpy	Yeats
wagon	wince	Yemen
waist	winch	yield
waive	windy	yodel
waked	wined	yoked
waken	wiped	yokel
waled	wiper	young
Wales	wired	yours
waltz	wised	youth
waned	wiser	yo-yos
wanly	wispy	yucca
waste	witch	Yukon
watch	witty	yummy
water	wives	
waved	wizen	
waver	woken	Zaire
waxed	woman	zebra
waxen	women	zeros
weary	woody	zesty
weave	wooer	zippy
weber	Woolf	zonal
		zoned

abacus	advise	amnion
abased	Aegean	amoeba
abated	aerate	amoral
abbess	aerial	amount
abduct	aeries	ampere
abided	aerobe	ampule
abject	affair	Amtrak
abjure	affect	amulet
ablate	affirm	amused
ablaze	afford	analog
Abnaki	affray	anchor
aboard	Afghan	anemia
abound	afield	anemic
abrade	aflame	angina
abroad	afloat	angler
abrupt	afraid	angora
abseil	afresh	animal
absent	ageing	animus
absorb	ageism	anklet
absurd	ageist	annals
abused	agency	anneal
abuser	agenda	annual
acacia	aghast	anoint
accede	agleam	anorak
accent	agreed	answer
accept	airbus	anthem
access	airily	anther
accord	airing	antler
accost	airing	anyhow
accrue	airman	anyone
accuse	airmen	anyway
acetic	airway	aortal
aching	akimbo	aortic
acidic	Alaska	Apache
acquit	albeit	apathy
across	albino	apexes
acting	alcove	apiary
action	alexia	apical
active	alight	apices
actual	alkali	apiece
acuity	allege	aplomb
acumen	alleys	apogee
adagio	allied	appall
addend	allied	appeal
addict	allies	appear
adduce	allude	append
adhere	allure	appose
adieus	almond	Arabic
adieux	almost	arable
adjoin	alpaca	arcade
adjure	alpine	arcane
adjust	alumna	archer
admire	alumni	archly
adored	always	arcing
adrift	amazed	Arctic
adroit	Amazon	arctic
adsorb	ambled	ardent
advent	ambush	argosy
adverb	amerce	argued
advert	amidst	argyle
advice	amigos	aright

arisen	avenge	barmen
armada	avenue	barony
armful	averse	barred
armies	aviary	barrel
arming	avidly	barren
armory	avowal	barrow
armpit	avowed	barter
around	awaked	baryon
arouse	awaken	baryta
arrant	aweigh	basalt
arrear	awhile	basing
arrest	awhirl	basket
arrive	awning	Basque
arroyo	azalea	bassos
artery	Azores	basted
artful		bathed
artist		bather
ascend	babble	bathos
ascent	babied	bating
ashier	babies	batman
ashore	baboon	batmen
ashram	backer	batted
asleep	backup	batten
aspect	back-up	batter
aspire	badger	batter
assail	baffle	battle
assent	bagful	bauble
assert	bagged	bazaar
assess	bagnio	beacon
assign	bakery	beaded
assist	baking	beagle
assize	baldly	beaker
assort	baleen	beamed
assume	baling	bearer
assure	Balkan	beaten
astern	ballad	beater
asthma	ballet	beatup
astral	ballot	beauty
astray	balsam	beaver
astute	Baltic	becalm
asylum	bamboo	became
Athens	banana	beckon
atomic	bandit	become
atonal	bangle	bedbug
atoned	banish	bedded
atrium	banker	bedlam
attach	banned	bedpan
attack	banner	beduin
attain	bantam	beetle
attend	banter	beeves
attest	banyan	befall
attire	banzai	befell
attune	baobab	before
auburn	barbed	beggar
august	barbel	begged
August	barber	begone
au pair	barely	behalf
aurora	barged	behave
author	barium	behead
autism	barley	beheld
autumn	barman	behest

behind	bitchy	botchy
behold	biting	bother
behove	bitten	bo tree
Beirut	bitter	bottle
belfry	bladed	bottom
belied	blamed	bouclé
belief	blanch	bought
bellow	blared	bought
belong	blazed	bounce
belted	blazer	bounty
bemire	bleach	bourse
bemoan	bleary	bovine
bemuse	blight	bowery
Bengal	blithe	bowing
benign	blonde	bowleg
benumb	bloody	bowler
benzol	blotch	boxcar
berate	blouse	boxful
Berber	blower	boxing
bereft	bluest	boyish
Berlin	bluing	braced
beside	bluish	bracer
bestir	blurry	braces
bestow	boater	Brahma
betake	bobbed	brainy
bethel	bobbin	braise
betide	bobble	branch
betook	bobcat	brandy
betray	bodega	brassy
betted	bodice	bratty
better	bodies	braved
bettor	bodily	brawny
bettor	boding	brazen
bevies	bodkin	Brazil
bewail	boggle	breach
beware	boiler	breast
beyond	boldly	breath
biased	bolero	breech
biceps	bolted	breeze
bicker	Bombay	breezy
bidden	bomber	Breton
bidder	bonbon	brevet
biding	bonded	brewer
bigamy	bonier	bribed
bigger	boning	bridal
bigwig	bon mot	bridge
bijoux	bonnet	bridle
bikini	bonsai	bright
billed	boodle	Briton
billet	bookie	broach
billow	bootee	broken
binary	bootie	broken
binder	boozer	broker
bionic	border	bronco
biopsy	boring	bronze
biotin	Borneo	brooch
birdie	borrow	broody
bisect	borsch	broque
bishop	borzoi	browse
bisque	Boston	bruise
bistro	botany	brunch

brunet
brutal
bubble
bubbly
bucket
buckle
budded
Buddha
budget
buffer
buffet
bugged
bugger
bugler
bulged
bulgur
bullet
bummed
bumper
bunchy
bundle
bungle
bunion
bunker
bunkum
burble
burden
bureau
burgle
burial
buried
burlap
burned
burner
burred
burrow
bursar
busboy
bushel
busied
busier
busily
bustle
butane
butler
butter
button
buying
buzzer
byelaw
bygone
byline
bypass
byplay
byword

cabana
cabbie
cabled
cached

cachet
cachou
cackle
cactus
caddie
cadged
Caesar
caftan
cagier
cagily
caging
caiman
cajole
caking
calico
caliph
callow
callus
calmly
calved
calves
camber
camera
camper
campus
Canada
canapé
canard
canary
cancan
cancel
cancer
candid
candle
candor
canine
caning
canker
canned
cannon
cannot
canoed
canopy
canter
canton
cantor
Canuck
canvas
canyon
capful
capped
captor
carafe
carbon
carboy
careen
career
caress
caries
caring
carnal

carpel
carpet
carrel
carrob
carrot
cartel
carton
carved
casaba
cashew
casing
casino
casket
caster
castle
castor
casual
catchy
catgut
Cathay
catkin
catnap
catnip
catsup
cattle
caucus
caught
causal
caused
caveat
cavern
caviar
cavies
caving
cavity
cavort
cayman
cayuse
ceased
ceding
celery
cellar
Celtic
cement
censer
censor
census
center
cereal
cerise
cerium
cervix
cesura
Ceylon
cha-cha
chafed
chalet
chalky
chance
chancy
change

chapel	clench	conies
charge	clergy	conned
chased	cleric	consul
chaser	clever	contra
chaste	clevis	convex
chatty	cliché	convey
cheeky	client	convoy
cheery	climax	cookie
cheese	clinch	cooler
cherry	clinic	coolie
cherub	clique	coolly
chesty	cloaca	cootie
chewer	cloned	copied
chichi	closed	copier
chicle	closet	copies
chided	clothe	coping
chilli	cloudy	copper
chilly	cloven	Coptic
chintz	clover	copula
chirpy	clumsy	coquet
chisel	clutch	cordon
chivvy	coarse	coring
choice	cobalt	cornea
choked	cobble	corner
choker	cobnut	cornet
choler	cobweb	corona
choose	coccyx	corpse
choosy	cockle	corpus
choppy	cocoon	corral
choral	coddle	corset
chorea	codger	cortex
chorus	codify	cosier
chosen	coding	cosily
chosen	coerce	cosine
Christ	coffee	cosmic
chrome	coffer	cosmos
chubby	coffin	cosset
chummy	cogent	co-star
chunky	cognac	costly
church	cohere	cotter
cicada	cohort	cotton
cilium	coitus	cougar
cinder	coldly	county
cinema	collar	couple
cipher	collie	coupon
circle	colony	course
circus	column	cousin
cirrus	combat	covert
cities	comber	coward
citing	comedy	cowboy
citron	comely	cowpox
citrus	coming	cowrie
civics	comity	coyote
clammy	commit	cozily
clamor	common	crabby
claque	compel	cradle
claret	comply	crafty
classy	concur	craggy
clause	condom	craned
clayey	condor	crania
cleave	confer	cranky

cranky
cranny
crated
crater
cravat
craved
craven
crayon
crazed
creaky
creamy
crease
creasy
create
crèche
credit
creepy
Creole
cretin
crewed
cringe
crises
crisis
crispy
critic
croaky
crocus
crouch
cruces
cruise
crummy
crunch
crusty
crutch
crying
cubing
cubism
cuckoo
cuddle
cudgel
cumber
cumuli
cupful
cupola
cupped
curare
curate
curdle
curfew
curing
curler
curlew
cursed
curtly
curtsy
curved
cuspid
cussed
custom
cutest
cutlet

cutoff
cycled
cygnet
cygnet
cylist
cymbal
cypher
cystic

dabbed
dabble
da capo
Dacron
dactyl
dagger
dahlia
dainty
Dakota
damage
damask
dammed
damned
dampen
damper
damsel
damson
danced
dander
dandle
danger
dangle
Danish
Danube
daphne
dapper
dapple
daring
darken
darkly
dating
dative
dawdle
Day-Glo
dazing
dazzle
deacon
deaden
deadly
deafen
dealer
dearly
dearth
debark
debase
debate
debris
debtor
debunk
decade
decamp

decant
deceit
decent
decide
decode
decree
deduce
deduct
deepen
deeply
deface
defame
defeat
defect
defend
defied
defile
define
deform
defray
deftly
defuse
degree
deiced
deicer
déjà vu
de jure
delete
delude
deluge
deluxe
demand
demean
demise
demote
demure
dengue
denial
denied
denier
denote
dentin
denude
depict
deploy
deport
depose
depute
deputy
derail
deride
derive
dermis
descry
desert
desert
design
desire
desist
despot
detach

detail
detain
detect
detest
detour
de trop
device
devise
devoid
devote
devour
devout
dewier
dewlap
diadem
dialed
dialog
diaper
dicier
dicing
dickey
dictum
diesel
differ
digest
digger
dilate
dilute
dimity
dimmed
dimmer
dimple
dinghy
dining
dinned
dinner
dipped
direct
dirndl
disarm
disbar
discus
dismal
dismay
disown
dispel
distil
disuse
dither
divers
divert
divest
divide
divine
diving
docile
docket
doctor
dodder
dodoes
doesn't

dogged
dogged
dogmas
doling
dollar
dollop
domain
doming
domino
donate
donjon
donkey
donned
doodle
doping
dories
dormer
dorsal
dosage
do-si-do
dosing
dotage
doting
dotted
double
doubly
douche
doughy
doused
dowsed
dozing
drachm
drafty
dragee
dragon
draped
drawer
dreamt
dreamy
dreary
dredge
dreggy
drench
dressy
driest
drippy
drivel
driven
drolly
droned
droopy
dropsy
drowse
drowsy
drudge
dryest
drying
dubbed
dubbin
Dublin
dueled

duenna
duffel
duffer
duffle
dugong
dugout
dulcet
dunlin
dunned
duping
duplex
duress
during
duster
duties
dyeing
dynamo

eaglet
earful
earthy
earwig
easier
easily
easing
Easter
eatery
eating
ebbing
echoed
echoes
eclair
eczema
eddied
eddies
edgier
edging
edible
editor
educed
eerily
efface
effect
effete
effigy
effort
effuse
eggnog
egoism
egoist
egress
eighth
eighty
either
elapse
elated
eldest
eleven
elicit
elided

elixir	eolith	exposé
eloped	epical	expose
eluded	epilog	expose
embalm	equate	extant
embark	equine	extend
emblem	equity	extent
embody	erased	extoll
emboss	eraser	extort
embryo	erbium	exuded
emceed	ermine	eyeful
emerge	eroded	eyeing
emeses	erotic	eyelet
emesis	errand	
emetic	errant	
émigré	errata	fabled
emoted	ersatz	fabric
empire	escape	facade
employ	eschew	facial
enable	escort	facile
enamel	escrow	facing
enamor	escudo	factor
en bloc	Eskimo	fading
encamp	espied	faecal
encase	estate	faeces
encode	esteem	fagged
encore	Esther	faggot
endear	estrus	faille
ending	ethics	fairly
endive	ethnic	faking
endued	euchre	falcon
endure	eulogy	fallen
energy	eunuch	fallow
enfold	eureka	falter
engage	Europe	family
engine	evaded	famine
engulf	evenly	famish
enigma	evilly	famous
enjoin	evince	fanged
enlist	evoked	fanned
enmesh	evolve	farced
enmity	exceed	farina
enough	except	faring
enrage	excess	farmer
enrapt	excise	farrow
enrich	excite	fasces
enroll	excuse	fascia
ensign	exempt	fasten
ensued	exhale	father
ensure	exhort	fathom
entail	exhume	fating
entice	exiled	fatted
entire	exodus	fatten
entity	Exodus	fatter
entomb	exotic	faucet
entrap	expand	faulty
entrée	expect	faunae
envied	expend	faunas
envies	expert	fazing
enzyme	expire	fealty
Eocene	expiry	fecund
eolian	export	fedora

feeble	fixing	forbid
feebly	fixity	forced
feeder	fizzle	forego
feeler	flabby	forest
feisty	flacon	forged
feline	flagon	forger
fellow	flaked	forget
felony	flakey	forgot
female	flambé	forked
femora	flamed	formal
fenced	flange	format
fencer	flared	former
fender	flashy	forums
Fenian	flatly	fossil
fennel	flatus	foster
ferret	flaunt	fought
ferule	flavor	foul-up
fervid	flawed	fourth
fervor	flaxen	foxier
festal	fledge	foxily
fester	fleece	fracas
fêting	fleecy	framed
fetish	fleshy	France
fetter	flight	frappé
fettle	flimsy	freaky
feudal	flinch	freely
fezzes	flinty	freest
fiancé	floozy	freeze
fiasco	floppy	French
fibbed	florae	frenzy
fibber	floral	fresco
fibril	floret	friary
fibula	florid	Friday
fickle	flossy	fridge
fiddle	floury	friend
fidget	flower	frieze
fierce	fluent	fright
fiesta	fluffy	frigid
figure	flunky	frilly
filial	flurry	fringe
filing	fluted	frisky
filler	flying	frizzy
fillet	flyman	frolic
fillip	flymen	frosty
filter	fobbed	frothy
filthy	fo'c'sle	frowzy
finale	fodder	frozen
finely	foetal	frugal
finery	foetid	fruity
finest	foetus	frumpy
finger	fogged	frying
finish	fogies	fuddle
finite	foible	fudged
finned	folder	fueled
firing	folksy	führer
firkin	follow	fulcra
firmly	foment	fumble
fiscal	fondle	fuming
fitful	fondly	fungal
fitted	fondue	fungus
fitter	forage	funnel

furies
furore
furred
furrow
fusing
fusion
futile
future

gabbed
gabble
gabled
gadded
gadfly
gadget
Gaelic
gagged
gaggle
gaiety
gainer
gaiter
galaxy
galley
Gallic
gallon
gallop
galore
Galway
Gambia
gambit
gamble
gambol
gamete
gamily
gamine
gaming
gammon
gander
Gandhi
Ganges
gangly
gannet
gantry
gaoler
gaping
gapped
garage
garble
garçon
garden
gargle
garish
garlic
garner
garnet
garret
garter
gasbag
gasify
gasket

gassed
gasses
gather
gauche
gaucho
gauged
gayety
gazebo
gazing
Gdansk
geisha
gelded
gelled
Gemini
gemmed
gender
genera
Geneva
genial
genius
gentle
gently
gentry
gerbil
German
gerund
gewgaw
geyser
ghetto
gibber
gibbet
gibbon
giblet
Gideon
gifted
giggle
giggly
gigolo
gilded
gimlet
ginger
Giotto
girder
girdle
girlie
giving
gladly
glamor
glance
glared
glassy
glazed
gleamy
glibly
glided
global
gloomy
glossy
glower
gluing
glumly

gluten
gnawed
gneiss
gnomic
gnomon
goaded
goalie
goatee
gobbet
gobble
goblet
goblin
go-cart
goddam
godson
Goethe
goggle
goiter
golden
golfer
good-by
goodly
gooier
goosed
gopher
gorged
gorgon
gorier
goring
gospel
gossip
Gothic
gotten
gouged
govern
gowned
graced
graded
graham
grainy
gramme
grange
granny
grassy
grated
grater
gratis
graved
gravel
graven
graver
Graves
grazed
grease
greasy
Greece
greedy
grieve
grille
grilse
grimly

gringo
griped
griper
grippe
grisly
gritty
grocer
groggy
groove
groovy
groped
grotto
grouch
ground
ground
grouse
grovel
grower
growth
grubby
grudge
grumpy
guffaw
guided
guidon
guilty
guinea
guitar
gullet
gummed
gundog
gunman
gunmen
gunned
gunner
gunshy
gurgle
gusher
gusset
gutted
gutter
Guyana
guzzle
gypped
gypsum
gyrate
gyrose

hackle
Haggai
haggis
haggle
hairdo
haling
hallow
halter
halvah
halved
halves
halves

hamlet
hammed
hammer
hamper
handed
Handel
handle
hangar
hanged
hanger
hanker
hansom
happen
Harare
harass
harbor
harden
hardly
haring
harken
harlot
harrow
hassle
hasten
hating
hatred
hatter
haunch
Havana
haven't
having
Hawaii
hawker
hawser
hazard
hazier
hazily
hazing
healer
health
heaped
hearer
hearse
hearth
hearty
heated
heater
heaved
heaven
Hebrew
heckle
hectic
hector
hedged
hedger
hegira
heifer
height
hejira
helium
helmet

helper
hemmed
herald
herbal
hereby
herein
heresy
Hermes
hermit
hernia
heroes
heroic
heroin
herpes
hewing
hiatus
hiccup
hidden
hiding
hijack
hiking
hinder
hinged
hipped
hippie
hiring
hither
Hitler
hitter
hiving
hoarse
hoaxer
hobble
hobnob
hoboes
hockey
hoeing
hogged
hogtie
holier
holing
hollow
homage
hombre
homely
homily
hominy
honest
honing
honkey
honkie
hooded
hoodoo
hoofed
hooked
hooker
hookey
hooped
hoopla
hooray
Hoover

hooves
hoping
hopped
hopper
hopper
Horace
horded
horned
hornet
horrid
horror
horsed
horses
horsey
hosing
hostel
hotted
hotter
hourly
housed
houses
howdah
howler
hoyden
hubbub
hubris
huddle
hugely
hugged
hugger
humane
humble
humbly
humbug
humeri
hummed
hummer
humped
hunger
hungry
hunter
hurdle
hurler
hurrah
hurray
hurtle
husker
hussar
hustle
hutzpa
huzzah
hyaena
hybrid
hymnal
hyphen
hyping

iambic
ibidem
iceman

icemen
icicle
iciest
ideate
idiocy
idlest
idling
ignite
ignore
iguana
imaged
imbibe
imbued
immune
immure
impact
impair
impala
impale
impart
impede
impend
import
impose
impugn
impure
impute
inborn
inbred
incest
incise
incite
income
incubi
indeed
indent
Indian
indict
indigo
indium
indoor
induce
induct
infamy
infant
infect
infest
infirm
inflow
influx
inform
infuse
ingest
Ingres
inhale
inhere
inject
injure
injury
inkier
inlaid

inland
inmate
inmost
innate
inning
Innuit
inpour
inroad
insane
inseam
insect
insert
inside
insist
in situ
insole
instal
instep
instil
insult
insure
intact
intake
intend
intent
intern
intomb
intone
intuit
inured
invade
invent
invert
invest
invite
invoke
inward
inwove
iodine
ionize
ipecac
irises
ironer
ironic
irrupt
Isaiah
island
isobar
Israel
issued
italic

jabbed
jabber
jackal
jacket
jading
jagged
jagged
jaguar

jailer
jalopy
jammed
jammer
jangle
jarful
jargon
jarred
jaunty
jawalk
jeerer
jejune
Jekyll
jerkin
jersey
jester
Jesuit
jetlag
jetsam
jetted
Jewish
jibbed
jigged
jiggle
jiggly
jigsaw
jilter
jingle
jitney
jitter
jiving
jobbed
jobber
jockey
jocose
jocund
jogged
jogger
joggle
joiner
jojoba
joking
Jordan
Joshua
jostle
jotted
jovial
Jovian
joyful
joyous
Judaic
judged
jugged
juggle
juicer
jujube
jumble
jumper
jungle
junior
Junker

junket
junkie
juries
jurist
justly
jutted

Kabuki
kaftan
kaiser
Kansas
kaolin
karate
kedged
keenly
keeper
kegler
kelpie
kelvin
kennel
Kenyan
kernel
ketone
kettle
khalif
kibosh
kidded
kiddie
kidnap
kidney
killer
kilter
kimono
kindle
kingly
kipper
kirsch
kismet
kiting
kitsch
kitten
klatch
Klaxon
knifed
knight
knives
knobby
knotty
knurly
kookie
kopeck
Korean
kosher
kowtow
kroner
kronor
kumiss
kümmel
kungfu
kurled

Kuwait

laager
labial
labile
labium
lacier
lacing
lackey
lactic
lacuna
ladder
laddie
la-di-da
ladies
lading
ladled
lagged
lagoon
Lahore
Lamaze
lament
laming
lammed
lanced
lancet
landau
landed
lapful
lapped
lappet
lapsed
larder
larger
lariat
larvae
larval
larynx
Lascar
lastly
lateen
lately
latent
latest
lather
Latino
latter
Latvia
launch
laurel
lavish
lawful
lawyer
laxity
laying
layman
laymen
layoff
layout
lazier

lazily
lazing
leaden
leader
lead-in
league
lean-to
leaped
learnt
leased
leaven
leaves
leaves
lecher
ledger
leeway
legacy
legate
legato
legend
legged
legion
legume
lender
length
lenity
Lenten
lentil
lesion
lessee
lessen
lesser
lesson
lessor
lethal
letter
Levant
levied
levies
levity
lewdly
liable
liaise
libido
Libyan
lichee
lichen
lidded
lieder
likely
liking
lilies
limber
liming
limner
limpet
limpid
limply
linage
linden
lineal

linear
lineup
linger
lining
linked
linker
linnet
lintel
liquid
liquor
Lisbon
lissom
listen
litany
litchi
litchi
litmus
litter
little
live-in
lively
livery
living
lizard
loaded
loafer
loathe
loaves
lobbed
locale
locate
locker
locket
lockup
locust
lodged
lodger
logged
logger
loggia
loggie
loiter
lollop
London
lonely
loofah
loosed
loosen
looser
looter
loping
lopped
lordly
lordly
lories
losing
lotion
lotted
louche
loudly
lounge

louver
lovely
loving
loving
lowboy
lubber
lugged
lugger
lumbar
lumber
lummox
lunacy
lunate
lunged
lupine
luring
lurker
Lusaka
luster
Luther
luxury
lyceum
lychee

macing
macron
madame
madden
madder
madman
madmen
madras
Madrid
maggot
magnet
magnum
magpie
Magyar
Mahler
mahout
maiden
mainly
make-up
making
malady
Malaga
malice
malign
mallet
mallow
mammal
mammon
manage
mañana
manege
manful
manger
mangle
maniac
manioc

manito	medley	minute
manitu	meekly	minute
manned	mellow	mirage
manned	melody	miring
manner	melted	mirror
manqué	member	miscue
mantel	memoir	misdid
mantis	memory	misery
mantle	menace	misfit
mantle	ménage	mishap
mantra	menial	mislay
manual	mensal	misled
manure	mensch	missal
Maoism	menses	missis
mapped	mental	missus
maquis	mentor	Mister
maraca	merely	misuse
maraud	merged	mitten
marble	merger	mixing
marcel	merino	mizzen
margin	merman	moaner
marina	mermen	mobbed
marine	Mersey	mobile
marked	mescal	mocker
marker	meteor	mock-up
market	method	modern
marlin	métier	modest
marmot	meting	modify
maroon	metric	modish
marred	mettle	module
marrow	Mexico	mohair
marshy	miasma	Mohawk
marten	micron	moiety
martin	midday	molder
martyr	middle	molest
marvel	midget	molten
mascot	midway	molter
masked	miffed	moment
masque	mighty	Monaco
massif	mikado	Monday
master	milady	monger
mating	mildew	Mongol
matins	mildly	monied
matrix	milieu	monies
matron	milker	monism
matted	miller	monkey
matter	millet	monody
mature	miming	moping
maxima	mimosa	mopped
mayfly	minced	moppet
mayhem	mincer	morale
mazing	minded	morass
meadow	minder	morbid
meager	mingle	morgue
meanly	minima	Mormon
measly	mining	morose
meddle	mining	morrow
medial	minion	morsel
median	minnow	mortal
medium	Minoan	mortar
medlar	minuet	mosaic

Moscow	mythic	nobler
Moslem		nobody
mosque		nodded
mostly	nabbed	noddle
mother	nagged	nodule
motile	nagger	noggin
motion	namely	noised
motive	naming	nonage
motley	napalm	noncom
mottle	napkin	noodle
mouser	Naples	Nordic
mousey	napped	normal
mousse	narrow	Norman
mouthy	Nassau	nosier
mouton	natant	nosily
moving	nation	nosing
mowing	native	notary
Mozart	natter	notice
mucous	nature	notify
mudded	naught	noting
muddle	nausea	notion
muffin	Navaho	nougat
muffle	Navajo	nought
Mugabe	navies	novena
mugged	Nazism	novice
mugger	nearby	nowise
mukluk	nearly	nozzle
mulish	neatly	nuance
mullah	nebula	nubbin
mullet	nectar	nubile
mumble	needle	nuclei
mummed	negate	nudged
mummer	nephew	nudism
Munich	nerved	nudist
murder	nestle	nudity
murmur	nether	nugget
muscat	netted	nuking
muscle	nettle	number
museum	neural	numbly
musing	neuron	nuncio
musket	neuter	nursed
Muslim	Nevada	nutmeg
muslin	newish	nuzzle
mussel	newton	
muster	niacin	
mutant	nibble	oafish
mutate	nicely	object
mutely	nicety	oblate
muting	nickel	oblige
mutiny	niggle	oblong
mutter	nimble	oboist
mutton	nimbly	obsess
mutual	nimbus	obtain
muumuu	nimrod	obtuse
muzzle	ninety	obvert
myopia	nipped	occult
myopic	nipper	occupy
myriad	nipple	ocelot
myrtle	Nippon	ochery
myself	nitric	o'clock
mystic	nitwit	octane

octave
octavo
ocular
oddity
Odessa
odious
odored
offend
office
offing
offset
ogling
ohmage
oilier
oilman
oilmen
Ojibwa
oldest
oldish
omelet
one-way
oniony
onward
oodles
oozing
opaque
opener
openly
opiate
opined
oppose
oppugn
optics
option
opuses
oracle
orally
orange
orated
orator
orchid
ordain
ordeal
ordure
Oregon
orgasm
orgies
orient
origin
oriole
orison
ormolu
ornate
ornery
orphan
osmium
osprey
ossify
otiose
ouster
outbid

outcry
outdid
outfit
outfox
outing
outlaw
outlay
outlet
output
outran
outrun
outset
outwit
overdo
overly
owlish
oxford
oxtail
oxygen
oyster

pacify
pacing
packer
packet
padded
paddle
paella
paging
pagoda
palace
palate
palely
paling
paling
palled
pallet
pallid
pallor
paltry
pampas
pamper
panama
pander
pandit
panned
pantie
pantry
panzer
papacy
papaya
papery
papyri
parade
parcel
pardon
parent
pariah
paring
parish

parity
parlay
parley
parlor
parody
parole
parrot
parsed
parson
parted
partly
passed
passim
pasted
pastel
pastor
pastry
patchy
patent
pathos
patina
patois
patrol
patron
patted
patter
paunch
pauper
paused
paving
Pavlov
Pawnee
pawpaw
paying
payoff
payola
peachy
peahen
peaked
peanut
pearly
pebble
pebbly
pectin
pedant
peddle
peeved
peewit
pegged
Peking
pelage
pellet
pelota
pelvic
pelvis
pencil
penned
pentup
penult
penury
peoage

people
peplum
pepped
pepper
pepsin
peptic
Pequot
period
perish
permit
person
pertly
peruke
peruse
peseta
pester
pestle
petard
petite
petrel
petrol
petted
pewter
peyote
phalli
phased
phlegm
phobia
phobic
phoebe
pholox
phoned
phonic
phooey
phrase
phylum
physic
piazza
pickax
picked
picker
picket
pickle
pickup
picnic
piddle
pieced
pierce
piffle
pigeon
pigged
piglet
pigsty
pilaff
pilfer
piling
pillar
pillow
pimple
pimply
pining

pinion
pinkie
pinned
Pinyin
piping
pipped
pippin
piqued
piracy
pirate
Pisces
pistil
pistol
piston
pitchy
pitied
pitman
pitted
pizazz
placed
placer
placid
plague
plaice
plaint
planed
planet
plaque
plasma
plated
platen
player
pleach
please
pledge
Pleiad
plenty
plexus
pliant
pliers
plight
plover
plower
plucky
plumed
plunge
plural
plushy
plying
pocket
podded
podium
poetic
poetry
pogrom
poised
poison
pokier
poking
Poland
polder

poleax
police
policy
poling
Polish
polish
polite
polity
pollee
pollen
poller
pomade
pomelo
pommel
Pompey
pom-pom
pompon
poncho
ponder
pongee
ponies
poodle
poorly
popery
popish
poplar
poplin
popped
popper
poring
porker
porous
portal
porter
portly
poseur
posies
posing
possum
postal
poster
potash
potato
poteen
potent
potion
potted
potter
pouchy
pouffe
pounce
powder
powwow
Prague
praise
prance
prated
prayer
preach
précis
prefer

prefix
prepay
preppy
presto
pretty
prewar
preyer
priced
pricey
prided
priest
primal
primal
primed
primer
primly
prince
priory
prison
prissy
privet
prized
probed
profit
prolix
prompt
pronto
propel
proper
pro tem
proton
Proust
proved
proven
pruned
prying
pseudo
psyche
psycho
public
pucker
puddle
pueblo
puffin
puking
pullet
pulley
pulpit
pulsar
pulsed
pumice
pummel
pumper
punchy
pundit
punier
punish
Punjab
punned
puppet
purdah

purely
purged
purify
purify
purism
purist
purity
purity
purple
pursed
purser
pursue
purvey
pusher
putrid
putsch
putted
puttee
putter
puzzle
pye-dog
python

quaint
quaked
Quaker
quanta
quarry
quarto
quartz
quasar
quaver
queasy
Quebec
quench
queued
quiche
quince
quinsy
quirky
quiver
quorum
quoted

rabbet
rabbis
rabbit
rabble
rabies
raceme
racial
racier
racily
racing
racism
racist
racket
racoon
radial

radish
radium
radius
raffia
raffle
rafter
ragbag
ragged
ragged
ragged
raging
raglan
ragout
ragtag
raider
raised
raisin
raking
rakish
rallie
ramble
ramify
rammed
ramrod
rancid
rancor
random
ranged
ranger
rankle
ransom
ranter
rapier
rapine
rapist
rapped
rapper
raptly
rarefy
rarely
rarest
raring
rarity
rascal
rasher
rashly
rather
ratify
rating
ration
ratios
rattan
ratted
ratter
rattle
ravage
ravine
raving
ravish
razing
reader

Reagan
really
realty
reamer
reaper
reason
rebate
reborn
rebuff
rebuke
recall
recant
recast
recede
recent
recess
recipe
recite
reckon
recoil
record
record
recoup
rectal
rector
rectum
redden
redder
redeem
redoes
redone
reduce
reecho
reefer
refill
refine
reflex
reform
refuge
refund
refuse
refuse
refute
regain
regale
regard
regent
reggae
regime
region
regret
rehash
reject
rejoin
relaid
relate
relent
relict
relied
relief
relish

relive
reload
remade
remain
remake
remand
remark
remedy
remind
remiss
remote
remove
rename
rended
render
renege
rennet
Renoir
renown
rental
reopen
repaid
repair
repast
repeal
repeat
repent
replay
report
repose
repute
rescue
reseat
resell
resent
reside
resign
resist
resold
resort
result
resume
resume
retail
retain
retake
retard
retell
retina
retire
retold
retook
retort
return
revamp
reveal
revere
revert
review
revile
revise

revive
revoke
revolt
revved
reward
rewind
rewire
rework
rhesus
rheumy
Rhodes
rhymed
rhythm
Rialto
ribald
riband
ribbed
ribbon
riches
richly
ridded
ridden
riddle
ridged
riding
riffle
rifled
rigged
rigger
riling
rimmed
ringed
ringer
rinsed
rioted
rioter
rip-off
ripped
ripper
ripple
rising
risque
ritual
Riyadh
robbed
robber
robing
robust
rocker
rocket
rococo
rodent
roller
Romany
Romish
romper
rookie
ropier
roping
rosary
rosier

roster	saliva	scummy
rostra	sallow	scurry
rotate	salmon	scurvy
rotted	saloon	scythe
rotten	salted	seaman
rotter	salute	seamen
rotund	salved	séance
rouble	salver	search
rouged	sampan	season
roused	sample	secant
routed	Samuel	secede
roving	sandal	second
rubbed	sander	secret
rubber	sanely	sector
rubble	sanity	secure
Rubens	sapped	sedate
rubies	sarong	seduce
rubric	sashay	seeing
ruched	sateen	seemly
ruckus	sating	seesaw
rudder	satiny	seethe
rudely	satire	seined
rueful	Saturn	seized
ruffle	saucer	seldom
rugged	savage	select
ruling	savant	seller
rumble	saving	selves
rumple	savior	Semite
rumpus	savory	senary
runnel	sawing	senate
runner	saying	sender
runway	scabby	senile
russet	scaled	senior
Russia	scampi	senora
rustic	scanty	senors
rustle	scarab	sensed
rutted	scarce	sensor
Rwanda	scared	sentry
	scarfs	sepsis
	scathe	septet
Sabine	scenic	septic
sachet	schema	sequel
sacred	scheme	sequin
sacrum	schism	serape
sadden	school	seraph
sadder	sconce	serene
saddle	scorch	serial
sadism	scored	series
sadist	scorer	sermon
safari	scotch	serous
safely	scrape	served
safest	scrawl	server
safety	scream	sesame
sagely	screen	settee
sagged	screwy	setter
Sahara	scribe	settle
sailor	script	Seurat
salaam	scroll	severe
salami	scrota	sewage
salary	scruff	sewing
saline	sculpt	sexier

sexism	shucks	slaver
sexist	shying	Slavic
sextet	Sicily	sleazy
sexton	sicken	sledge
sexual	sickle	sleepy
shabby	sickly	sleety
shaded	siding	sleeve
shadow	sidled	sleigh
shaggy	sienna	sleuth
shaken	sierra	sliced
shaker	siesta	slight
shaman	sieved	slinky
shamed	sifter	slippy
shamus	signal	sliver
shandy	signet	slogan
shanty	Signor	sloped
shaped	silage	sloppy
shaper	silent	sloshy
shared	silica	slouch
sharer	silken	slough
shaved	siloed	Slovak
shaven	silver	sloven
shaver	simian	slowly
sheath	simile	sludge
sheeny	simmer	sludgy
sheikh	simper	sluice
shelly	simple	slummy
shelve	simply	slurry
Sherpa	sinewy	slushy
sherry	sinful	smarmy
shield	singed	smeary
shifty	singer	smelly
Shiite	single	smiled
shiksa	singly	smirch
shikse	sinker	smithy
shimmy	sinned	smoggy
shined	sinner	smoked
shiner	sinner	smoker
Shinto	Siouan	smooch
shiver	siphon	smooth
shlock	sipped	smudge
shoddy	siring	smudgy
shored	Sirius	smugly
should	sister	smutty
shoved	sitcom	Smyrna
shovel	siting	snaggy
showed	sitter	snaked
shower	sizing	snappy
shrank	sizzle	snared
shrewd	skated	snarly
shriek	skater	snatch
shrift	sketch	snazzy
shrike	skewer	sneaky
shrill	skiing	sneeze
shrimp	skimpy	sneezy
shrine	skinny	sniffy
shrink	slaked	sniped
shrive	slalom	sniper
shroud	slangy	snippy
shrove	slated	snitch
shrunk	slaved	snivel

snobby	spiced	stated
snoopy	spider	static
snooty	spiffy	stator
snooze	spigot	statue
snored	spiked	status
snotty	spinal	staved
snuffy	spinet	stayed
snugly	spiral	steady
sobbed	spired	steamy
soccer	spirit	steely
social	splash	stench
socket	spleen	steppe
sodded	splice	stereo
sodden	spoilt	sterna
sodium	spoken	sticky
sodomy	sponge	stifle
soften	spongy	stigma
softie	spooky	stingy
softly	sporty	stinky
soigné	spotty	stitch
soirée	spouse	stocky
solace	sprain	stodge
solder	sprang	stodgy
solely	sprawl	stoked
solemn	spread	stolen
soling	spring	stolid
soloed	sprint	stoned
solute	sprout	stooge
solved	spruce	stored
Somali	sprung	stormy
somber	spumed	stoved
sonant	spunky	strafe
sonata	sputum	strain
sonnet	spying	strait
soothe	squall	strata
sopped	square	streak
sorbet	squash	stream
sordid	squawk	street
sorely	squeak	stress
sorest	squeal	strewn
sorrel	squint	striae
sorrow	squire	strict
sortie	squirm	stride
sotted	squirt	strife
sought	squish	strike
source	stable	string
sourly	stadia	stripe
soused	staged	stripy
soviet	staked	strive
sowing	stalag	strobe
spaced	Stalin	strode
spaded	stalky	stroke
spared	stamen	stroll
sparse	stance	strong
spavin	stanza	strove
specie	staple	struck
speech	starch	strung
speedy	stared	stubby
spewer	starry	stucco
sphere	starve	studio
sphinx	stasis	stuffy

stumpy	swerve	taster
stupid	swiped	tatted
stupor	swirly	tattle
sturdy	swishy	tattoo
styled	switch	taught
stylus	swivel	taught
stymie	Sydney	Taurus
subbed	sylvan	tauten
subdue	symbol	tautly
sublet	syntax	tavern
submit	syphon	tawdry
suborn	syrupy	teased
subtle	system	teasel
subtly		teaser
suburb		Te Deum
subway	tabard	tedium
succor	tabbed	teeing
sucker	tabled	teepee
suckle	tablet	teeter
sudden	tacked	teethe
suffer	tackle	Tehran
suffix	tagged	teller
sugary	Tahiti	temper
suitor	tailed	temple
sulfur	tailor	tenant
sullen	Taiwan	tender
sultan	taking	tendon
sultry	talcum	tennis
summed	talent	tensed
summer	talker	tenure
summit	talkie	terror
summon	tallow	terser
sundae	Talmud	testes
Sunday	tamale	testis
sunder	tamely	tetchy
sundry	taming	tether
sunken	tamper	Teuton
sunned	tampon	Thames
suntan	tandem	thatch
superb	tangle	theirs
supine	tanker	theism
supped	tanned	theist
supper	tannic	thence
supple	tannin	theory
supply	Taoism	theses
surely	Taoist	thesis
surest	taping	thieve
surety	tapped	thinly
surfer	tappet	thirst
surged	target	thirty
surrey	tariff	thorax
surtax	Tarmac	thorny
survey	tarpon	though
suttee	tarred	thrall
suture	tartan	thrash
svelte	Tartar	thread
swampy	tartar	threat
swanky	tartly	thresh
swathe	Tarzan	thrice
sweaty	tassel	thrift
Sweden	tasted	thrill

thrive	tomato	troupe
throat	tomboy	trowel
throne	tomcat	truant
throng	tomtit	trudge
throve	tom-tom	truest
thrown	tongue	truism
thrush	tonsil	trusty
thrust	toothy	trying
thwack	toping	tubing
thwart	topped	tubule
thymus	topper	tufted
ticker	topple	tugged
ticket	torero	tumble
tickle	torpid	tumult
tidbit	torpor	tundra
tidied	torque	tuning
tidier	torrid	tunnel
tidily	torten	turban
tiling	toting	turbid
tiller	totted	turbot
tilted	totter	tureen
timbal	toucan	turgid
timber	touché	turkey
timbre	touchy	Turkey
timely	toupee	turnip
timing	tousle	turret
tinder	touter	turtle
tinged	towage	turves
tingle	toward	tusked
tingly	toxoid	tussle
tinier	traced	tuxedo
tinker	tracer	twangy
tinkle	traded	tweedy
tinned	trader	tweeze
tinsel	tragic	twelve
tinter	trance	twenty
tipped	trashy	twiggy
tippet	trauma	twilit
tipple	travel	twined
tiptoe	treaty	twinge
tiptop	treble	twirly
tirade	trebly	twisty
tiring	tremor	twitch
tissue	trench	two-ply
titbit	trendy	tycoon
tithed	trepan	typhus
titian	tribal	typify
titled	tricky	typing
titter	trifle	typist
Tivoli	trimly	tyrant
Tobago	triple	
tocsin	triply	
toddle	tripod	Uganda
toeing	trivet	uglier
toffee	trivia	uglily
togged	troche	ulster
toggle	troika	ultimo
toiler	Trojan	umlaut
toilet	trophy	umpire
toling	tropic	unable
tolled	trough	unbend

unbent
unbind
unbolt
unborn
unbred
unclad
uncoil
uncork
undoes
undone
unduly
unease
uneasy
uneven
unfair
unfold
unfurl
unholy
unhook
unhurt
unique
unisex
unison
united
unjust
unkind
unless
unlike
unload
unlock
unmade
unmake
unmask
unpack
unpaid
unpick
unplug
unread
unreal
unrest
unroll
unruly
unsafe
unsaid
unseal
unseat
unseen
unshod
unsnap
unsold
unstop
unsung
unsure
untidy
untied
untold
untrue
unused
unveil
unwary
unwell

unwind
unwise
unwrap
upbeat
update
upheld
uphill
uphold
upkeep
upland
upmost
upping
uppish
uppity
uprear
uproar
uproot
upshot
uptake
uptown
upturn
upward
Uranus
urbane
urchin
uremia
ureter
urgent
urging
urinal
usable
useful
usurer
uterus
utmost
Utopia

vacant
vacate
vacuum
vagary
vagina
vainly
valise
Valium
valley
valued
valuer
vandal
vanish
vanity
varied
varied
vassal
vastly
vatted
vector
veiled
Velcro
vellum

velour
velvet
vender
vendor
veneer
venial
venous
vented
verbal
verged
verger
verify
verily
verity
vermin
vernal
versed
versus
vertex
vessel
vestal
vested
vestry
vetoed
vetoer
vetoes
vetted
vexing
viable
viably
victim
victor
vicuna
viewer
Viking
vilely
vilest
vilify
vinery
vinous
violet
violin
virago
virgin
virile
virtue
visage
viscid
Vishnu
vision
visual
vitals
vivify
vizier
voiced
volley
volume
volute
voodoo
vortex
votary

voting
votive
voyage
voyeur
vulgar

wabble
wadded
waddle
waddly
wading
waffle
wagged
waggle
waging
Wagner
wahine
waiter
waived
waiver
waking
waling
walker
walk-up
wallet
wallop
wallow
walnut
walrus
wampum
wander
wangle
waning
wanner
wanton
warble
warden
warder
warier
warily
warmer
warmly
warmth
warred
warren
Warsaw
washer
wasted
waster
watery
wattle
wavier
wavily
waving
waxier
waxing
waylay
way-out
weaken
weakly

weapon
weasel
weaved
weaver
webbed
wedded
wedged
weekly
weevil
weight
weirdo
welder
welter
wetted
wetter
whacky
whaled
whaler
wheeze
wheezy
whence
wherry
whiled
whimsy
whined
whinny
whisky
whited
whiten
whiter
wholly
whoosh
wicked
wicker
wicket
widely
widest
wieldy
wiener
wifely
wigged
wiggle
wiggly
wigwag
wigwam
wildly
wilful
wilier
wilily
willed
willow
wimple
winded
window
windup
winery
winged
wining
winkle
winner
winnow

winter
wintry
wiping
wirier
wiring
wisdom
wisely
wisest
wising
withal
wither
within
wizard
wobble
wobbly
woeful
wolves
wombat
wonder
wonted
wonton
wooded
wooden
woodsy
woofer
woolen
woolly
worker
worsen
worthy
wraith
wreath
wrench
wretch
wriest
wright
writer
writhe

Xanadu
Xerxes
xyloid

yammer
Yankee
yanqui
yapped
yarrow
yasmak
yearly
yeasty
yellow
Yemeni
yenned
yeoman
yeomen
yes-man
yes-men
yipped

yippee	zanier	zinnia
yogurt	zanies	zipped
yoking	zanily	zipper
yonder	zapped	zircon
Yoruba	zealot	zither
yuppie	zenith	zodiac
	zephyr	zombie
	zeroes	zoning
	zigzag	zonked
Zambia	zinced	zygote

abalone	acutely	airship
abandon	adamant	airsick
abashed	adapter	airwave
abasing	adaptor	à la King
abating	addenda	à la mode
abaxial	address	Alaskan
abdomen	adenoid	albinos
abeting	adeptly	albumen
abetted	adhered	albumin
abetter	adipose	alchemy
abettor	adjourn	alcohol
abeyant	adjudge	alfalfa
abiding	adjunct	algebra
ability	adjured	Algeria
abjured	admiral	Algiers
ablated	admired	aliases
abolish	admirer	aliment
aborted	adopter	alimony
abraded	adoring	aliquot
Abraham	adrenal	allayed
abreast	adulate	alleged
abridge	advance	allegro
abscess	adverse	allergy
abscond	advised	all-over
absence	adviser	all-star
absinth	aeonian	all-time
absolve	aerated	alluded
abstain	aerator	allured
abusing	aerobic	alluvia
abusive	aerosol	allying
abutted	affable	almanac
abysmal	affably	already
academy	afflict	alright
Acadian	affront	also-ran
acanthi	African	altered
acceded	against	alumina
acclaim	ageless	alumnae
account	agenged	alumnus
accrual	aggress	alyssum
accrued	agilely	amalgam
accurst	agility	amateur
accused	agitate	amatory
accuser	agonies	amazing
acerbic	agonize	ambient
acetate	aground	ambling
acetify	aileron	amenity
acetone	ailling	America
achieve	ailment	amiable
acidify	aimless	amiably
acidity	aircrew	ammeter
acolyte	airdrop	ammonia
aconite	airfoil	amnesia
acquire	airhead	amnesic
acreage	airiest	amnesty
Acrilan	airiier	amoebae
acrobat	airless	amoebas
acronym	airlift	amoebic
acrylic	airline	amongst
actress	airmail	amorous
actuary	airplay	amphora
actuate	airport	amplify

ampoule
amputee
amusing
anagram
analogy
analyst
analyze
anapest
anarchy
anatomy
anchovy
ancient
andante
andiron
android
anemone
aneroid
angelic
angling
angrily
anguish
angular
aniline
animate
animism
aniseed
annelid
annuity
annular
anodize
anodyne
anomaly
another
antacid
antenna
anthill
anthrax
antigen
antilog
antique
antonym
Antwerp
anxiety
anxious
anybody
anymore
anywise
aphasia
aphides
aplenty
apocope
apology
apostle
apparel
appease
applaud
applied
appoint
apposed
apprise
approve

apricot
a priori
apropos
aptness
aquaria
aquatic
aqueous
Arabian
Aramaic
Arapaho
arbiter
arbutus
archaic
archery
archive
archway
arcuate
arduous
arguing
aridity
arising
armhole
armoire
armored
arousal
aroused
arraign
arrange
arrayal
arrival
arrived
arsenal
arsenic
article
artisan
artiste
artless
artwork
ascetic
ascribe
asepsis
aseptic
asexual
ashamed
ashiest
ashtray
Asiatic
asinine
askance
asocial
asperse
asphalt
aspirin
assault
assayer
assegai
assuage
assumed
assured
astound
astride

asunder
atavism
atelier
atheism
atheist
athirst
athlete
athwart
atlases
atomism
atomize
atoning
atrophy
attaché
attaint
attempt
attired
attract
attuned
auction
audible
audibly
auditor
augment
augured
aurally
aureate
aureole
auricle
aurorae
auspice
austere
Austria
autopsy
avarice
avenger
average
averred
aviator
avidity
avocado
awaking
awesome
awfully
awkward
azimuth

babbitt
babbled
babying
babyish
baby-sat
babysit
bacilli
backing
backlog
badland
badness
baffled
baggage

baggier
bagging
bagging
Baghdad
bagpipe
Bahamas
bailiff
balance
balcony
balding
baleful
ballast
ballboy
balloon
balmier
baloney
bambino
bandage
Band-Aid
bandana
bandbox
bandied
baneful
Bangkok
banking
banning
banquet
banshee
baptism
Baptist
baptize
barbell
bargain
barging
barmaid
baronet
baroque
barrack
barrage
barrier
barring
barroom
barytes
basally
baseman
basemen
bashful
bassoon
bastard
basting
bathing
bathtub
batiste
battery
battier
batting
battled
Bauhaus
bauxite
Bavaria
bawdier

bawdily
bayonet
bazooka
beadier
beading
beanbag
bearded
bearing
bearish
beastly
beatify
beating
beatnik
because
becloud
bedding
be-devil
bedouin
bedpost
bedrock
bedroll
bedroom
bedside
bedsore
bedtime
beefier
beehive
beeline
beeswax
begging
begonia
begrime
beguile
beguine
behaved
behoove
behoved
Beijing
belabor
belated
belayed
Belfast
Belgian
Belgium
believe
bellboy
bellhop
bellied
bellies
bellows
beloved
beltway
belying
bemired
bemused
bending
beneath
benefit
Bengali
benzene
benzine

bequest
berated
bereave
Bermuda
berries
berserk
beseech
besides
besiege
besmear
bespeak
bespoke
bestial
betaken
betided
betoken
betroth
betting
between
betwixt
beveled
bewitch
bezique
biasing
biaxial
bibelot
bicycle
bidding
bifocal
biggest
biggish
bigoted
bigotry
bilious
billing
billion
billowy
bindery
binding
biology
bionics
biplane
bipolar
biretta
biscuit
bismuth
bittern
bittier
bitumen
bivalve
bivouac
bizarre
blabbed
blabber
blacken
blackly
bladder
blaming
blandly
blanket
blankly

blaring
blarney
blasted
blatant
blazing
bleakly
blemish
blender
blessed
blessed
blinder
blindly
blinker
blister
bloated
blooper
blossom
blotchy
blotted
blotter
blouson
blow-dry
blowfly
blowier
blowing
blubber
blunder
bluntly
blurred
blushed
blusher
bluster
boarder
boating
boatman
boatmen
bobbing
bobbled
bobsled
boggled
bogyman
bogymen
Bolivia
bollard
bologna
boloney
bolster
bombard
bombast
bonanza
bondage
bondman
bondmen
bonfire
bonuses
bookend
bookish
booklet
boorish
booster
bootleg

boozier
boredom
borough
borscht
botanic
bottled
boudoir
boulder
bounced
bouncer
bouquet
bourbon
bowknot
bowlful
bowline
bowling
boycott
boyhood
bracing
bracken
bracket
bradded
brading
bragged
Brahman
Brahmin
braille
braised
braking
bramble
brambly
brander
bravado
bravely
bravery
braving
bravura
brawler
brazier
breaded
breadth
breaker
break-up
breathe
breathy
breeder
brevity
brewery
bribery
bribing
bridled
briefly
brigade
brigand
brimful
brimmed
brioche
briquet
brisket
briskly
bristle

bristly
Britain
British
brittle
broaden
broadly
brocade
broiler
bromide
bronchi
bronzed
brothel
brother
brought
brownie
browsed
bruised
bruiser
brusque
brutish
bubbled
bubonic
buckram
bucolic
buddies
budding
buffalo
buffoon
bugbear
buggery
buggies
bugging
bugling
builder
bulbous
bulgier
bulging
bulkier
bulkier
bulldog
bullied
bullies
bullion
bullock
bulrush
bulwark
bumming
bumpier
bumpkin
bundled
bungled
bungler
bunnies
bunting
buoyant
burbled
bureaus
bureaux
burgeon
burgess
burgher

burglar
burgled
burlier
Burmese
burning
burnish
burnous
burring
bursary
burying
busbies
Bushido
bushier
bushing
bushman
bushmen
bustard
bustled
busying
butcher
buttery
buttock
buzzard

cabaret
cabbage
cabinet
cabling
caboose
caching
cackled
cadaver
caddied
caddies
caddish
cadence
cadenza
cadging
cadmium
caesura
cagiest
caisson
caitiff
cajoled
calcify
calcium
calculi
caldron
calends
caliber
caliper
calling
callous
caloric
calorie
calumny
Calvary
calving
calyces
calypso

camphor
canasta
candela
candied
candied
candies
candled
cannery
cannily
canning
cantata
canteen
canvass
capable
capably
capital
capping
caprice
capsize
capstan
capsule
captain
caption
captive
capture
caracul
caramel
caravan
caraway
carbide
carbine
carcass
cardiac
careful
caribou
carmine
carnage
caroled
carotid
carouse
carport
carried
carrier
carrion
carroty
carsick
cartage
cartoon
carving
cascade
cascara
caseous
cashier
Caspian
cassaba
cassava
cassock
casting
casting
casuist
catalog

catarrh
Catawba
catcall
catcher
catchup
caterer
catfish
cathode
catmint
cat's-eye
cattery
cattier
catwalk
causing
caustic
cautery
caution
cavalry
caveman
cavemen
caviare
caviled
cayenne
ceasing
cedilla
ceiling
cellist
Celsius
censure
centaur
central
century
ceramic
certain
certify
cesspit
cesurae
Chablis
chafing
chagrin
chalice
chamber
chamois
chanced
changed
channel
chantey
Chanuka
chaotic
chapeau
chapped
chapter
charade
charged
charger
charier
chariot
charity
charmer
charred
charter

chasing	citadel	codicil
chassis	citizen	coequal
chasten	civilly	coerced
château	clamber	coexist
chatted	clammed	cogency
chattel	clamper	cognate
chatter	clangor	cohabit
cheapen	clapped	cohered
cheaply	clapper	coinage
cheater	clarify	coition
cheddar	clarion	colicky
cheetah	clarity	colitis
chemise	classic	collage
chemist	clatter	collate
cherish	clausal	collect
cheroot	cleaner	colleen
cherubs	cleanly	college
chevron	cleanse	collide
chewier	clearly	colloid
Chianti	cleaved	collude
chicane	cleaver	cologne
Chicano	clement	colonel
chicken	climate	colored
chicory	climber	coltish
chiding	clinker	combine
chiefly	clipped	comfort
chiffon	clipper	comical
chigger	cloacae	command
chignon	clobber	commend
chimera	clogged	comment
chiming	cloning	commode
chimney	closely	commons
Chinese	closest	commune
chinned	close-up	commute
Chinook	closing	compact
chintzy	closure	company
chinwag	clothed	compare
chipped	clotted	compass
chipper	cloture	compeer
chivied	clouded	compete
chmaera	clubbed	compile
Choctaw	cluster	complex
choking	clutter	comport
cholera	coarsen	compose
chopped	coastal	compost
chopper	coaster	compote
chorale	coating	compute
chorale	coaxial	comrade
chortle	cobbler	concave
chowder	cocaine	conceal
chronic	cockade	concede
chuckle	cockeye	conceit
churish	cockier	concept
chutney	cockily	concern
chutzpa	cockney	concert
ciliary	cockpit	concise
circled	coconut	concoct
circlet	coddled	concord
circuit	codeine	concuss
cissoid	codfish	condemn
cistern	codices	condign

condole	cornice	crewmen
condone	cornier	cribbed
conduce	corolla	cricket
conduct	coroner	crimson
conduit	coronet	cringed
confess	corpora	crinkle
confide	correct	crinkly
confine	corrode	cripple
confirm	corrupt	crisply
conflux	corsage	crochet
conform	corsair	cronies
confuse	Corsica	crooked
confute	cortege	crooner
congeal	cossack	cropped
congest	costive	croquet
conical	costume	crossly
conifer	coterie	crouton
conjoin	cottage	crowbar
conjure	cottony	crucial
connect	council	crucify
conning	counsel	crudely
connive	counter	crudest
connote	country	crudity
conquer	coupler	cruelly
consent	couplet	cruelty
consign	courage	cruised
consist	courier	cruiser
console	coursed	cruller
consort	courser	crumble
consult	courtly	crumbly
consume	couture	crumpet
contact	covered	crumple
contain	coverup	crunchy
contend	cowhand	crusade
content	cowslip	crusher
contest	coxcomb	cryptic
context	coyness	crystal
contort	cozener	cubical
contour	crabbed	cubicle
control	cracker	cuckold
contuse	crackle	cuddled
convene	crack-up	cuisine
convent	cradled	culprit
convert	cragged	cultist
convict	crammed	culture
convoke	crampon	culvert
cookery	craning	cumulus
cooking	cranium	cunning
coolant	crassly	cupping
coolish	crating	curable
copilot	craving	curaçao
copious	crazier	curator
coppery	crazing	curbing
coppice	creased	curdled
copying	created	curiosa
coracle	creator	curious
cordage	creeper	curlier
cordial	cremate	curling
cordite	crested	currant
corncob	crevice	current
corneal	crewman	curried

currish
cursing
cursive
cursory
curtail
curtain
curving
cushier
cushion
custard
custody
cutback
cuticle
cutlass
cutlery
cut-rate
cutting
cyanide
cycling
cyclone
cynical
cypress

dabbing
dabbled
dabbler
daddies
dailies
dairies
daisies
dallied
damaged
damming
dancing
dandies
dandify
dandled
dangled
dappled
darkish
darling
dashing
dastard
datable
dauphin
dawdled
dawdler
dawning
daytime
dazedly
dazzled
deadend
dead-eye
deadpan
dealing
deanery
deathly
debacle
debased
debated

debater
debauch
debited
debrief
Debussy
decagon
decapod
decease
deceive
decency
decibel
decided
decimal
declaim
declare
decline
decoded
decoder
decorum
decreed
decrial
decried
defaced
de facto
defamed
default
defense
defiant
deficit
defiled
defined
deflate
deflect
defraud
defrock
defrost
defunct
defused
defying
degauss
degrade
deicing
deified
deistic
deities
deleted
delight
delimit
deliver
delouse
deltoid
deluded
deluged
delving
demerit
Demerol
demesne
demigod
demised
demonic
demoted

demotic
denizen
Denmark
densely
density
dentine
denture
denuded
denying
deplete
deplore
deposed
deposit
deprave
depress
deprive
deputed
deraign
derange
derbies
derived
derrick
dervish
descant
descend
descent
deserve
desired
despair
despise
despite
despoil
despond
dessert
destine
destiny
destroy
détente
detract
devalue
develop
deviant
deviate
deviled
devilry
devious
devisal
devised
devisee
devisor
devolve
devoted
devotee
dewiest
diagram
dialect
dialing
diamond
diaries
diarist
diciest

dictate
diction
diehard
dietary
diffuse
digging
digital
dignify
dignity
digress
dilated
dilemma
diluted
dimming
dimness
dinette
dinning
diocese
diorama
dioxide
diploma
dipping
diptych
dirtied
dirtily
disable
disavow
disband
discard
discern
discoid
discord
discuss
disdain
disease
disgust
dishier
disjoin
dislike
dismiss
disobey
display
disport
dispose
dispute
disrobe
disrupt
dissect
dissent
distaff
distant
distend
distill
distort
disturb
disused
dittany
diurnal
diverge
diverse
divided

divider
divisor
divorce
divulge
divvied
dizzied
dizzily
doddery
dodging
dogging
doggone
doilies
doleful
dollies
dolphin
doltish
donated
donator
Don Juan
donning
doorman
doormen
dormant
dormice
dossier
dotting
doubled
doublet
douched
doughty
dousing
dowager
dowdily
doweled
dowries
dowsing
doyenne
dozenth
drachma
draftee
dragged
dragnet
dragoon
drapery
draping
drastic
draught
drawing
dreamed
dreamer
dredged
dredger
Dresden
dressed
dresser
dribble
driblet
drifter
drinker
dripped
driving

drizzle
drizzly
droning
droplet
dropped
dropper
drought
drowned
drubbed
drugged
drummed
drummer
drunken
dryades
dryness
dualism
duality
dubbing
dubiety
dubious
duchess
ductile
dudgeon
dueling
duelist
dukedom
dullard
dummies
dumpier
dungeon
dunnage
dunning
durable
durance
dustier
duteous
dutiful
dwelled
dwindle
dynamic
dynasty

eagerly
earache
eardrum
earldom
earlier
earlobe
earmark
earnest
earring
earshot
earthen
earthly
easiest
eastern
eatable
echelon
echidna
echoing

eclipse
eclogue
ecology
economy
ecstasy
ectopic
Ecuador
eddying
edgiest
edifice
edified
edition
educate
educing
effaced
effendi
effused
egotism
egotist
ejector
elapsed
elastic
elating
elation
elderly
elector
elegant
elegiac
elegies
elegize
element
elevate
eliding
elision
elitism
elitist
ellipse
eloping
eluding
elusion
elusive
elusory
Elysium
emanate
embargo
embassy
embolus
embrace
embroil
embryos
emerald
emerged
eminent
emirate
emitted
emoting
emotion
emotive
empanel
empathy
emperor

emplane
emporia
empower
empress
emptied
empties
emulate
emulous
enabled
encased
enchant
enclave
enclose
encoded
encomia
encored
encrust
endemic
endless
endorse
enduing
enemies
enforce
engaged
England
English
engorge
engrave
engross
enhance
enlarge
enliven
en masse
ennoble
enplane
enquire
enquiry
enraged
en route
enslave
ensnare
ensuing
en suite
ensured
entente
enteric
enthral
enthuse
enticed
entitle
entozoa
entrain
entrant
entreat
entries
entropy
entrust
entwine
envelop
envious
envious

environ
envying
epaulet
epergne
epicure
epigram
episode
epistle
epitaph
epithet
epitome
epochal
epsilon
equable
equably
equaled
equally
equated
equator
equerry
equinox
erasing
erasure
erectly
erector
eremite
eroding
erosion
erosive
erotica
erratic
erratum
erudite
escaped
escapee
escheat
esparto
espouse
espying
esquire
essence
esthete
Estonia
estuary
etching
eternal
ethanol
ethical
eugenic
euphony
evacuee
evading
evasion
evasive
evening
evictor
evident
evinced
evoking
evolved
exactly

exalted	fallacy	feudist
examine	falling	fiancée
example	fallout	fibbing
excerpt	falsely	fibered
excised	falsify	fibroid
excited	falsity	fibrous
exclaim	fanatic	fibulae
exclude	fancied	fiction
excreta	fancier	fiddled
excrete	fancies	fiddler
excused	fancily	fidgety
execute	fanfare	fielder
exhaled	fanning	fierier
exhaust	fantail	fierily
exhibit	fantasy	fifteen
exhumed	faraday	fifties
exigent	faraway	fighter
exiling	farcing	figment
exogamy	farming	figured
exotica	farrago	fillies
expanse	farrier	filling
expense	farther	filmier
expiate	fascism	finagle
expired	fascist	finally
explain	fashion	finance
explode	fatally	finding
exploit	fateful	fineess
explore	fatigue	finesse
exposed	fatless	finical
exposer	fatness	finicky
expound	fattest	Finland
express	fattier	finless
expunge	fatties	finning
extinct	fatting	Finnish
extract	fatuity	Finnish
extreme	fatuous	firearm
extrude	faux pas	firefly
exuding	favored	fireman
exurbia	fearful	firemen
eyeball	feather	firstly
eyebrow	feature	fishery
eyesore	febrile	fishier
eyewash	federal	fishing
Ezekiel	feebler	fission
	feeding	fissure
	feeling	fistful
faceted	feigned	fitness
faction	feigner	fittest
factory	femoral	fitting
factual	fencing	fitting
faculty	ferment	fixable
faddier	fermium	fixated
faddist	ferried	fixedly
fagging	ferries	fixings
faggoty	ferrous	fixture
faience	ferrule	fizzier
failing	fertile	fizzled
failure	fervent	flaccid
faintly	festive	flagged
fairies	festoon	flakier
fairway	fetlock	flaking

flaming
flanker
flannel
flapped
flapper
flare-up
flaring
flatted
flatten
flatter
flatter
flaunty
fleabag
fledged
fleeced
fleeing
fleetly
Flemish
fleshly
flexure
flicker
flighty
flipped
flipper
flitted
flitter
floater
flocked
flogged
flogger
flopped
flopper
Florida
florist
flotsam
flounce
flouter
flowery
flubbed
fluency
flummox
flunkey
fluster
fluting
flutist
flutter
fluxion
flyleaf
foamier
fobbing
focally
focused
focuses
foggier
foggily
fogging
fogyish
foliage
foliate
follies
fondant

fondled
foolery
foolish
footage
footman
footmen
foppery
foppish
foraged
forbade
forbear
forbore
forceps
forcing
forearm
foreign
foreleg
foreman
foremen
foresaw
foresee
forever
forfeit
forgave
forgery
forging
forgive
forgone
forlorn
Formica
formula
forsake
forsook
forties
fortify
fortune
forward
forwent
foulard
founder
foundry
foxiest
fox-trot
fragile
frailty
framing
frankly
frantic
fraught
frazzle
freckle
freckly
freebie
freedom
freeman
freemen
freesia
freeway
freezer
freight
freshen

freshet
freshly
fretful
fretsaw
fretted
friable
frigate
fringed
Frisbee
Frisian
frisson
fritter
frizzle
frogged
frogman
frogmen
frontal
frosted
froward
fuchsia
fuddled
fudging
fueling
fuelled
fulcrum
fulfill
fulsome
fumbled
fumbler
funeral
fungoid
funkier
funnier
funnies
funnily
furbish
furious
furlong
furnace
furnish
furrier
furring
further
furtive
fusible
fussier
fussily
fusspot
fustian
fustier
fuzzier
fuzzily

gabbing
gabbled
gabling
gadding
gagging
gainful
gainsay

gallant	gesture	Goliath
galleon	getting	gondola
gallery	ghastly	goodbye
galling	gherkin	goodish
gallium	ghostly	goofier
gallows	gibbous	gooiest
gambled	giblets	goosing
gambler	giddier	gorging
ganglia	giddily	goriest
gantlet	giggled	gorilla
gapping	gimmick	goshawk
garaged	gingery	gosling
garbage	gingham	gossipy
garbled	ginseng	gouache
gargled	gipsies	gouging
garland	giraffe	goulash
garment	girdled	gourmet
garnish	girlish	grabbed
garotte	gizzard	grabber
garrote	glacial	gracing
gaseous	glacier	grackle
gassier	gladden	grading
gassing	gladder	gradual
gastric	glamour	grafter
gaudier	glanced	grammar
gaudily	glaring	grampus
gauging	Glasgow	granary
Gauguin	glazier	grandee
gavotte	glazing	grandly
gawkier	gleaner	grandma
gawkily	gleeful	grandpa
gayness	gliding	granite
gazelle	glimmer	grannie
gazette	glimpse	granola
gearbox	glisten	granule
geckoes	glitter	graphic
gelatin	gloater	grapnel
gelding	globule	grapple
gelling	gloried	gratify
gemming	glories	grating
general	glorify	grating
generic	glottal	gravely
geneses	glottis	gravest
genesis	glowing	gravies
Genesis	glucose	graving
genetic	glueing	gravity
genital	glummer	grayish
Genoese	glutted	grazing
genteel	glutton	greased
gentian	gnarled	greatly
gentile	gnawing	Grecian
gentler	Gnostic	gremlin
genuine	go-ahead	Grenada
geodesy	gobbled	grenade
geology	gobbler	griddle
Georgia	goddamn	grieved
germane	goddess	griffin
Germany	godhead	griffon
gestalt	godless	grimace
gestapo	godsend	grimmer
gestate	goggled	grinder

grinned	habitat	haulage
griping	habitue	haunted
gripped	hackled	hauteur
gristle	hackney	have-not
gristly	hacksaw	hawkish
gritted	haddock	haziest
grizzle	hafnium	headier
grizzly	haggard	headily
grocery	haggled	heading
grogram	haggler	headman
grommet	hairier	headmen
grooved	Haitian	healthy
groover	halcyon	hearing
groping	halibut	hearken
grossly	halloes	hearsay
grouchy	halogen	hearten
groupie	halting	heathen
groused	halving	heather
growing	halyard	heavier
growler	Hamburg	heavily
grown-up	hamming	heaving
grubbed	hammock	Hebraic
grudged	hamster	Hebraic
gruffly	handbag	heckled
grumble	handful	heckler
grunted	handier	hectare
Gruyère	handily	hedging
gryphon	handled	heedful
guarded	hands-on	heftier
gudgeon	hanging	heinous
Guevara	hangman	heiress
guiding	hangmen	helical
Guignol	Hanover	helixes
guilder	hapless	hellion
gullies	happier	hellish
gumboil	happily	helpful
gumdrop	hardier	helping
gummier	hardily	hemlock
gumming	harelip	hemming
gumshoe	haricot	heretic
gunboat	harmful	hernial
gunfire	harmony	heroine
gunnery	harness	heroism
gunning	harpies	herring
gunshot	harpist	herself
gunwale	harpoon	hessian
guppies	harried	hexagon
gurgled	harrier	hibachi
gurnard	harshly	hickory
gushier	harvest	hideous
gushing	has-been	highway
gustier	hashish	hillier
gustily	Hasidic	hillock
gutless	Hasidim	himself
gutting	hassled	hinging
guzzled	hassock	hirsute
gymnast	hastier	history
gypping	hastily	hitting
gypsies	hatchet	hoarder
gyrated	hateful	hobbies
gyrator	haughty	hobbled

hobnail
hoedown
hogging
hoggish
hogwash
holdall
holding
holiday
holiest
Holland
holster
homburg
homonym
honesty
honeyed
hoodlum
hopeful
hophead
hopping
hording
horizon
hormone
hornier
horrify
horsier
horsing
hosanna
hosiery
hospice
hostage
hostess
hostile
hotfoot
hothead
hottest
hotting
housing
however
huddled
huffier
huffily
hugging
hulking
humanly
humbled
humdrum
humerus
humidor
humming
hummock
hundred
Hungary
hunting
hurdled
hurdler
hurried
hurtful
hurting
hurtled
husband
huskier

huskies
huskily
hussies
hustled
hustler
hutzpah
hydrant
hydrate
hydrous
hygiene
hymnary

Iberian
iceberg
Iceland
iciness
ideally
idiotic
idolize
idyllic
igneous
ignited
igniter
ignoble
ignobly
ignored
ill-bred
illegal
illicit
illness
imagery
imagine
imaging
imbibed
imbuing
imitate
immense
immerge
immerse
immoral
immured
impaled
impanel
impasse
impeach
impeded
imperil
impetus
impiety
impinge
impious
implant
implied
implode
implore
imposed
impound
impress
imprint
improve

impulse
imputed
inanely
inanity
inaptly
inbreed
inbuilt
incense
incised
incisor
incited
incline
include
incrust
incubus
Indiana
indices
indoors
indrawn
induced
indulge
inertia
inexact
infancy
inferno
infidel
infield
inflame
inflate
inflect
inflict
infused
ingénue
ingrain
ingrate
ingress
ingrown
inhabit
inhaled
inhered
inherit
inhibit
inhuman
initial
injured
inkblot
inkblot
inkling
innards
inquest
inquire
inquiry
inshore
insider
insight
insipid
insofar
inspect
inspire
install
instant

instate	jawbone	justify
instead	jazzier	jutting
instill	jazzily	
insular	jealous	
insulin	Jehovah	Kampala
insured	jellied	kaoline
insurer	jellies	Karachi
integer	jellify	karakul
intense	Jericho	Kashmir
interim	jerkier	katydid
interne	jerkily	kedging
intoned	jetties	keelson
intrude	jetting	keeping
inuring	jeweled	keratin
invaded	jeweler	kestrel
invader	jewelry	ketchup
invalid	Jezebel	keyhole
invalid	jibbing	keynote
inveigh	jiffies	kibbutz
inverse	jigging	kickoff
invited	jiggled	kidding
invoice	jimmied	kiddish
invoked	jimmies	killing
involve	jingled	killjoy
inwards	jitters	kindest
inweave	jittery	kindled
inwoven	jobbing	kindred
Iranian	jobless	kinetic
Ireland	jocular	kinfolk
iridium	jodhpur	kingdom
irksome	jogging	kingpin
ironies	joggled	kinkier
Islamic	joinery	kinship
isolate	jointed	kinsman
isotope	jointly	kinsmen
Israeli	jollier	Kirghiz
issuing	jollity	kitchen
isthmus	jonquil	kitties
Italian	jostled	Kleenex
itemize	jotting	knavery
iterate	journal	knavish
ivories	journey	kneecap
	joyless	kneeing
	joyride	kneeled
	joyrode	knifing
jabbing	jubilee	knitted
jacinth	Judaism	knitter
jackass	judging	knobbed
jackdaw	juggled	knocker
jackpot	juggler	knotted
Jacuzzi	jugular	know-how
jagging	juicier	knowing
jai alai	jujitsu	knuckle
Jakarta	jukebox	kookier
Jamaica	jumbled	Koranic
jamming	jumpier	Koumiss
jangled	jumping	Kremlin
janitor	Jungian	krimmer
January	juniper	Krishna
jarring	Jupiter	krypton
jasmine	justice	kumquat
javelin		

Kurdish
Kuwaiti

labeled
labeler
labiate
labored
laborer
laciest
laconic
lacquer
lactate
lacteal
lactose
ladling
ladybug
laggard
lagging
Lamaism
Lamaist
lambent
lamming
lamplit
lampoon
lamprey
lancing
landing
languid
languor
lankier
lanolin
lantern
lanyard
Laotian
Lapland
lapping
lapsing
lapwing
larceny
largely
largess
largest
largish
lashing
lassoes
lasting
latency
lateral
lathery
lathing
latrine
lattice
Latvian
launder
laundry
lawless
lawsuit
laxness
layette
layover

laziest
leading
leafage
leaflet
leakage
leakier
leaning
leaping
learned
learner
leasing
leather
leaving
Lebanon
lechery
lectern
lecture
leeward
lefties
leftism
leftist
legally
legatee
leggier
legging
leghorn
legible
legibly
legless
Leipzig
leisure
lemmata
lemming
lending
lengthy
lenient
leonine
leopard
leotard
leprosy
leprous
lesbian
Lesotho
letdown
letting
lettuce
leveled
levelly
leveret
levying
lexical
lexicon
liaised
liaison
libeled
libeler
liberal
Liberia
liberty
library
license

lift-off
lighten
lighter
lightly
lignite
likable
lilting
limeade
limited
Lincoln
lineage
lineman
linemen
lingoes
lingual
linkage
linseed
lintier
lioness
lionize
lip-read
lip-sync
liquefy
liqueur
lissome
listing
literal
lithium
litotes
liturgy
livable
lividly
loathed
lobbied
lobbies
lobbing
lobelia
lobster
locally
located
locator
lockjaw
lockout
lodging
loftier
loftily
logbook
logging
logical
longbow
longing
lookout
loonier
loonies
loosely
loosest
loosing
lopping
lorries
losable
lottery

lotting
lounged
louring
lousier
loutish
lovable
lovably
lowborn
lowbrow
lowdown
lowland
lowlier
loyally
loyalty
lozenge
Lucerne
lucidly
Lucifer
luckier
luckily
Luddite
luggage
lugging
lullaby
lumbago
lumpier
lunatic
lunging
luridly
lustful
lustier
lustily
lying-in
lyrical

maadies
macabre
macadam
macaque
machete
machine
macramé
maddest
Madeira
madness
Madonna
maestro
magenta
maggoty
magical
magnate
magneto
magnify
mahatma
mailbox
maillot
mailman
mailmen
majesty
Majorca

makable
malacca
Malachi
malaise
malaria
malefic
mallard
malmsey
malodor
Maltese
maltose
mammary
mammoth
manacle
managed
manager
Managua
manakin
manatee
mandate
mandrel
mangled
mangoes
manhole
manhood
man-hour
manhunt
manikin
manilla
manitou
mankind
manlier
manlike
man-made
manning
mannish
mansard
mansion
mapping
marabou
marbled
marcher
marimba
mariner
marital
marking
marline
marquee
marquis
married
marring
marrowy
Marsala
marshal
marshal
martial
Martian
martini
marxism
marxist
mascara

masonic
masonry
massage
masseur
massive
mastery
mastiff
mastoid
matador
matinee
Matthew
matting
matting
mattock
matured
maudlin
Maugham
mawkish
maximal
maximum
mayoral
mazurka
meander
meaning
measles
measure
meatier
medaled
meddled
meddler
mediate
medical
mediums
meeting
megaton
meiosis
mélange
melanin
melodic
melting
memento
menaced
menfolk
menthol
mention
mercies
mercury
merging
merited
mermaid
merrier
merrily
meshuga
message
Messiah
messier
messily
mestizo
metaled
Metazoa
methane

Mexican	mistime	mottoes
microbe	mistook	mourner
middies	mistral	mousier
midland	misused	mouthed
midmost	mitosis	movable
midriff	mixture	movably
midterm	mobbing	Mubarak
Midwest	mobbish	muckier
midwife	mobster	muddied
midyear	mockery	muddier
migrant	modally	mudding
migrate	modeled	muddled
mildewy	modesty	muddler
mileage	modicum	muezzin
milieux	modiste	muezzin
militia	modular	muffled
milkier	Mohican	muffler
milkman	moisten	mugging
milksop	moldier	mugwump
milling	molding	mulatto
million	Molière	mullion
mimical	mollify	mumbled
mimicry	mollusk	mumbler
minaret	Mombasa	mummies
mincing	monadic	mummify
mindful	monarch	mumming
mineral	moneyed	mundane
mingier	mongrel	murkier
mingled	moniker	murrain
minimal	monitor	muscled
minimum	monkeys	Muscovy
mintage	monkish	musical
minuend	monocle	muskrat
minuted	monodic	mustang
minutia	monolog	mustard
Miocene	monsoon	mustier
miracle	monster	mustily
miscall	montage	mutable
miscast	Montana	mutably
miscued	monthly	mutated
misdeal	moocher	muzzled
misdeed	moodier	Mycenae
misdone	moodily	mystery
miserly	moonlit	mystify
misfire	mooring	
mishear	Moorish	
mislaid	mopping	nab-bing
mislead	moraine	Nabokov
mismate	morally	nacelle
misname	mordant	nagging
misplay	morning	Nahuatl
misread	morocco	naiades
misrule	Morocco	Nairobi
missile	moronic	naively
missing	morphia	naivete
mission	mortify	naivety
missive	mortise	nakedly
misstep	moselle	Namibia
mistake	moseyed	nankeen
mistier	mossier	nannies
mistily	mottled	naphtha

napping
narcism
narrate
narwhal
nasally
nascent
Nasiism
nastier
nastily
nattier
nattily
natural
naughty
nebulae
nebular
necktie
needful
needier
needled
negated
neglect
Negress
Negroes
Negroid
neither
nemesis
neology
neonate
Neptune
nerving
nervous
nestled
netting
nettled
network
neurone
neutral
neutron
newborn
newness
newsman
newsmen
Niagara
nibbled
Nicosia
Nigeria
niggard
niggled
nightie
nightly
ninnies
niobium
nipping
nirvana
nitpick
nitrate
nitrous
noblest
nodding
nodular
noisier

noisily
noising
noisome
nomadic
nominal
nominee
noniron
nonplus
nonstop
noonday
norther
nosegay
nosiest
nostril
nostrum
notable
notably
notched
notepad
nothing
noticed
no-trump
nourish
novelty
nowhere
noxious
nuclear
nucleon
nucleus
nudging
nullify
nullity
numeral
nunnery
nuptial
Nureyev
nursery
nursing
nurture
nuttier
nuzzled

oarlock
oarsman
oarsmen
oatmeal
Obadíah
obelisk
obesity
obliged
oblique
obloquy
obscene
obscure
obsequy
observe
obtrude
obverse
obviate
obvious

ocarina
occlude
Oceania
oceanic
octagon
October
octopus
oculist
oddball
oddment
oddness
odorous
odyssey
Oedipus
offbeat
offense
offerer
offhand
officer
offload
offside
ogreish
oiliest
oilskin
oldness
oldster
Olympic
Olympus
ominous
omitted
omnibus
onerous
oneself
ongoing
onshore
Ontario
opacity
opening
operate
opinion
opossum
opposed
opposer
oppress
optical
optimal
optimum
opulent
orating
oration
oratory
orbital
orchard
ordered
orderly
ordinal
oregano
organdy
organic
orifice
origami

orotund
ortolan
osmosis
osmotic
ostrich
ottoman
ourself
outcast
outcome
outdone
outdoor
outface
outflow
outgrew
outgrow
outlast
outline
outlive
outlook
outpost
outrage
outrank
outsell
outside
outsize
outsold
outstay
outvote
outward
outwear
outworn
ovarian
ovaries
ovation
overact
overage
overall
overate
overawe
overdue
overeat
overlap
overlay
overran
overrun
oversaw
oversea
overtax
overtly
ovulate
oxidize

pabulum
pacific
Pacific
package
packing
paddies
padding
paddled

paddock
padlock
pageant
pageboy
pailful
painful
painter
paisley
pajamas
palaver
palette
palling
palmate
palmist
palpate
palsied
panacea
panache
pancake
paneled
panicky
pannier
panning
panoply
panpipe
pansies
panther
paperer
papilla
papoose
paprika
papyrus
parable
paraded
paradox
paragon
parapet
parasol
parboil
paresis
parfait
parlous
paroled
parolee
parotid
parquet
parried
parsing
parsley
parsnip
partake
partial
partied
parties
parting
partite
partner
partook
parvenu
paschal
passage

passing
passion
passive
Pasteur
pastier
pastime
pasting
pasture
patella
patency
pathway
patient
patriot
patsies
pattern
patties
patting
paucity
paunchy
pausing
payable
payload
payment
payroll
peacock
peafowl
peasant
pebbled
peccary
pedagog
pedaled
peddled
peddler
peeling
peerage
peeress
peeving
peevish
Pegasus
pegging
pelagic
pelican
penalty
penance
pendant
pendent
pending
penguin
pennant
pennies
penning
pension
pensive
peonies
peopled
peppery
peppier
pepping
percale
percent
percept

per diem
perfect
perfidy
perform
perfume
pergola
perhaps
perigee
periled
perinea
periwig
perjure
perjury
perkier
Permian
permute
perplex
Perrier
Persian
persist
persona
pertain
perturb
perusal
perused
pervade
pervert
peskier
pessary
petaled
petiole
petrify
pettier
pettily
petting
pettish
petunia
pfennig
phaeton
phalanx
phallic
phallus
phantom
pharaoh
pharynx
phasing
philter
phoenix
phoneme
phonics
phonier
phonies
phoning
phrasal
phrased
physics
pianist
picador
Picasso
piccolo
pickier

picking
pickled
picture
piddled
piebald
piecing
pie-eyed
pierced
Pierrot
piggery
pigging
piggish
pigment
pigmies
pigtail
pilgrim
pillage
pillion
pillory
piloted
pimento
pimpled
pinball
pincers
pincher
pinhead
pinkish
pinnate
pinning
pioneer
pipette
pipping
piquant
piquing
piranha
pirated
pirogue
Piscean
pit-a-pat
pitcher
piteous
pitfall
pithead
pithier
pitiful
pitting
pitying
pivotal
pivoted
pizzazz
placard
placate
placebo
placing
placket
plagued
plainly
planing
planish
planned
planner

planter
plaster
plastic
plateau
plating
platoon
•platted
platter
plaudit
playboy
playful
playlet
play-off
pleaded
pleased
pleated
pledged
pledgee
plenary
pliable
pliably
pliancy
plodded
plodder
plopped
plosive
plotted
plotter
plowman
plowmen
plugged
plumage
plumber
pluming
plummet
plumply
plunder
plunged
plunger
pluvial
plywood
poacher
podding
podlike
poesies
poetess
poetize
pointed
pointer
poising
pokiest
Polaris
polecat
polemic
policed
politic
polkaed
pollard
pollute
poloist
polygon

polymer
pompano
Pompeii
pompous
poniard
pontiff
pontoon
poorish
popcorn
popeyed
poppies
popping
porcine
portage
portend
portent
portico
portion
portray
posited
possess
postage
postern
postman
postmen
posture
postwar
potable
potency
potheen
potherb
pothole
potluck
pottage
pottery
potties
potting
pouched
poultry
pounced
poverty
powdery
prairie
praised
praline
pranced
prating
prattle
prawner
preachy
precede
precept
precise
precook
predate
predict
preempt
preface
prefect
preform
preheat

prelate
prelude
premier
premise
premium
prepaid
prepare
preplan
preppie
prepuce
presage
present
present
preside
presume
pretend
pretest
pretext
pretzel
prevail
prevent
preview
pricier
pricing
prickle
prickly
priding
primacy
primary
primate
priming
primmed
primmer
primula
printer
privacy
private
privies
prizing
probate
probing
probity
problem
proceed
process
proctor
procure
prodded
prodder
prodigy
produce
product
profane
profess
proffer
profile
profuse
progeny
program
project
prolong

promise
promote
pronoun
propane
prophet
propose
propped
prorata
prorate
prosaic
prosier
prosper
protean
protect
protégé
protein
protest
proudly
proverb
provide
proving
proviso
provoke
provost
prowess
prowler
proxies
proximo
prudent
prudery
prudish
pruning
prussic
Psalter
psychic
puberty
publish
puckish
pudding
puddled
puerile
puffier
Pullman
pulsate
pulsing
pumpkin
pungent
puniest
Punjabi
punning
punster
puppies
purging
puritan
purloin
purport
purpose
pursing
pursued
pursuer
pursuit

purview	raggedy	rebuild
pushier	ragging	rebuilt
pushily	ragtime	rebuked
pussies	ragweed	receded
pustule	railing	receipt
put-down	railway	receive
putrefy	raiment	recency
putting	rainbow	recital
putting	rainier	recited
puzzled	rainily	reclaim
puzzler	raising	recline
Pygmies	rake-off	recluse
pyramid	Raleigh	recount
pyretic	rallied	recover
pyrites	Ramadan	recruit
Pyrrhic	rambled	rectify
	rambler	rectory
	ramming	recycle
quaking	rampage	reddish
qualify	rampant	redhead
quality	rampart	redness
quantum	rancher	redoing
quarrel	randier	redoubt
quarter	ranging	redound
quartet	Rangoon	redress
Quechua	rankled	reduced
queenly	ransack	reducer
queerly	Raphael	redwood
queried	rapidly	reedier
queries	rapping	reelect
queuing	rapport	reenact
quibble	rapture	reenter
quicken	rarebit	reentry
quickie	ratable	referee
quickly	ratafia	refined
quieted	rat-a-tat	reflect
quietly	ratchet	refract
quinine	rattier	refrain
quintet	ratting	refresh
quipped	rattled	refried
quitted	rattler	refugee
quitter	raucous	refusal
qui vive	raunchy	refused
Quixote	ravaged	refuted
quizzed	ravager	regaled
quizzes	raveled	regalia
quondam	ravioli	regally
Quonset	rawhide	regatta
quoting	rawness	regency
	reactor	regimen
	readied	regress
rabidly	readily	regroup
raccoon	reagent	regular
raciest	realism	rehouse
radiant	realist	reissue
radiate	reality	rejoice
radical	realize	relapse
radicle	realtor	related
radioed	rebated	release
raffish	rebirth	reliant
raffled	rebound	relieve

relievo	retract	risotto
relived	retread	ritzier
relying	retreat	rivaled
remarry	retrial	rivalry
remnant	retrial	riveted
remodel	Réunion	riveter
remorse	reunion	riviera
remount	reunite	Riviera
removal	revalue	roaches
removed	reveled	roadbed
remover	reveler	roadway
renamed	revelry	roaster
rending	revenge	robbery
reneged	revenue	robbing
renewal	revered	robotic
replace	reverie	rockier
replete	reverse	Rockies
replica	reviled	roguery
replied	revised	roguish
replies	revisit	roister
repoint	revival	rollick
reposed	revived	romaine
repress	revoked	Romance
reprint	revolve	romance
reproof	revulet	Romania
reprove	revving	Romansh
reptile	rewaken	röntgen
repulse	rewired	roofing
reputed	rewound	rooftop
request	rewrite	rookery
requiem	rewrote	roomful
require	rhenium	roomier
requite	rhizome	rooster
reredos	rhodium	rorqual
reroute	rhombus	roseate
rescind	rhubarb	rosette
rescued	rhyming	rosiest
rescuer	ribbing	Rossini
reserve	rickets	rostrum
resided	rickety	rotated
residue	ridding	rottary
resolve	riddled	rotting
resound	ridging	rotunda
respect	riffled	roughen
respire	rifling	roughly
respite	rigging	rouging
respond	rightly	rounded
restate	rigidly	rounder
restful	rimless	roundly
restive	rimming	roundup
restock	ringing	rousing
restore	ringlet	routine
resumed	rinsing	routing
retaken	rioting	rowboat
rethink	riotous	rowdier
retinae	ripiest	rowdies
retinal	riposte	rowdily
retinue	ripping	royally
retired	rippled	royalty
retouch	risible	rubbery
retrace	riskier	rubbing

rubbish
rubella
Rubicon
ruching
ruction
ruddier
ruffian
ruffled
ruinous
rumbled
rummage
rumpled
runaway
rundown
runnier
running
rupture
rurally
Russell
Russian
rustier
rustled
rustler
rutting

Sabaoth
Sabbath
sackful
sacking
saddest
saddled
saddler
sadness
saffron
sagging
sailing
sainted
saintly
salable
salient
sallied
salsify
saltier
saltine
saluted
salvage
salving
salvoes
samovar
Samoyed
sampled
sampler
samurai
sanctum
sandbag
sandier
sangria
San José
sapient
sapling

Sapphic
sapping
Saracen
sarcasm
sarcoma
sardine
sashimi
satanic
satchel
satiate
satiety
satisfy
satsuma
satyric
saucier
saunter
sausage
sauteed
savaged
savanna
sawmill
scabbed
scabies
scaling
scallop
scalpel
scalper
scamper
scandal
scanned
scanner
scapula
scarier
scarify
scaring
scarlet
scarred
scarves
scathed
scatted
scatter
scenery
scepter
schemer
scherzo
schmalz
scholar
sciatic
science
scoffer
scollop
scooper
scooter
scoring
scorner
Scorpio
scottie
scourer
scourge
scraggy
scraped

scraper
scrapie
scrappy
scratch
scrawny
screech
scribed
scrimpy
scrooge
scrotum
scrubby
scruffy
scrunch
scruple
scudded
scuffle
scupper
scuttle
scythed
seafood
seagull
sealant
seaport
seasick
seaside
seating
Seattle
seaward
seaweed
seceded
seclude
secrecy
secrete
section
secular
secured
sedated
seduced
seducer
seedier
seedily
seeking
seeming
seepage
seeress
seethed
segment
seining
seismic
seizing
seizure
selfish
selling
sellout
seltzer
selvage
seminal
seminar
Semitic
senator
sending

send-off	sheaves	siemens
Senegal	shebang	sieving
sensate	shekels	sighing
sensing	shellac	sighted
sensory	shelled	sightly
sensual	Shelley	signify
sequoia	shelter	Signora
seraphs	shelved	Signore
Serbian	shelves	Signori
serfdom	sherbet	Sikhism
serious	sheriff	silence
serpent	shiatsu	silicon
serrate	shimmer	silkier
serried	shindig	silkily
servant	shingle	sillier
service	shingly	sillily
servile	shinier	siloing
serving	shining	silvery
session	shining	similar
setback	shinned	simpler
setting	shipped	simplex
settled	shipper	sincere
settler	shirker	sine die
seventh	shivery	singing
seventy	shocker	singled
several	shoeing	sinking
severed	shopped	sinless
Seville	shopper	sinning
sexiest	shoring	sinuate
sexless	shorten	sinuous
sextant	shortly	sipping
shackle	shotgun	sirloin
shadier	shoving	sirocco
shadily	showery	sissies
shading	showier	sistine
shadowy	showily	sit-down
shagged	showing	sitting
shagged	showman	sitting
shakier	showmen	situate
shakily	show-off	sixpack
shaking	shrilly	sixteen
shallot	shrived	sixties
shallow	shrivel	sizable
shamble	shriven	sizably
shaming	shudder	sizzled
shammed	shudder	skating
shammer	shuffle	skeptic
shampoo	shunned	sketchy
shapely	shunner	skidded
shaping	shut-eye	skilled
sharing	shutter	skillet
sharpen	shuttle	skimmed
sharper	shylock	skinned
sharpie	shyness	skipped
sharply	shyster	skipper
shatter	Siamese	skitter
Shavian	Siberia	skulker
shaving	sibling	sky-high
Shawnee	sickbed	skyjack
sheared	sidecar	skyward
sheathe	sidling	slabbed

slacken	snaffle	sophism
slacker	snafued	sophist
slaking	snagged	soppier
slammed	snakier	sopping
slammer	snakily	soprano
slander	snaking	sorcery
slapped	snapped	sorghum
slasher	snapper	sorirly
slating	snaring	sorrier
slatted	snatchy	soufflé
slavery	sneaker	soulful
slaving	sneezed	soundly
slavish	snicker	soupçon
slaying	sniffer	soupier
sledded	sniffle	sourish
sledged	snifter	sousing
sleeper	snigger	soybean
sleeved	sniping	sozzled
sleight	snipped	spacial
slender	snippet	spacing
slicing	snooker	spackle
slicker	snooper	spading
sliding	snoozed	spangle
slimier	snoring	spaniel
slimmed	snorkel	Spanish
slimmer	snorted	spanned
slipped	snowier	spanner
slipper	snowman	sparing
slipway	snowmen	sparkle
slither	snubbed	sparred
slobber	snuffle	sparrow
slogged	snugged	Spartan
sloping	snugger	spastic
slopped	snuggle	spatial
slotted	soaking	spatted
slouchy	soaring	spatter
sloughy	sobbing	spatula
slugged	soberly	speaker
sluiced	society	special
slumber	sockeye	species
slummed	sodding	specify
slumped	soggier	speckle
slurred	soignée	specter
slyness	sojourn	spectra
smarten	solaced	specula
smartly	soldier	speeded
smelled	solicit	spelled
smelter	solidly	speller
smidgen	soloing	spender
smiling	soloist	spering
smiting	Solomon	sphered
smitten	soluble	spheric
smokier	solubly	spicier
smoking	solvent	spicily
smolder	solving	spicing
smoochy	Somalia	spicule
smoothy	somatic	spidery
smother	somehow	spikier
smudged	someone	spiking
smugger	sonnies	spilled
smuggle	soothed	spinach

spindle
spindly
spinner
spin-off
Spinoza
spiring
spiting
spittle
splashy
spliced
splotch
splurge
spoiled
spoiler
spondee
sponged
sponger
sponsor
spotlit
spotted
spotter
sprayer
springy
spruced
spumous
spurner
spurred
sputnik
sputter
squalid
squally
squalor
squared
squashy
squatty
squawky
squeaky
squeeze
squelch
squiffy
squinty
squirmy
squishy
stabbed
stabber
stabile
stabled
stadium
stagged
stagger
stagier
staging
stained
staking
stalked
stalled
stamina
stammer
standby
stapled
stapler

starchy
stardom
starkly
starlet
starred
starter
startle
starved
stately
stating
station
statism
statist
stature
statute
staunch
staving
staying
stealth
steamer
steepen
steeple
steeply
stellar
stemmed
stencil
stepped
sterile
sternly
sternum
steroid
stetson
stetted
steward
sticker
stiffen
stiffly
stifled
stilted
Stilton
stimuli
stipend
stipple
stir-fry
stirred
stirrer
stirrup
stoical
stoking
stomach
stonier
stoning
stopgap
stopped
stopper
storage
storied
storied
stories
storing
stoutly

stoving
stowage
strafed
strange
stratum
stratus
Strauss
streaky
stretch
strewed
striate
striker
stringy
striped
striven
stroked
strudel
stubbed
stubble
stubbly
studded
student
studied
studied
studies
stuffer
stumble
stunned
stunner
stunted
stupefy
stutter
Stygian
styling
stylish
stylist
stylize
stymied
styptic
styrene
suavely
suavity
subbing
subdued
subject
subjoin
sublime
subrosa
subside
subsidy
subsiol
subsist
subsume
subteen
subtend
subvene
subvert
succeed
success
succumb
suckled

sucrose
suction
sudsier
suffice
suffuse
suggest
suicide
suiting
sulfate
sulfide
sulkier
sulkily
sullied
sultana
Sumatra
summary
summery
summing
summons
sunbeam
sunburn
sundial
sundown
sunfish
sunless
sunnier
sunning
sunspot
supping
support
suppose
supreme
surface
surfeit
surfing
surgeon
surgery
surging
surlier
surlily
surmise
surname
surpass
surplus
surreal
survive
suspect
suspend
sustain
sutured
swabbed
swaddle
swagger
Swahili
swallow
swapped
swarthy
swathed
swatted
swatter
swearer

sweater
Swedish
sweeten
sweetie
sweetly
swelled
swelter
swerved
swiftly
swigged
swimmer
swindle
swinger
swinish
swiping
swizzle
swollen
swooned
swopped
syllabi
symptom
syncope
synodal
synonym
syringe
systole

Tabasco
tabbies
tabbing
tableau
tabling
tabloid
tabooed
taboret
tabular
tacitly
tackier
tacking
tackled
tackler
tactful
tactics
tactile
tadpole
taffeta
tagging
tainted
takeoff
talkier
tallied
tallies
tallish
tallowy
tallyho
taloned
tamable
tambour
tanager
tanbark

tangelo
tangent
tangier
Tangier
tangled
tangoed
tankage
tankard
tannery
tanning
tannish
tantrum
tapioca
tapping
tardier
tardily
tarnish
tarried
tarring
tartare
tastier
tasting
tatters
tattier
tatting
tattled
Taurean
tawnier
taxable
taxicab
teacher
tearful
tearing
teasing
teddies
tedious
teeming
teenage
teenier
teethed
Tel Aviv
teleran
telling
temblor
tempera
tempest
tenable
tenably
tenancy
tendril
tenfold
tensely
tensile
tensing
tension
tensity
tensive
tenuity
tenuous
tenured
tequila

terbium
termini
termite
ternary
terrace
terrain
terrier
terrify
tersely
testate
testier
testify
testily
tetanus
textile
textual
texture
theater
theatre
theorem
therapy
thereby
therein
thereof
thermal
thermos
thicken
thicket
thickly
thieved
thieves
thimble
thinker
thinned
thinner
thirdly
thirsty
thistle
thither
thorium
thought
thready
thrifty
thrived
thriven
throaty
through
thruway
thudded
thulium
thunder
thyroid
thyself
Tibetan
ticking
tickled
tidiest
tidings
tidying
tighten
tightly

tigress
tillage
timbrel
timeout
timidly
timothy
timpani
tinfoil
tingled
tinkled
tinnier
tinnily
tinning
tinting
tipping
tippled
tippler
tipsier
tipsily
tipster
tiptoed
titanic
tithing
titular
toadies
toaster
tobacco
toccata
toddies
toddled
toddler
toehold
toenail
togging
toggled
tolling
tonally
tonight
tonnage
tonneau
tonsure
tontine
topcoat
topiary
topical
topknot
topless
topmost
topping
topping
toppled
topsail
topsoil
torment
tornado
Toronto
torpedo
torrent
torsion
tortoni
torture

tossing
totaled
totally
totemic
totting
touched
toughen
tourism
tourist
tourney
tousled
towards
towboat
toweled
towered
toxemia
tracery
trachea
tracing
tracker
tractor
trading
traduce
traffic
tragedy
trailer
trainee
trainer
traipse
traitor
trammel
trample
transit
transom
trapeze
trapped
trapper
travail
trawler
treadle
treason
trebled
trefoil
trekked
trellis
tremble
trembly
tremolo
tresses
trestle
triadic
tribune
tribute
triceps
trickle
trident
trifled
trifler
trigger
trilogy
trimmed

trimmer
Trinity
trinket
tripled
triplet
Tripoli
tripped
tripper
trisect
tritely
tritium
triumph
trivial
trochee
trodden
trolley
trollop
trooper
Trotsky
trotted
trotter
trouble
trounce
trouped
trouper
truancy
trucker
truckle
trudged
truffle
trumpet
trundle
trustee
trysail
tsarina
tsarist
T-square
tsunami
tubbier
tubular
Tuesday
tugging
tuition
tumbled
tumbler
tumbrel
tumbril
tummies
tunable
tuneful
Tunisia
tunnies
turbine
Turkish
turmoil
turning
turnkey
turnoff
turnout
Tuscany
tussled

tussock
tutored
twaddle
tweeter
tweezed
twelfth
twiddle
twilled
twinged
twining
twinkle
twinned
twirler
twister
twitchy
twiting
twitted
twitter
twofold
two-some
two-time
tympani
typeset
typhoid
typhoon
typical
tyranny
tzarina
tzarist

ugliest
ukelele
Ukraine
ukulele
ululate
umbrage
umpired
umpteen
unaided
unarmed
unasked
unaware
unbosom
unbound
unbowed
uncanny
unchain
uncivil
unclasp
unclean
unclear
uncouth
uncover
unction
undated
undergo
undoing
undress
undying
unearth

unequal
ungodly
unguent
unhandy
unhappy
unheard
unhinge
unicorn
unified
uniform
uniting
unkempt
unknown
unlearn
unleash
unloose
unloved
unlucky
unmaker
unmanly
unmoved
unnamed
unnerve
unquote
unravel
unready
unscrew
unsnarl
unsound
unstick
unstuck
untamed
untried
untruth
untying
unusual
unwaged
unwound
upbraid
updated
up-front
upgrade
upheave
upraise
upright
upsilon
upstage
upstart
upstate
upsurge
upswing
uptight
uptrend
upwards
uranium
urethra
urgency
urinary
urinary
urinate
urology

Uruguay
useless
usually
usurper
utensil
utility
utilize
Utopian
utterly

vacancy
vacated
vaccine
vacuity
vacuous
vaginal
vagrant
vaguely
valance
valence
valency
valiant
validly
valleys
valuing
vamoose
vampire
Vandyke
vanilla
vantage
vapidly
vaporer
vaquero
variant
variety
various
varmint
varnish
varsity
varying
Vatican
vatting
vaulted
vaulter
vaunter
veering
vegetal
vehicle
veiling
veining
velvety
venally
venison
venting
ventral
venture
veranda
verbena
verbose
verdant

verdict
verdure
verging
vermeil
vernier
verruca
versify
version
vertigo
vesicle
vespers
vestige
veteran
vetoing
vetting
viaduct
vibrant
vibrate
vibrato
viceroy
vicious
victory
victual
village
villain
villein
villous
vinegar
vintage
vintner
violate
violent
violist
virgule
virtual
viruses
vis-à-vis
viscera
viscose
viscous
visible
visibly
visited
visitor
vitally
vitamin
vitiate
vitrify
vitriol
vittles
vividly
vocalic
voguish
voicing
volcano
volleys
voltage
voltaic
voluble
volubly
vomited

voucher
voyaged
voyager
Vulgate
vulpine
vulture

wabbled
wackier
wackily
wadding
waddled
waddler
waffled
waggery
wagging
waggish
waggled
wagtail
Waikiki
waiting
waiving
wakeful
Waldorf
walkout
walkway
wallaby
wangled
wanness
wanting
warbled
warbler
warfare
warhead
wariest
warlike
warlock
warmest
warning
warpath
warrant
warring
warrior
warship
warthog
wartime
washing
washout
washtub
waspish
wassail
wastage
wasting
wastrel
watcher
watered
wattage
wattled
wavelet
waviest

waxiest
waxwing
waxwork
waylaid
wayside
wayward
wealthy
wearied
wearier
wearily
wearing
weather
weaving
webbing
wedding
wedging
wedlock
weedier
weekday
weekend
weenier
weeping
weighty
weirder
weirdly
welcome
welfare
well-fed
well-off
western
wetback
wetness
wettest
wetting
whaling
wharves
whatnot
wheedle
wheeled
wheezed
whereas
whereby
wherein
whereof
whereon
whereto
whether
whetted
whiling
whimper
whining
whipped
whippet
whirred
whisker
whiskey
whisper
whistle
whither

whiting
whitish
Whitman
Whitsun
whittle
whizzed
whizzes
whoever
whoopee
whopper
whorled
Wichita
widgeon
widower
wielder
wiggled
wildcat
wiliest
willful
willing
willowy
wimpier
wincing
windbag
windier
winding
Windsor
winning
winning
winsome
wintery
wiretap
wishful
wispier
wistful
without
witless
witness
wittier
wittily
witting
wizened
wobbled
wolfram
womanly
woodier
woolies
woollen
woozier
woozily
wordier
wordily
wording
workday
working
workman
workmen
workout
worldly

wormier
worn-out
worried
worrier
worries
worship
worsted
would-be
wounded
wrangle
wrapped
wrapper
wreathe
wrecker
wrestle
wriggle
wriggly
wringer
wrinkle
wrinkly
writhed
writing
written
wronged
wrongly
wrought
Wyoming

Yangtze
yapping
yardage
yardarm
yashmak
yenning
yeshiva
Yiddish
yipping
yodeled
yodeler
yoghurt
younger
yttrium
Yucatán

Zambezi
zaniest
zapping
zealous
zestful
zestier
zincing
zincked
Zionism
Zionist
zippier
zipping
zonally
zoology

aardvark
abattoir
abdicate
abductor
aberrant
abetment
abeyance
abhorred
abjectly
abjuring
ablating
ablation
ablative
ablution
abnegate
abnormal
abortion
abortive
abrading
abrasion
abrasive
abridged
abrogate
abruptly
abscissa
absentee
absently
absinthe
absolute
absolved
abstract
abstruse
absurdly
abundant
abutment
abutting
academic
acanthus
a capella
acceding
accepted
accepter
acceptor
accident
accolade
accredit
accruing
accuracy
accurate
accursed
accusing
accustom
acerbity
achieved
achiever
acidosis
acoustic
acquaint
acquired
acridity
acrimony

acrostic
actinide
actinium
activate
actively
activism
activist
activity
actually
actuated
actuator
adaptive
addendum
addicted
addition
additive
adequacy
adequate
adherent
adhering
adhesion
adhesive
adjacent
adjudged
adjuring
adjuster
adjustor
adjutant
adlibbed
admiring
admitted
admonish
adoption
adoptive
adorable
adorably
adroitly
adultery
advanced
advising
advisory
advocaat
advocacy
advocate
aerating
aeration
aerobics
aesthete
affected
afferent
affiance
affinity
afflatus
affluent
affright
agencies
aggrieve
agitated
agitator
agitprop
agnostic

agonized
agrarian
agreeing
agronomy
aigrette
airborne
airbrush
aircraft
Airedale
airfield
airiness
airliner
airplane
airspace
airstrip
airtight
à la carte
alacrity
alarming
alarmist
albacore
albinism
alderman
alfresco
Algonkin
alienate
alienism
alienist
alighted
aliquant
alkalies
alkaline
alkalize
alkaloid
allaying
alleging
allegory
allegros
alleluia
allergen
allergic
alleyway
alliance
allocate
allotted
allowing
all-round
allspice
alluding
alluring
allusion
allusive
alluvial
alluvium
almighty
alopecia
alphabet
Alsatian
alter ego
altering
although

altitude
altruism
altruist
aluminum
alveolar
amarylis
ambiance
ambience
ambition
ambrosia
ambulant
ambulate
amenable
amenably
American
amethyst
amicable
amicably
ammoniac
ammonium
amnesiac
amniotic
amoeboid
amortize
amperage
amphorae
amputate
anabolic
anaconda
analogue
analyses
analysis
analytic
analyzed
anarchic
anathema
ancestor
ancestry
androgen
anecdote
aneurism
aneurysm
Angeleno
angelica
Anglican
angström
animated
animator
anisette
ankylose
annalist
annotate
announce
annually
annulled
anorexic
anserine
anteater
antecede
antedate
antelope

antennae
antennas
anterior
anteroom
antibody
antidote
antihero
antimony
antipode
antipope
antiqued
antlered
anyplace
anything
anywhere
aperient
aperitif
aperture
aphorism
aphorist
apiarian
apiaries
apiarist
apoplexy
apostasy
apostate
apothegm
appalled
apparent
appeased
appeaser
appendix
appetite
applause
apple-pie
appliqué
applying
apposing
apposite
appraise
apprised
approach
approval
approved
après-ski
aptitude
aqualung
aquanaut
Aquarian
aquarium
Aquarius
aqueduct
aquiline
arachnid
Arapahoe
arbalest
arboreal
arboreta
archaism
archduke
archival

ardently
arguable
arguably
argument
armament
armature
armchair
Armenian
armories
aromatic
arousing
arpeggio
arranged
arrester
arriving
arrogant
arrogate
arsonist
arterial
arteries
artesian
artfully
artifact
artifice
artiness
artistic
artistry
asbestos
asbestus
ascribed
asperity
aspersed
asphyxia
aspirant
aspirate
aspiring
assassin
assemble
assembly
assessor
assonant
assorted
assuaged
assuming
assuring
asterisk
asteroid
astonish
astutely
Atabrine
Athenian
athletic
Atlantic
atomical
atomized
atomizer
atrocity
atrophic
attached
attacker
attiring

attitude
attorney
attrited
attuning
atypical
audacity
audience
audition
auditory
au gratin
auguring
augustly
au revoir
auspices
Austrian
autistic
autobahn
autocrat
auto-da-fé
automata
automate
autonomy
autumnal
Ave Maria
avenging
averaged
averment
averring
aversely
aversion
aviaries
aviation
aviatrix
avowedly

babbling
babushka
babyhood
baccarat
bachelor
bacillus
backache
backbite
backbone
backcomb
backdate
backdoor
backdrop
backfire
backhand
backlash
backless
backlist
backmost
backpack
backrest
backsent
backside
backspin
backstop

backtalk
backward
backwash
backyard
Baconian
bacteria
badinage
badmouth
baffling
baguette
bailable
bailsman
Bakelite
bakeries
balanced
balancer
baldhead
baldness
balkiest
ballcock
balletic
balloted
ballpark
ballroom
ballyhoo
balmoral
baluster
banality
bandaged
bandanna
bandeaux
banditry
bandsman
bandsmen
bandying
banister
bankbook
bankroll
bankrupt
baptized
barathea
Barbados
barbaric
barbecue
barbican
barbital
bareback
barefoot
bareness
baritone
barnacle
barnyard
baroness
baronial
baronies
barreled
barrenly
barrette
barterer
basaltic
baseball

baseborn
baseless
baseline
basement
baseness
basilica
basilisk
basketry
bassinet
bathetic
bathrobe
bathroom
battiest
battle-ax
battling
bawdiest
bayberry
bdellium
beadiest
beadlike
bearable
bearably
bearskin
beatific
beauties
beautify
becoming
bedazzle
bedecked
bedimmed
bedstead
beechnut
beefcake
beefiest
befallen
befitted
befogged
befriend
befuddle
beggarly
beginner
begotten
begotten
begrudge
beguiled
behaving
behavior
behemoth
beholden
beholder
behoving
belaying
belfries
believed
believer
belittle
bellyful
bellying
Bel Paese
bemiring
bemusing

benedict
benefice
benignly
bequeath
berating
bereaved
bergamot
beriberi
berretta
besieged
besieger
besmirch
besotted
besought
bespoken
bestowal
bestride
bestrode
betaking
betatron
bête noir
betiding
betrayal
betrayer
beveling
beverage
bewilder
biannual
biathlon
Biblical
bibulous
bicuspid
bicycled
bicycler
biddable
biennial
biennium
bifocals
bigamist
bigamous
bilabial
bilberry
billeted
billowed
bindweed
binnacle
binomial
biometry
biopsies
biracial
bird-bath
birdcage
birdlime
birdseed
bird's-eye
birthday
bisector
bisexual
bitchier
bitchily
bitterly

bittiest
bivalent
biweekly
blabbing
blackout
blacktop
blamable
blandish
blastoff
blatancy
bleacher
bleeding
Blenheim
blessing
blinding
blissful
blithely
blizzard
blockade
blockage
bloodied
bloodier
bloodily
bloomers
blooming
blotting
blowiest
bludgeon
bluebell
bluebird
blueness
blurring
blushing
blustery
boastful
bobbling
bobby pin
bobolink
bobwhite
bodywork
boggling
bohemian
boldface
boldness
bollworm
bona fide
bonehead
bonhomie
bookcase
bookmark
bookworm
booziest
Bordeaux
bordered
borrower
bossiest
botanist
botanize
bottling
botulism
bouffant

bouillon
bouncing
boundary
bounties
boutique
boweries
boyishly
bracelet
brackish
bradding
braggart
bragging
brainier
braising
branched
brandied
brandies
brandish
brand-new
brassier
brattish
brawnier
breakage
breaking
breakout
breathed
breather
breeches
breeding
breeding
brethren
breviary
bribable
bridling
briefing
brighten
brightly
brimming
bringing
Brisbane
bristled
britches
Brittany
broached
Broadway
brocaded
broccoli
brochure
bronchus
bronzing
broodier
brooding
brougham
brouhaha
browbeat
browsing
bruising
brush-off
Brussels
brutally
bubblier

bubbling
buckaroo
buckshot
buckskin
Budapest
Buddhism
Buddhist
Bulgaria
bulgiest
bulkhead
bulkiest
bulldoze
bulletin
bullfrog
bullring
bull's-eye
bullying
bumpiest
buncombe
bundling
bungalow
bungling
buoyancy
burbling
burglary
burgling
Burgundy
burliest
burnoose
bursitis
bursting
bush-baby
bushiest
business
bustling
busybody
butchery
buttress
buzzword

caballed
cackling
caddying
caduceus
caesurae
caffeine
cajoling
calabash
calamine
calamity
calculus
Calcutta
calendar
calicoes
calliope
calmness
calories
Cambodia
Cambrian
camellia

camisole
camomile
campaign
campfire
campuses
camshaft
Canadian
canaries
Canberra
canceled
candidly
candling
canister
cannabis
cannibal
canoeing
canoeist
canonize
canopied
canopies
capacity
capriole
capsicum
capsular
captious
captured
Capuchin
capybara
caracole
carbolic
cardamom
cardigan
cardinal
carefree
careless
careworn
carillon
carnally
carnival
Carolina
caroling
carousal
caroused
carousel
carpeted
carriage
carrying
caryatid
Casanova
cascaded
case-book
caseload
casement
casework
cashmere
cassette
castanet
castaway
cast iron
castrate
casually

casualty
catacomb
catalyst
catalyze
catapult
cataract
catchier
catching
category
catheter
catholic
Catholic
cattiest
caucuses
cauldron
causeway
cautious
cavalier
caviling
cavities
celerity
celibacy
celibate
cellular
cemetery
cenotaph
Cenozoic
censured
censurer
centered
cephalic
ceramics
cerebral
cerebric
cerebrum
ceremony
cerulean
cervical
cervices
cesarean
cesspool
cetacean
chairman
chairmen
chalkier
chambray
champion
chancier
chancing
chandler
changing
Channuka
chaperon
chaplain
chapping
charcoal
charging
chariest
charisma
charming
charring

chastise
chastity
châteaux
chattier
chattily
chatting
checkers
checkout
cheekier
cheerful
cheerier
cheerily
chemical
chenille
Cherokee
cherries
cherubic
chessman
chessmen
chestier
chestnut
chewiest
Cheyenne
chick-pen
childish
children
chillier
chilling
chinning
chipmunk
Chippewa
chipping
chirpier
chiseled
chiseler
chitchat
chivalry
chivvied
chivying
chloride
chlorine
choirboy
choleric
choosier
choosing
choppier
chopping
chop suey
chorally
chortled
choruses
chow chow
chow mein
christen
chromium
chubbier
chuckker
chunkier
churning
chutzpah
cicatrix

cicerone
cinchona
cincture
cinnabar
cinnamon
circling
circular
circuses
citation
citreous
civilian
civility
civilize
claimant
clambake
clammier
clamming
clannish
clansman
clansmen
clapping
clap-trap
clarinet
classier
classify
clavicle
clean-cut
cleansed
cleanser
clear-cut
clearing
cleavage
cleaving
clematis
clemency
clergies
clerical
cleverly
climatic
clincher
clinging
clinical
clipping
cliquish
clitoris
cloddish
clogging
cloister
closeted
clothier
clothing
clothing
clotting
cloudier
clownish
clubable
clubbing
clubfoot
clumsier
clumsily
coachman

coachmen
coalesce
coarsely
coattail
coauthor
cockatoo
cockcrow
cockerel
cockeyed
cockiest
cocksure
cocktail
coddling
codified
coercing
coercion
coercive
coextend
cogently
cogitate
coherent
cohering
cohesion
cohesive
coiffeur
coiffure
coincide
colander
coldness
coleslaw
coliseum
collapse
collated
collided
colliery
colloquy
Colombia
colonial
colonies
colonist
colonize
Colorado
colorful
coloring
colorist
colossal
colossus
Columbia
columnar
Comanche
comatose
combated
combined
comeback
comedian
comedies
commando
commence
commerce
commoner
commonly

communal
communed
commuted
commuter
compared
competed
compiled
compiler
complain
complete
complied
composed
composer
compound
compress
comprise
computed
computer
conceded
conceive
concerti
concerto
conclave
conclude
concrete
condense
condoled
condoned
conduced
confetti
confided
confined
conflate
conflict
confound
confront
confused
confuted
congress
conjoint
conjugal
conjured
conjurer
conjuror
connived
connoted
conquest
conserve
consider
consoled
consommé
conspire
constant
construe
consular
consumed
consumer
contempt
continue
contract
contrary

contrast
contrite
contrive
contused
convened
convener
convenor
converge
converse
conveyer
conveyor
convince
convoked
convulse
coolness
coonskin
copulate
copybook
coquetry
coquette
cordless
cordovan
corduroy
cornball
corniest
cornmeal
coronary
corporal
corpsman
corridor
corroded
cortical
cortices
corundum
corvette
cosecant
cosiness
cosmetic
costlier
costumed
costumer
couchant
countess
counties
coupling
coursing
courtesy
courtier
covenant
Coventry
coverage
coverall
covering
coverlet
covertly
covetous
cowardly
cowering
co-worker
coxswain
coziness

crabbing
cracking
crackled
cradling
craftier
craftily
cramming
cranefly
crankier
crankily
crannied
crannies
cratered
crawfish
crayfish
craziest
creakier
creakily
creamery
creamier
creasing
creating
creation
creative
creature
credence
credenza
credible
credibly
creditor
creepier
creeping
cremated
creosote
crescent
cretonne
crevasse
cribbage
cribbing
criminal
cringing
crinkled
crippled
crispier
criteria
critical
critique
croakier
crockery
cropping
crossbar
crossbow
crossing
croupier
crucible
crucifix
crudités
cruising
crumpled
crusader
crushing

crustier
crustily
cucumber
cuddling
cudgeled
cul-de-sac
culinary
culottes
culpable
culpably
cultural
cultured
cumbrous
cum laude
cumulate
cumulous
cupboard
cupidity
curative
curdling
curlicue
curliest
currency
currying
curtness
curtsied
curtsies
cushiest
cuspidor
customer
cuteness
cyclamen
cyclical
cylinder
cynicism
cynosure
Cyrillic
czarrina

dabbling
dactylic
Dadaiism
daffodil
daintier
daintily
daiquiri
dairyman
dairymen
dallying
damaging
Damascus
damnably
Damocles
dampness
dandling
dandruff
dandyism
dangling
dankness
danseuse

dappling
daringly
darkling
darkness
darkroom
dateless
dateline
daughter
dauphine
dawdling
daybreak
daydream
daylight
dazzling
deadbeat
deadhead
deadlier
deadline
deadlock
deadwood
deafmute
deafness
deanship
dearness
deathbed
debarred
debasing
debating
debility
debiting
debonair
debugged
decadent
decagram
decanter
deceased
decedent
deceived
deceiver
December
decently
deciding
decimate
decipher
decision
decisive
declared
declined
decoding
decorate
decorous
decrease
decrepit
decrying
dedicate
deepness
defacing
defaming
defecate
defector
defender

deferred
defiance
defiling
defining
definite
deflated
deflower
deforest
deformed
defrayal
deftness
defusing
de Gaulle
degraded
deifying
deionize
dejected
Delaware
delegate
deleting
deletion
delicacy
delicate
delirium
delivery
deloused
deluding
deluging
delusion
delusive
delusory
demagogy
demeanor
demented
dementia
demijohn
demising
democrat
demolish
demoniac
demoting
demotion
demurely
demurred
denazify
denoteed
denoting
denounce
denuding
depicted
depleted
deplored
deposing
depraved
deprived
deputate
deputies
deputing
deputize
deranged
derelict

deriding	dietetic	dissolve
derision	diffused	dissuade
derisive	diggings	distance
derisory	digitize	distaste
deriving	dihedral	distinct
derogate	dilating	distract
describe	dilation	distrait
descried	dilatory	distress
deserted	diligent	district
deserter	dilution	distrust
deserved	diluvial	disunion
designed	diminish	disunite
designer	dinghies	disunity
desiring	dinosaur	disusing
desirous	diocesan	dittoing
desolate	diplomat	diuretic
despatch	directly	divagate
despised	director	divalent
despotic	direness	diverged
destined	dirtying	dividend
detached	disabled	dividing
detainee	disabuse	divinely
detainer	disagree	divinity
detector	disallow	division
deterred	disarray	divisive
dethrone	disaster	divorcee
detonate	disburse	divulged
detritus	disciple	divvying
deviance	disclaim	dizziest
deviated	disclose	dizzying
deviling	discolor	djellaba
devilish	discount	docilely
devilled	discover	docility
deviltry	discreet	docketed
devising	discrete	doctoral
devolved	diseased	doctrine
Devonian	disfavor	document
devoting	disgorge	dogeared
devotion	disgrace	dogfight
devoutly	disguise	doggedly
dewiness	dishiest	doggerel
dewy-eyed	dishonor	dogmatic
dextrose	disinter	do-gooder
dextrous	disjoint	dogwatch
diabetes	disliked	doldrums
diabetic	dislodge	dolomite
diabolic	disloyal	dolorous
diagnose	dismally	domestic
diagonal	dismount	domicile
dialogue	disorder	dominant
dialysis	dispatch	dominate
diamanté	dispense	domineer
diameter	disperse	dominion
diapason	displace	dominoes
diarrhea	disposal	donating
diastole	disprove	donation
diatonic	disputed	doomsday
diatribe	disquiet	doorjamb
dictated	Disraeli	doorknob
dictator	disrobed	dopiness
didactic	disserve	dormancy

dormered
dormouse
dotterel
doubling
doubloon
doubtful
douching
doughier
doughnut
dourness
dovecote
dovetail
doweling
downtown
doxology
drabness
drachmae
drachmai
draftier
dragging
drainage
dramatic
dreadful
dreamily
dreaming
drearier
drearily
dredging
dressage
dressing
dribbled
driftage
drilling
drinking
dripping
driveled
drizzled
drollery
dropping
droughty
drowsily
drowsing
drubbing
drudgery
drudging
drugging
druggist
drumming
drunkard
duckiest
duckling
ductless
dulcimer
dullness
dumbbell
dumbness
dumfound
dumpling
dungaree
dunghill
duodenal

duodenum
duologue
duration
dustless
Dutchman
Dutchmen
dutiable
dwarfish
dwelling
dwindled
dyestuff
dynamics
dynamism
dynamite
dynastic
dynatron
dyslexia
dyslexic

earliest
earnings
easement
easiness
easterly
eastward
eateries
eau-de-vie
eclectic
eclipsed
ecliptic
ecologic
economic
ecstatic
ecumenic
edacious
edentate
edginess
edifying
educable
educated
educator
educible
eduction
eeriness
effacing
efficacy
effigies
effluent
effusing
effusion
effusive
eggplant
egoistic
egomania
Egyptian
eighteen
eighties
Einstein
ejection
elapsing

El Dorado
election
elective
electric
electron
elegance
elegancy
elephant
elevated
elevator
eleventh
eligible
ellipses
ellipsis
elliptic
elongate
eloquent
emaciate
emanated
embalmer
embattle
embedded
embezzle
embitter
emblazon
embodied
embolden
embolism
emceeing
emergent
emerging
emeritus
emersion
emigrant
emigrate
eminence
eminency
emissary
emission
emissive
emitting
Emmental
empathic
emphases
emphasis
emphatic
emplaned
employee
employer
emporium
emptying
empyreal
empyrean
emulsify
emulsion
emulsive
enabling
enameled
enamored
encasing
enceinte

encircle	enuresis	Ethiopia
enclosed	envelope	ethnical
encoding	enviable	etiology
encomium	enviable	Etruscan
encoring	envisage	eugenics
encroach	envision	eulogies
encumber	Eolithic	eulogize
endanger	epicycle	euphonic
endeavor	epidemic	euphoria
endorsee	epidural	euphoric
endorser	epigraph	Eurasian
enduring	epilepsy	European
energies	epilogue	europium
energize	Epiphany	eurythmy
enervate	episodic	evacuate
enfeeble	equaling	evaluate
enforced	equality	evanesce
engaging	equalize	eventful
engender	equalled	eventual
engineer	equating	eversion
engorged	equation	everyday
engraved	equipage	everyone
engraver	equipped	eviction
enhanced	equities	evidence
enlarged	erasable	evildoer
enlarger	erectile	evilness
enlisted	erection	evincing
enmities	erection	evolving
ennobled	erective	exacting
enormity	errantry	examined
enormous	erringly	examiner
enplaned	eruption	exampled
enquired	eruptive	excavate
enquirer	escalade	exceeded
enraging	escalate	excelled
enrolled	escallop	exchange
ensconce	escapade	excising
ensemble	escaping	excision
enshrine	escapism	exciting
enshroud	escapist	excluded
ensilage	escargot	excretal
enslaved	escarole	excreted
ensnared	eschewal	excusing
ensuring	esophagi	execrate
entangle	esoteric	executed
entering	espalier	executer
enthrall	especial	executor
enthrone	espousal	exegeses
enthused	espoused	exegesis
enticing	espresso	exemplar
entirely	essayist	exercise
entirety	esthetic	exertion
entities	estimate	ex gratia
entitled	estivate	exhaling
entozoan	Estonian	exhuming
entracte	estrange	exigency
entrails	estrogen	exiguous
entrance	et cetera	existent
entreaty	eternity	ex libris
entrench	eternize	exorcise
entwined	ethereal	exorcism

exorcist
exorcize
expander
expedite
expelled
expertly
expiated
expiring
explicit
exploded
explorer
exponent
exporter
exposing
exposure
exposure
expunged
extended
extensor
exterior
external
extolled
extorter
extruded
exultant
eyepiece
eyesight
eyeteeth
eyetooth

fabulist
fabulous
faceless
facelift
facetted
facially
facilely
facility
factotum
faddiest
fadeless
failsafe
fairness
faithful
falconer
falconry
falderal
fallible
falsetto
familial
familial
familiar
families
famished
famously
fanciest
fanciful
fancying
fandango
fanlight

fantasia
farcical
farewell
farthest
fascicle
fastener
fastness
fatalism
fatalist
fatality
fatherly
fatigued
fattiest
faultier
faultily
favoring
favorite
fealties
fearless
fearsome
feasible
feasibly
feathery
featured
February
feckless
federate
feedback
feigning
feldspar
felicity
felinity
fellatio
felonies
feminine
feminism
feminist
feminize
ferocity
ferreted
ferrying
fervency
festival
fetching
feticide
feverfew
feverish
feverous
fiascoes
fiddling
fidelity
fiendish
fiercely
fieriest
fiftieth
fighting
figurine
figuring
filament
filially
filigree

Filipino
filleted
filmiest
filthier
finagled
finagler
finalist
finality
finalize
financed
fineries
finespun
finessed
finished
finisher
finitely
fireball
firebomb
fireplug
firetrap
firewood
firework
firmness
fiscally
fishiest
fishwife
fissured
fitfully
fivefold
fixation
fixative
fizziest
fizzling
flabbier
flabbily
flagging
flagrant
flakiest
flamenco
flamingo
flapping
flashier
flatfeet
flatfoot
flatiron
flatness
flattery
flattest
flatting
flatware
flatworm
flaunted
flautist
flavored
flawless
flaxseed
fleabane
fleabite
flection
fledging
fleecing

fleeting
fleshier
flexible
flexibly
flimflam
flimsier
flimsily
flinging
flipflop
flippant
flipping
flitting
floating
flogging
floodlit
flooring
floozies
floppier
floppies
flopping
Florence
flotilla
flounced
flounder
flourish
flowered
floweret
flubbing
fluently
fluffier
fluidity
flunkies
fluoride
flurried
flurries
fluttery
flyblown
flypaper
flywheel
foamiest
focalize
focusing
focussed
fogbound
foggiest
folderol
foliated
folklore
follicle
follower
fomenter
fondling
fondness
foolscap
football
footfall
foothold
footling
footnote
footpath
footsore

footstep
footwear
footwork
foraging
forborne
force-fed
forceful
forcible
forcibly
fordable
forebear
forebode
forecast
foredeck
forefeet
forefoot
foregoes
foregone
forehand
forehead
foreknew
foreknow
forelock
foremast
foremost
forename
forenoon
forensic
forepart
foreplay
foresail
foreseen
foreskin
forester
forestry
foretell
foretold
forewarn
forewent
forewing
foreword
forgiven
forgoing
forklift
formally
formerly
formless
formulae
formulas
forsaken
forsooth
forswear
forswore
forsworn
fortieth
fortress
fostered
fountain
fourfold
foursome
fourteen

fourthly
foxglove
foxhound
foxiness
fraction
fracture
fragment
fragrant
frazzled
freakier
freakish
freckled
freckled
freedman
freedmen
freezing
frenetic
frenzied
frenzies
frequent
frescoed
frescoes
freshman
fretting
fretwork
Freudian
friaries
friction
friendly
frighten
frillier
fringing
frippery
friskier
frizzier
frizzled
frogging
frontage
frontier
front man
front men
frostbit
frostier
frostily
frosting
frothier
froufrou
fructify
fructose
frugally
fruit fly
fruitful
fruitier
fruition
frumpish
fuddling
fuelling
fugitive
Fujiyama
fullback
fullness

fumbling
fumigate
fumingly
function
funerary
funereal
funkiest
funneled
funniest
furbelow
furlough
furriest
furthest
fuselage
fussiest
fustiest
futility
futurism
futurity
fuzziest

gabbling
gadabout
gadgetry
gaieties
gainsaid
galactic
galaxies
Galilean
galloped
galoshes
galvanic
gambling
gamboled
gamester
gaminess
gangland
gangling
ganglion
gangrene
gangster
gantries
gapeworm
garaging
garbling
gardener
gardenia
gargling
gargoyle
garishly
garotted
garrison
garroted
gasified
gaslight
gasolene
gasoline
gassiest
gasworks
gaudiest

gauntlet
gawkiest
gazpacho
gelatine
gelation
gelidity
geminate
gemology
gemstone
gendarme
generate
generous
genetics
genially
genitals
genitive
geniuses
genocide
gentlest
geodesic
geologic
geometry
Georgian
geranium
Germanic
germinal
gestated
gestural
gestured
Ghanaian
ghettoes
ghoulish
gibingly
giddiest
gigantic
giggling
gimcrack
gimmicky
gingerly
girdling
girlhood
giveaway
gladdest
gladiola
gladioli
gladness
glancing
glasnost
glassful
glassier
glassily
glaucoma
gleaming
gleaning
glibbest
glibness
glimpsed
glittery
gloaming
gloating
globally

globular
gloomier
gloomily
glorious
glorying
glossary
glossier
glossily
glowworm
glummest
glutting
gluttony
glycerin
goalpost
goatherd
goatskin
gobbling
god-awful
godchild
Goebbels
gogetter
goggling
goings-on
goldfish
goodness
goofiest
gorgeous
gossamer
gossiped
gourmand
governor
grabbing
graceful
gracious
gradient
graduate
graffiti
graftage
grafting
grandeur
grand mal
grandson
grannies
granular
graphite
grappled
grappler
grasping
grassier
grateful
gratuity
gravamen
graveled
gravelly
grayling
grayness
greasier
greasing
greedier
greedily
greenery

greening
greenish
greeting
greyness
gridiron
grieving
grievous
grillage
grimaced
Grimaldi
grimmest
grimness
grinding
grinning
gripping
grittier
gritting
grizzled
groggier
groggily
groovier
grooving
grottoes
grouping
grousing
groveled
growling
grubbier
grubbing
grudging
grueling
gruesome
grumbled
grumpier
grumpily
grunting
guaranty
guardian
guerilla
guernsey
guessing
guidance
guileful
guiltier
guiltily
gullible
gullibly
gummiest
gumption
gunfight
gunmetal
gunpoint
gunsmith
gurgling
gushiest
gustiest
guttural
guzzling
gymkhana
gyrating
gyration

Habakkuk
habitual
hacienda
hackling
haggling
hairball
hairiest
half-life
hallmark
hallowed
handball
handbill
handcuff
handicap
handiest
handling
handmade
handmaid
handrail
handsome
handyman
handymen
hanger-on
hangnail
hangover
Hannibal
Hanukkah
happiest
harakiri
ha-rangue
hardball
hardener
hardiest
hardware
hardwood
harebell
harlotry
harmless
harmonic
harridan
harrying
hasheesh
hassling
hastiest
hatchery
hatchway
haunches
haunting
hausfrau
Hawaiian
hawthorn
hazelnut
haziness
headache
headgear
headiest
headless
headline
headlong
headword
heartier

heartily
heatedly
heavenly
heaviest
heckling
hedgehog
hedgepig
hedgerow
hedonism
hedonist
heedless
heftiest
hegemony
heighten
heirloom
heliport
Hellenic
helmeted
helmless
helmsman
helpless
Helsinki
hemstich
henchman
henchmen
heptagon
heraldic
heraldry
herdsman
herdsmen
heredity
heresies
herewith
heritage
hermetic
hesitant
hesitate
hexagram
hibiscus
hiccough
hiccuped
high-ball
highbrow
higher-up
highness
high-rise
high-tech
hijacker
hilarity
hilliest
Himalaya
hinderer
hindmost
Hinduism
hireling
Hispanic
historic
hitherto
hoarding
hoarsely
hobbling

hobbyist	hungrily	immodest
hogshead	huntress	immolate
hoisting	huntsman	immortal
holiness	huntsmen	immunity
holiness	hurdling	immunize
hologram	hurrying	immuring
Holstein	hurtling	impacted
homeless	huskiest	impaling
homespun	hustings	impeding
homeward	hustling	impelled
homework	hyacinth	imperial
homicide	hydrated	impetigo
homilies	hydrogen	impinged
hominess	hygienic	implicit
Honduras	hymeneal	imploded
honestly	hypnosis	implored
honeydew	hypnotic	implying
Hong Kong	hysteria	impolite
Honolulu	hysteric	importer
honorary		imposing
hoodwink		impostor
hooligan	ice cream	impotent
hopeless	ice-skate	imprison
hormonal	idealism	improper
horniest	idealist	improved
horology	idealize	impudent
horrible	ideation	impugner
horribly	idée fixe	impunity
horridly	identify	impurity
horrific	identity	imputing
horsefly	ideology	inaction
horseman	idiocies	inactive
horsemen	idleness	incensed
horsiest	idolater	inchoate
hospital	idolatry	incident
hostelry	idolized	incising
hotelier	igniting	incision
hothouse	ignition	incisive
houseman	ignominy	inciting
housemen	ignorant	inclined
hovering	ignoring	included
howitzer	ill-fated	incoming
huckster	ill-timed	increase
huddling	illumine	incubate
huffiest	ill-usage	incurred
hugeness	illusion	indebted
Huguenot	illusive	indecent
hula-hula	illusory	indented
humanely	imagined	indicate
humanism	imagines	indigent
humanity	imbecile	indirect
humanize	imbedded	indolent
humanoid	imbibing	inducing
humbling	imitated	inductee
humidify	imitator	indulged
humidity	immanent	industry
humility	immature	inedible
humorist	immerged	inequity
humorous	immersed	inerrant
humpback	imminent	inertial
hungrier	immobile	inexpert

infamies	interior	jalousie
infamous	intermit	jamboree
infantry	intermix	jangling
inferior	internal	Japanese
infernal	internee	jaundice
infernos	Interpol	jauntily
inferred	interred	Javanese
infinite	interval	jazziest
infinity	intimacy	jealousy
inflamed	intimate	jeopardy
inflated	intimate	jeremiad
informal	intonate	Jeremiah
informed	intoning	jerkiest
informer	intrench	jetliner
infra dig	intrepid	jettison
infrared	intrigue	jewelled
infringe	intruded	jeweller
infusing	intruder	jew's-harp
infusion	intuited	jiggling
inhalant	inundate	jim-dandy
inhaling	invading	jimmying
inherent	invasion	jingling
inhering	invasive	jingoism
inhumane	inveigle	jocosely
inimical	inventor	jocosity
iniquity	inverted	joggling
initiate	investor	jokester
injector	inviting	jokingly
injuries	invoiced	jolliest
injuring	invoking	jostling
inlaying	involute	jovially
innately	involved	joyfully
innocent	inwardly	joyously
innovate	inweaved	joystick
innuendo	Irishman	jubilant
inquired	Irishmen	Judaical
inquirer	ironclad	judgment
insanely	ironical	judicial
insanity	ironware	juggling
inscribe	ironwork	juiciest
insecure	Iroquois	julienne
inserter	irrigate	jumbling
insignia	irritant	jumpiest
insolent	irritate	junction
insomnia	Islamism	juncture
insomuch	islander	Jurassic
inspired	isolated	justness
inspirit	isotherm	juvenile
instable	isotonic	
instance	isotopic	
instated	issuance	kamikaze
instinct	Istanbul	kangaroo
instruct	itemized	Katmandu
insulate		kedgeree
insuring		keelhaul
intaglio	jackboot	keenness
integral	jacketed	keepsake
intently	Jacobean	kenneled
interact	jacquard	Kentucky
intercom	jailbird	kerchief
interest	jalopies	kerosene

keyboard
keypunch
keystone
Khartoum
kibitzer
kickback
kidnaped
kidnaper
killdeer
kilobyte
kilogram
kilovolt
kilowatt
kindling
kindness
kinetics
kingbolt
king-size
Kingston
kinkiest
kinsfolk
Kinshasa
Kiribati
kissable
knapsack
kneedeep
kneeling
knickers
knightly
knitting
knitwear
knobbier
knockout
knothole
knotless
knottier
knotting
knowable
knuckled
kohlrabi
kolinsky
kookiest
Krakatoa

labeling
labelled
Labrador
laburnum
lacerate
lacrosse
lactated
ladylike
ladyship
laid-back
lakeside
lamasery
lambaste
lambskin
lameness
laminate

lamppost
landfall
landlady
landless
landlord
landmark
landmass
landslip
landward
lang syne
language
languish
lankiest
lankness
lapidary
larboard
largesse
larkspur
larynges
Las Vegas
latchkey
lateness
latently
Latinate
latitude
latterly
latticed
laudable
laudably
laudanum
laughing
laughter
launcher
laureate
Lausanne
lavatory
lavender
lavishly
lawfully
lawmaker
laxative
layabout
laziness
leafless
leakiest
leanness
leapfrog
learning
leathery
Lebanese
lectured
lecturer
leftover
leftward
left-wing
legacies
legalism
legalist
legality
legalize
legation

leggiest
lemonade
lengthen
lenience
leniency
lenitive
lethally
lethargy
lettered
letterer
leukemia
leveling
levelled
leverage
levitate
lewdness
liaising
libation
libeling
libelled
libelous
liberate
Liberian
libretti
libretto
licensed
licensee
licenser
licorice
lierally
lifeboat
lifebuoy
lifeless
lifelike
lifeline
life-size
lifetime
lifework
ligament
ligature
lighting
lighting
likeable
likelier
likewise
limerick
limiting
linchpin
linesman
linesmen
lingerie
linguist
liniment
linoleum
Linotype
lionized
lipstick
lip-synch
listener
listless
litanies

literacy	luckiest	malignly
literary	luckless	malinger
literate	lukewarm	maltreat
literati	luminary	manacled
litigant	luminous	managing
litigate	lumpiest	mandamus
littoral	lunacies	mandarin
liturgic	luncheon	mandated
liveable	lunkhead	mandible
livelier	luscious	mandolin
livelong	lushness	mandrake
liveried	lustiest	mandrill
liveries	lustrous	man-eater
liverish	lutanist	maneuver
lividity	lutetium	manfully
loathing	Lutheran	mangling
lobbying	luxuries	mangrove
lobbyist	lychgate	maniacal
lobotomy	lynching	manicure
locality	lynchpin	manifest
localize	lyricism	manifold
locating	lyricist	Manitoba
location		manliest
lockable		mannered
locution	macaroni	mannerly
lodestar	macaroon	mannikin
lodgment	macerate	man-of-war
loftiest	machined	manorial
logician	machismo	manpower
logistic	mackerel	man-sized
loiterer	mackinaw	mantilla
lollipop	madrigal	manually
lolloped	madwoman	marabout
lonelier	madwomen	marathon
lonesome	magazine	marauder
longhair	magician	marbling
longhand	magicked	marginal
long-term	magnesia	mariachi
looker-on	magnetic	marigold
looniest	magnolia	marinade
loophole	maharani	marinate
lopsided	mah-jongg	maritime
lordosis	mahogany	marjoram
lordship	mailable	markedly
lothario	mainland	marketed
loudness	mainline	marksman
lounging	mainmast	marksmen
lousiest	mainsail	marmoset
loveable	mainstay	marquess
lovebird	maintain	marquise
loveless	majestic	Marrakes
loveless	majolica	marriage
lovelier	majority	marrying
lovingly	makeable	marshier
lowering	Malagasy	martinet
lowkeyed	malaprop	martyred
low-level	malarial	marveled
lowliest	malarkey	Maryland
low-lying	Malaysia	marzipan
loyalist	mal de mer	massacre
lucidity	Maldives	massaged

masseuse
masterly
masthead
mastodon
material
materiel
maternal
matrices
matronly
mattress
maturate
maturing
maturity
maverick
maximize
mayflies
mayoress
mea culpa
meanness
meantime
measlier
measured
measurer
meatiest
mechanic
meddling
mediated
mediator
Medicaid
Medicare
medicate
medicine
medieval
mediocre
meditate
meekness
megabyte
megalith
megawatt
melamine
melanoma
melodeon
melodies
meltable
membrane
memorial
memories
memorize
memsahib
menacing
mendable
menially
meniscus
men-of-war
menswear
mentally
mephitic
merchant
merciful
mergence
meridian

meringue
meriting
merriest
mesdames
mesdames
meshugge
meshwork
mesmeric
Mesozoic
mesquite
messiest
metaling
metalize
metalled
metallic
metaphor
meteoric
methanol
metonymy
metrical
miasmata
microdot
middling
midnight
midpoint
midwives
mightier
mightily
migraine
migrated
migrator
miladies
mildness
militant
military
militate
milkiest
milkmaid
milkweed
milliner
millpond
mimicked
mimicker
minatory
mindless
mingiest
mingling
minimize
minister
ministry
minority
minotaur
minstrel
minutely
minutest
minutiae
minuting
mirrored
misapply
miscarry
mischief

miscible
miscount
miscuing
misdealt
misdoing
miserere
miseries
misfired
misguide
misheard
mishmash
misjudge
mismatch
mismated
misnamed
misnomer
misogamy
misogyny
misplace
misprint
misprize
misquote
misruled
misshape
Missouri
misspell
misspelt
misspend
misspent
misstate
mistaken
mistiest
mistimed
mistreat
mistress
mistrial
mistrust
misusage
misusing
misvalue
mitigate
mnemonic
mobility
mobilize
moccasin
modality
modeling
modelled
moderate
modestly
modified
modifier
modishly
modulate
Mohammed
moisture
molasses
moldable
Moldavia
moldiest
molecule

molehill	motorcar	mystical
moleskin	motorist	mystique
molester	motorize	mythical
momentum	motorman	
monarchy	mottling	
monastic	mountain	nacreous
monaural	mounting	nainsook
monetary	mournful	nameless
monetize	mourning	namesake
Mongolia	mousiest	Napoleon
mongoose	moussaka	narcissi
monistic	mouthful	narcosis
monition	moveable	narcotic
monkeyed	movement	narrated
monodist	movingly	narrator
monogamy	muchness	narrowly
monogram	mucilage	narwhale
monolith	muckiest	nasality
monomial	muckrake	nasalize
monopoly	mucosity	nascence
monorail	muddiest	nascency
monotone	muddling	nastiest
monotony	muddying	natality
Monotype	mudguard	national
monoxide	muffling	natively
Monrovia	Muhammad	nativism
monsieur	mulberry	nativist
Montreal	muleteer	nativity
monument	mulligan	nattiest
moodiest	multiple	nauseate
moonbeam	multiply	nauseous
moonless	mumbling	nautical
mootness	munition	nautilus
moquette	muralist	navigate
moralist	murderer	Nazarene
morality	murkiest	Nazareth
moralize	murmurer	nearness
morbidly	muscatel	neatness
mordancy	muscling	Nebraska
moreover	muscular	nebulous
moribund	mushroom	necklace
Moroccan	musicale	neckline
morosely	musician	neediest
morpheme	musketry	needless
Morpheus	musquash	needling
morphine	mustache	negating
mortally	mustiest	negation
mortgage	Musulman	negative
mortised	Musulmen	negligee
mortoria	mutating	Nehemiah
mortuary	mutation	neighbor
moseying	muteness	nematode
mosquito	mutilate	neonatal
mossback	mutineer	neophyte
mossiest	mutinied	neoprene
mosslike	mutinies	nepotism
mothball	mutinous	nepotist
motherly	muttered	nestling
motility	mutually	nestling
motivate	muzzling	nettling
motorbus	mycology	neuritic

neuritis
neuroses
neurosis
neurotic
newcomer
newlywed
newsreel
newsroom
Nez Perce
nibbling
niceness
niceties
nickname
nicotine
niftiest
niftiest
niggling
nightcap
nihilism
nihilist
Nijinsky
nineteen
nineties
nitrogen
nobelium
nobility
nobleman
noblemen
nobodies
nocturne
noisiest
nomadism
nominate
nonesuch
nonevent
nonhuman
nonmetal
nonsense
nonstick
nonunion
nonwhite
noontime
normalcy
normally
Normandy
Norseman
northern
nosedive
nosiness
nota bene
notaries
notarize
notation
notebook
noticing
notified
notional
novelist
November
novocain
nowadays

nucleate
nudeness
nugatory
nuisance
numbness
numeracy
numerate
numerous
numskull
nurtured
nuthatch
nutrient
nutshell
nuttiest
nuzzling

obduracy
obdurate
obedient
obeisant
obituary
objector
oblation
obligate
obliging
oblivion
obscured
observed
observer
obsesive
obsidian
obsolete
obstacle
obstruct
obtruded
obviated
obvolute
occasion
occident
occluded
occupant
occupied
occupier
occurred
octoroon
oddities
odometer
odorless
offcolor
offender
offering
official
offshoot
offshore
offstage
ohmmeter
oilcloth
oilfield
oiliness
ointment

Oklahoma
old-timer
old-world
oleander
oligarch
Olympiad
Olympian
omelette
omission
omitting
oncoming
one-piece
one-sided
onlooker
ooziness
opaquely
openness
openwork
operable
operably
operated
operatic
operator
operetta
opponent
opposing
opposite
optician
optimism
optimist
optimize
optional
opulence
oracular
orangery
oratorio
ordainer
ordinand
ordinary
ordnance
organdie
organism
organist
organize
orgasmic
Oriental
original
ornament
ornately
orthodox
osculate
ossified
outboard
outbound
outbrave
outbreak
outburst
outclass
outcries
outdated
outdoing

outdoors	overstep	parallel
outfield	overtake	paralyze
outflank	overtime	paramour
outgoing	overtone	paranoia
outgrown	overtook	paranoid
outhouse	overture	paraquat
outlined	overturn	parasite
outlived	overview	par avion
outlying	overwork	parceled
outmoded	ovulated	pardoned
outraged	owlishly	parental
outrange	oxidized	Parisian
outrider	oxymoron	parlance
outright		parlayed
outshine		parleyed
outshone	pacified	Parmesan
outsider	pacifier	parodied
outsmart	pacifism	parodist
outstrip	pacifist	paroling
outvoted	packaged	paroxysm
outwards	packager	parroted
outweigh	paddling	parrying
ovalness	Paganini	partaken
overcame	paganism	partaker
overcast	paginate	Parthian
overcoat	painless	particle
overcome	painting	partisan
overdoes	Pakistan	partying
overdone	palatial	passable
overdose	palatine	passably
overflow	paleness	passerby
overhand	palimony	Passover
overhang	palisade	passport
overhaul	palliate	password
overhead	palmetto	pastiche
overhear	palomino	pastiest
overheat	palpable	pastille
overhung	palpably	pastoral
overkill	palpated	pastrami
overlaid	pamphlet	pastries
overland	panatela	pastured
overleaf	pancaked	patchier
overload	pancreas	patellae
overlook	pandemic	patentee
overlord	panderer	patently
overmuch	paneling	paternal
overpaid	panelist	pathetic
overpass	panicked	patience
overplay	panorama	pavement
overrate	pantheon	pavilion
override	pantiles	paycheck
overrode	pantries	peaceful
overrule	Pap smear	peachier
overseas	parabola	pebblier
overseen	paradigm	pebbling
overseer	parading	pectoral
oversell	paradise	peculate
overshoe	paraffin	peculiar
overshot	Paraguay	pedagogy
oversize	parakeet	pedaling
oversold	parallax	pedalled

pedantic
pedantry
peddling
pederast
pedestal
pedicure
pedigree
pediment
pedology
peekaboo
peephole
peerless
peignoir
Pekinese
pellagra
pell-mell
pellucid
pemmican
penalize
penchant
penciled
pendency
pendulum
penitent
penknife
penology
pentacle
pentagon
pentomic
penumbra
peopling
per annum
perceive
perforce
perfumed
periling
perilous
perineum
periodic
perjured
perjurer
perkiest
permeate
perorate
peroxide
personae
personal
perspire
persuade
pertness
perusing
Peruvian
pervaded
pervader
perverse
pervious
peskiest
petition
pettiest
pettifog
petulant

phantasm
phantasy
pharisee
pharmacy
pheasant
phonemic
phonetic
phoniest
phrasing
physical
physique
picayune
pickerel
picketed
picketer
pickiest
pickling
pick-me-up
pictured
piddling
piercing
pigsties
pilaster
pilferer
pillaged
pillager
pillared
pilotage
piloting
pinafore
pince-nez
pinch-hit
pinecone
pinewood
pingpong
pinioned
pinnacle
pinochle
pinprick
pintsize
pinwheel
pipeline
piquancy
pirating
Pissarro
pistoled
pithiest
pitiable
pitiably
pitiless
pittance
pivoting
pixieish
pizzeria
placable
placably
placated
placenta
placidly
plagiary
plaguing

plaiting
plangent
planking
plankton
planless
planning
plantain
plateaux
plateful
platelet
platform
platinum
platonic
platting
platypus
playback
playbill
playmate
playroom
pleading
pleasant
pleasing
pleasure
plebeian
plectrum
pledging
Pleiades
plethora
pleurisy
pliantly
Pliocene
plodding
plopping
plotting
plowable
pluckier
pluckily
plugging
plumbing
plummier
plumpish
plunging
plurally
plushier
pocketed
pockmark
podiatry
poetical
poignant
poisoned
poisoner
polarity
polarize
Polaroid
poleless
policies
policing
polisher
politely
politico
politics

polities
polkaing
polliwog
pollster
polluted
polluter
polonium
poltroon
polygamy
polyglot
polygyny
pomander
pommeled
pony tail
pooh-pooh
poopular
popinjay
Popsicle
populace
populate
populism
populist
populous
porosity
porphyry
porpoise
porridge
portable
portably
portaged
porthole
portlier
portrait
Port Said
Portugal
positing
position
positive
positron
possible
possibly
postcard
postdate
postlude
postmark
postpaid
postpone
postured
potatoes
potbelly
potently
potsherd
poultice
pouncing
poundage
pourable
powerful
practice
praedial
praising
prancing

prankish
pratfall
prattled
preacher
preamble
preceded
precinct
precious
preclude
predator
preexist
prefaced
pregnant
prejudge
premiere
premised
prenatal
prepared
presaged
prescibe
prescind
presence
preserve
presided
pressing
pressman
pressmen
pressure
prestige
presumed
pretense
preterit
Pretoria
prettier
prettify
prettily
previous
priciest
prickled
prie-dieu
priestly
priggish
primeval
primmest
primming
primness
primrose
primulae
princely
princess
printing
printout
prioress
priories
priority
prisoner
pristine
probable
probably
probated
proceeds

proclaim
procured
procurer
prodding
prodigal
produced
producer
profaned
profaner
profiled
profited
pro forma
profound
progress
prohibit
prolapse
prolific
prologue
promised
promoted
promoter
prompter
promptly
properly
property
prophecy
prophesy
proposal
proposed
proposer
propound
propping
prorated
proscibe
prosiest
prospect
prostate
protégée
protocol
protract
protrude
provable
provably
Provence
provided
provider
province
provoked
proximal
prudence
prurient
Prussian
psalmist
ptomaine
publican
publicly
puddling
puffball
puffiest
pugilism
pugilist

puissant
Pulitzer
pulmotor
pulsated
pulsator
pummeled
pumpable
punchier
punctual
puncture
pungency
puniness
punitive
puppetry
puppyish
purchase
purebred
pureness
purified
purifier
puristic
purlieus
purplish
purpoive
purposed
pursuant
pursuing
purulent
purveyor
pushcart
pushiest
pushover
pussycat
putative
puzzling
pyorrhea
Pyrenees

quackery
quadrant
quadrate
quadroon
quagmire
quaintly
qualmish
quandary
quantify
quantity
quarried
quarries
quatrain
quayside
queasier
queasily
querying
question
queueing
quibbled
quieting
quietism

quietude
quilting
quipping
quipster
quirkier
quisling
quitting
quivered
quixotic
quizzing
quotable
quotient

rabbeted
rabbited
racially
raciness
radially
radiance
radiancy
radiated
radiator
radioing
raffling
raggedly
raillery
railroad
raincoat
rainfall
rainiest
rallying
rambling
ramified
rampaged
rampancy
ranching
randiest
randomly
rankling
rapacity
rapidity
rarefied
rarefied
rarities
rascally
rashness
rateable
ratified
ratifier
rational
rattiest
rattling
ravaging
raveling
ravenous
rawboned
reaction
reactive
readable
readjust

readying
reaffirm
realized
reappear
rearmost
reasoner
reassert
reassume
reassure
rebating
rebelled
rebuking
rebuttal
rebutted
rebutter
recapped
receding
received
receiver
recently
recharge
recision
reciting
reckless
reclined
recliner
recommit
recorder
recourse
recovery
recreant
recreate
recurred
redeemer
redeploy
redirect
redolent
redouble
reducing
reechoes
reediest
reef knot
reemploy
reenlist
refereed
referent
referral
referral
referred
refinery
refinery
refining
refinish
refitted
reflated
reforest
reformed
reformer
reformer
refusing
refuting

regaling
regicide
regiment
regional
register
registry
regulate
rehearse
rehoused
reindeer
reinvest
rejoiced
rekindle
relapsed
relating
relation
relative
relaxant
relaying
released
relegate
relevant
reliable
reliably
reliance
relieved
religion
reliving
relocate
remaking
remedial
remedied
remedies
remember
reminder
remitted
remotely
removing
renaming
renegade
reneging
renounce
renovate
renowned
repartee
repaying
repeated
repeater
repelled
rephrase
replaced
replying
reporter
reposing
repotted
reprieve
reprisal
reproach
reproved
republic
repulsed

reputing
required
requital
rerouted
rescuing
research
resemble
reserved
resettle
resident
residing
residual
resigned
resinous
resister
resistor
resolute
resolved
resonant
resonate
resource
respired
response
restated
restless
restored
restorer
restrain
restrict
resuming
retailer
retainer
retaking
retarded
reticent
reticule
retiring
retraced
retrench
retrieve
returnee
reunited
reveille
reveling
revelled
reveller
revenged
revenuer
reverend
reverent
revering
reversal
reversed
reviewer
reviling
revising
revision
revivify
reviving
revoking
revolved

revolver
rewiring
rhapsody
rheostat
rhetoric
rhinitis
rhomboid
rhythmic
ribaldry
richness
rickshaw
ricochet
riddance
riddling
ridicule
Riesling
riffling
riffraff
rifleman
riflemen
rightful
rightism
rightist
rigidity
rigorous
ringside
ringworm
riparian
ripeness
riposted
rippling
riskiest
ritually
rivaling
rivalled
riveting
roadside
roadster
roadwork
robotics
robustly
rocketed
rocketry
rockiest
roentgen
roll call
roly-poly
romanced
Romanian
Romanies
Romansch
romantic
roofless
roomiest
roommate
rootless
rosaries
rosemary
rosewood
rosiness
Rotarian

rotating
rotation
roughage
roulette
Rousseau
rowdiest
rowdyism
royalist
rubbishy
rubicund
rubidium
rucksack
ruddiest
rudeness
rudiment
ruefully
ruffling
ruggedly
rumbling
ruminant
ruminate
rumpling
runabout
runner-up
runniest
runtiest
ruptured
rush hour
rustiest
rustling
rutabaga
ruthless
ruttiest
ryegrass

sabotage
saboteur
sacredly
sacristy
saddling
Sadducee
sadistic
sagacity
sageness
salaried
salaries
saleable
salesman
salesmen
salience
saliency
salinity
salivary
salivate
sallying
saltiest
salutary
saluting
salvaged
Salzburg

samarium
sameness
samizdat
sampling
sanctify
sanction
sanctity
sand-cast
San Diego
sandiest
sandwich
saneness
sanguine
sanitary
sanitize
Sanskrit
Santiago
sapience
sapiency
sapphire
saraband
sardonic
Satanism
Satanist
satiable
satiably
satiated
satirist
satirize
saturate
Saturday
saucepan
sauciest
sauterne
savagely
savagery
savaging
savannah
savories
savorily
scabbard
scabbing
scaffold
scalawag
scalding
scallion
scandium
scanning
scansion
scantier
scantily
scarcely
scarcity
scariest
scarring
scathing
scatting
scavenge
scenario
scenical
schedule

schemata
scheming
Schiller
schizoid
schmaltz
schnapps
schooner
Schubert
Schumann
sciatica
scimitar
scissors
scofflaw
scolding
scoopful
scorched
scorcher
scornful
Scorpian
scorpion
scot-free
Scotland
Scotsman
Scotsmen
Scottish
scourged
scouting
scrabble
scragged
scraggly
scramble
scrammed
scraping
scrapped
scrapper
scratchy
screamer
screener
screwier
scribble
scribing
scrofula
scrounge
scrubbed
scrutiny
scudding
scuffled
scullery
sculptor
scurried
scuttled
scything
seaboard
seaborne
seafarer
sea front
seagoing
seahorse
sealskin
seamless
seaplane

searcher	serenade	shocking
seascape	serenely	shoddier
seashell	serenity	shoddily
seashore	sergeant	shooting
seasonal	serially	shopping
seasoner	seriatim	shopworn
seceding	serrated	shortage
secluded	serviced	shortcut
seconder	set piece	Shoshone
secondly	settling	shoulder
secreted	severely	shouting
secretly	severest	shoveled
securely	severing	showcase
securing	severity	showdown
security	sewerage	showiest
sedately	sexiness	showroom
sedating	sextuple	shrapnel
sedation	sexually	shredded
sedative	shabbier	shredder
sediment	shabbily	shrewdly
sedition	shackled	shrewish
seducing	shadiest	shriving
sedulity	shafting	shrugged
sedulous	shaggier	shrunken
seedcake	shaggily	shuffled
seediest	shagging	shunning
seedling	shagreen	shutdown
seething	shakiest	shutting
selected	shambled	shuttled
selector	shambles	sibilant
selenium	shameful	Sicilian
selfless	shamming	sicklier
self-made	shamrock	sickness
self-pity	shandies	sickroom
selfsame	shanghai	sidekick
selvedge	shanties	sideline
semantic	shantung	sidereal
semester	sharpish	sideshow
semiarid	shearing	sidestep
seminary	sheathed	sidewalk
Seminole	sheather	sideways
semiotic	shedding	siftings
Semitism	sheepish	signaled
semitone	sheeting	signally
semolina	sheikdom	signpost
senility	shelving	silenced
senorita	shepherd	silencer
sensible	sherries	silently
sensibly	shiftier	silicone
sensuous	shiftily	silkiest
sentence	shilling	silkworm
sentient	shimmery	silliest
sentinel	shimmied	simonize
sentries	shingled	simplest
separate	shingles	simplify
Sephardi	shiniest	simulate
septuple	shinning	sinecure
sequence	shipmate	sinfully
sequined	shipment	singeing
seraphic	shipping	singling
seraphim	shlepped	singsong

singular
sinister
sinkable
sinkhole
Sinn Fein
sinuated
sisterly
situated
sixtieth
sizzling
skeletal
skeleton
skewbald
skidding
skillful
skimming
skimpier
skimpily
skin-deep
skin-dive
skinhead
skinnier
skinning
skipping
skirmish
skittish
skullcap
skylight
slabbing
slamming
slangier
slapdash
slapping
slashing
slattern
slatting
Slavonic
sleazier
sleazily
sledding
sledging
sleepier
sleepily
sleeping
sleeving
slightly
slimiest
slimmest
slimming
slimness
slinging
slinkier
slinking
slipknot
slippage
slippery
slipping
slipshod
slithery
slitting
slobbery

sloe-eyed
slogging
sloppier
sloppily
slopping
slothful
slotting
slovenly
slowdown
slowness
slowpoke
slowworm
sluggard
slugging
sluggish
sluicing
slummier
slumming
slurring
slushier
sluttish
smacking
smallish
smallpox
smarmier
smashing
smellier
smelling
smithies
smitting
smocking
smokiest
smoothen
smoothie
smoothly
smudgier
smudging
smuggest
smuggled
smuggler
smugness
smuttier
snagging
snakiest
snappier
snapping
snappish
snapshot
snazzier
sneakier
sneakily
sneaking
sneezing
sniffier
sniffily
sniffled
snipping
snitcher
sniveled
snobbery
snobbier

snobbish
snootier
snoozing
snottier
snowball
snowfall
snowiest
snowplow
snowshoe
snubbing
snuffbox
snuffled
snuggest
snugging
snuggled
snugness
soapsuds
sobriety
sociable
sociably
socially
societal
Socrates
Socratic
sodality
softball
softener
softness
software
softwood
soggiest
solacing
solarium
solarize
solecism
solemnly
soleness
solenoid
solidify
solidity
solitary
solitude
solstice
solution
solvable
solvency
somberly
sombrero
somebody
somewhat
songbird
songster
son-in-law
sonority
sonorous
soothing
soppiest
Sorbonne
sorcerer
soreness
sorority

sorriest
sortable
soulless
sounding
sourness
southern
southpaw
souvenir
spaceman
spacemen
spacious
spackled
spadeful
spangled
Spaniard
spanking
spanning
sparkled
sparkler
sparring
sparsely
spatting
speaking
specific
specimen
specious
speckled
spectral
spectrum
speculum
speedier
speedily
speeding
speedway
spelling
spending
sphagnum
spheroid
spiciest
spikiest
spillage
spilling
spindled
spinning
spinning
spinster
spiracle
spiraled
spirally
spirited
spiteful
spitting
spittoon
splatter
splendid
splendor
splicing
splinter
splotchy
splurged
splutter

spoilage
spoiling
spondaic
spongier
sponging
spookier
spoon-fed
spoonful
sporadic
sporting
sportive
spotless
spottier
spottily
spotting
sprained
spreader
springer
sprinkle
sprinter
sprocket
sprucely
sprucing
spryness
spunkier
spurious
spurring
spurtive
squabble
squadron
squander
squarely
squaring
squarish
squatted
squatter
squeaker
squealer
squeegee
squeezed
squeezer
squiggle
squinter
squirrel
Sri Lanka
stabbing
stabling
staccato
stagging
stagiest
stagnant
stagnate
stairway
stallion
stalwart
stampede
standard
standing
standoff
stapling
stargaze

starling
starring
starring
startled
starving
statuary
staysail
steadied
steadier
steadily
stealing
stealthy
steamier
stedfast
steerage
stemless
stemming
Stendhal
stepping
sterling
stetting
stickier
sticking
stickler
stickler
stickpin
stifling
stigmata
stiletto
stimulus
stingier
stinging
stingray
stinking
stinting
stippled
stirring
stockade
stockier
stockily
stocking
stodgier
stoicism
stolidly
stoniest
stopcock
stoppage
stopping
storeyed
stormier
stowaway
straddle
stradled
strafing
straggle
straggly
straight
strainer
straiten
stranger
stranger

strangle
strapped
strategy
stratify
straying
streaker
streamer
strength
stretchy
strewing
striated
stricken
stricken
strictly
stridden
strident
striding
striking
stripier
striping
stripped
stripper
striving
stroking
stroller
strongly
stropped
struggle
strummed
strumpet
strutted
stubbier
stubbing
stubbled
stubborn
stuccoed
studding
studious
studying
stuffing
stultify
stumbled
stumpier
stunning
stuntman
stuntmen
stupidly
sturdier
sturdily
sturgeon
stylized
subduing
subentry
subgroup
subhuman
sublease
submerge
submerse
subpoena
subsided
subsonic

subsumed
subtitle
subtlety
subtract
suburban
suburbia
succinct
succorer
suchlike
suckling
Sudanese
suddenly
sufferer
sufficed
suffrage
suffused
sufragan
suicidal
suitable
suitably
suitcase
sukiyaki
sulfuric
sulkiest
sullenly
sullying
sultrily
sunbathe
sunburnt
sundries
sunlight
sunniest
sunshade
sunshine
superbly
superego
superior
superman
supermen
supernal
supplant
supplest
supplied
supplier
supplies
supposed
suppress
surcease
sureness
sureties
surfaced
surgical
surliest
surmised
surmount
surplice
surprise
surround
surveyor
survival
survived

survivor
suspense
suturing
suzerain
sveltely
swabbing
swaddled
swampier
swan dive
swankily
swapping
swastika
swathing
swatting
swayable
swearing
sweatily
sweating
sweeping
sweetish
swelling
swerving
swigging
swimming
swimsuit
swindled
swindler
swinging
swiveled
swopping
sycamore
syllabic
syllable
syllabub
syllabus
symbolic
symmetry
sympathy
symphony
symposia
syndrome
synonymy
synopses
synopsis
synoptic
syphilis
Syracuse
syringed
systemic
systolic

tableaux
tabooing
tabulate
taciturn
tackiest
tackling
tactical
tactless
Tahitian

tailback	Teletype	thorough
tailgate	televise	thousand
tailless	telltale	thrasher
tailored	temerity	threaten
takeover	tempered	threnody
talented	temperer	thresher
talisman	template	thriller
talkiest	temporal	thriving
tallying	tempting	throbbed
Talmudic	tenacity	throttle
tamarack	tendency	throwing
tamarind	tenderly	thrummed
tamarisk	tenement	thudding
tameness	Tennyson	thuggery
tandoori	tentacle	thuggish
tangency	tenurial	thumping
tangible	tepidity	thundery
tangibly	teriyaki	Thursday
tangiest	terminal	Tiberius
tangling	terminus	tickling
tangoing	terraced	ticklish
Tanzania	terrapin	tideland
tapestry	terrazzo	tidemark
tapeworm	terrible	tidiness
tardiest	terribly	tigerish
targeted	terrific	tightwad
tarragon	tertiary	tillable
tarrying	testator	timbered
tartaric	testicle	Timbuktu
tartness	testiest	timeless
tasseled	Teutonic	timeworn
tasteful	textbook	timidity
tastiest	textural	timorous
tattered	textured	tincture
tattiest	Thailand	tingeing
tattling	thallium	tingling
tattooed	thankful	tininess
tautness	thatcher	tinkling
tawdrier	theistic	tinniest
tawdrily	thematic	tinseled
tawniest	theocrat	tippling
tax-ation	theology	tipsiest
taxonomy	theories	tiptoing
taxpayer	theorist	tireless
teaching	theorize	tiresome
teakwood	thespian	Tirolean
teammate	thiamine	titanium
teamster	thickish	titmouse
teamwork	thickset	toadying
teaseled	thievery	toadyism
teaspoon	thieving	toboggan
tectonic	thievish	toddling
teenager	thinking	together
teeniest	thinness	toggling
teething	thinnest	toiletry
teetotal	thinning	toilsome
tegument	thirteen	tokenism
telecast	thirties	tolerant
telegram	thoraces	tolerate
teletext	thoracic	tomahawk
telethon	thornier	tomatoes

commyrot
comorrow
conality
coneless
consured
coothier
cop-heavy
copology
coppling
coreador
cornadic
cornados
corpidly
corridly
cortilla
cortoise
cortuous
cortured
torturer
totaling
totality
totalled
totemism
totemist
touchier
touching
Toulouse
touristy
toweling
towelled
towering
township
toxicity
tracheae
trachoma
trackage
traction
tractive
traduced
tragical
training
traipsed
tramping
trampled
tranquil
transact
transect
transept
transfer
transfix
transmit
trapdoor
trapezia
trapping
Trappist
trashier
traveled
traveler
travelog
traverse
travesty

treading
treasure
treasury
treaties
treatise
trebling
treeless
trekking
trembled
trencher
trendier
trephine
trespass
triangle
Triassic
tribunal
trickery
trickier
trickily
trickled
tricolor
tricycle
trifling
trillion
trimaran
trimmest
trimming
trimness
Trinidad
tripling
tripping
triptych
trochaic
trombone
trophies
tropical
trotting
troubled
trounced
trouping
trousers
truantry
truckage
trucking
truckled
trudging
trueness
truistic
trumpery
truncate
trundled
trussing
trusteed
trustful
trustier
truthful
tubbiest
tubeless
tubercle
tuberose
tuberous

tumbling
tumidity
tumorous
tuneless
tungsten
tunneled
turbaned
turbofan
turbojet
turmeric
turncoat
turnover
turnpike
tussling
tutelage
tutorage
tutorial
tutoring
tweezers
tweezing
twenties
twiddled
twilight
twinging
twinkled
twinning
twittery
two-faced
two-sided
tympanic
tympanum
typecast
typeface
typified
typology
tyrannic
Tyrolean

ubiquity
ugliness
ulcerate
ulcerous
ulterior
ultimate
umbrella
umpiring
unafraid
unawares
unbacked
unbanned
unbarred
unbeaten
unbelief
unbended
unbiased
unbidden
unbroken
unbuckle
unburden
unbutton

uncapped	unnerved	vagabond
uncaring	unsaddle	vagaries
unclothe	unsavory	vagrancy
uncombed	unseeing	vainness
uncommon	unseemly	valanced
uncooked	unsettle	validate
uncouple	unshaded	validity
unctuous	unshaken	valorize
undenied	unshaven	valorous
underact	unsigned	valuable
underage	unsought	valuably
underarm	unspoilt	valvular
underbid	unspoken	vampiric
undercut	unstable	vanadium
underdog	unstated	vaneless
underfed	unsteady	vanguard
underlay	unstrung	vanities
underlie	unsuited	vanquish
underpin	untangle	vapidity
undersea	untapped	vaporish
undertow	untaught	vaporize
undulant	untidier	vaporous
undulate	untidily	variable
unearned	untimely	variably
uneasier	untiring	variance
uneasily	untoward	varicose
unending	unusable	varietal
unerring	unwanted	variorum
unevenly	unwieldy	vascular
unfairly	unwisely	Vaseline
unfasten	unwonted	vastness
unfetter	unworthy	vaulting
unfitted	unzipped	vegetate
unformed	upcoming	vehement
ungainly	updating	velocity
unharmed	upgraded	velveted
unheeded	upheaval	venality
unhinged	upholder	venation
unholily	upmarket	vendable
unicycle	uppercut	vendetta
unifying	upraised	vendible
unionism	uprising	venerate
unionist	upstaged	venereal
unionize	upstairs	Venetian
uniquely	upstream	vengeful
univalve	up-to-date	venially
universe	urbanely	venomous
unjustly	urbanity	venously
unkindly	urbanize	ventured
unlawful	urgently	veracity
unleaded	urinated	verandah
unlearnt	urologic	verbally
unlikely	usefully	verbatim
unlimber	usurious	verbiage
unlisted	utilized	verboten
unloosen	uxorious	verdancy
unlovely		verdured
unloving		verified
unmaking	vacantly	verifier
unmanned	vacating	verities
unmarked	vacation	verjuice

ermouth
ernally
ertebra
ertexes
ertical
ertices
resicant
vestment
restries
vexation

ibrancy
ibrated
vibrator
iburnum
icarage
icinity
igilant
ignette
igorous
ilified
illager
illainy
incible
inegary
ineries
vineyard
iolable
violated
violator
violence
virginal
Virginia
irility
virology
virtuosi
virtuoso
virtuous
virulent
visceral
viscidly
viscount
visitant
visiting
visually
vitality
vitalize
vitiated
vitreous
vivacity
vivarium
viva voce
vivified
vivisect
vocalist
vocalize
vocation
vocative
voidable
volatile
volcanic
volcanos

volition
volleyed
vomiting
voracity
vortexes
vortices
votaries
voyaging

wabbling
wackiest
waddling
waffling
waggling
wainscot
waitress
walkaway
walkover
walloped
wanderer
wangling
wantonly
warbling
wardress
wardrobe
war-horse
wariness
warranty
washable
washbowl
washroom
wasteful
watchdog
watchful
watchman
watchmen
watering
Waterloo
water-ski
waterway
watt-hour
wattling
waviness
waxiness
wayfarer
weaklier
weakling
weakness
weaponry
wearable
weariest
wearying
weeklies
weeniest
weirdest
welcomed
wellborn
well-bred
well-done
well-kept

well-nigh
well-paid
well-read
well-to-do
well-worn
Welshman
Welshmen
werewolf
westerly
westward
whackier
whackily
wharfage
whatever
wheedled
wheezier
wheezing
whenever
wherever
whetting
whimsies
whinnied
whiplash
whipping
whirring
whiskery
whiskeys
whiskies
whistled
whistler
white-hot
whitened
whiteout
whittled
whizzing
whodunit
whomever
whooping
whopping
wickedly
wide-eyed
wigglier
wiggling
wild-eyed
wildfire
wildfowl
wildlife
wildness
wildwood
wilfully
wiliness
wimpiest
windfall
windiest
windlass
windmill
windpipe
windward
wingspan
winnable
Winnipeg

wireless
wiriness
wishbone
wispiest
wisteria
witchery
witching
withdraw
withdrew
withheld
withhold
witicism
wittiest
wizardry
wobbling
woefully
womanish
wondrous
woodbine
woodcock
woodenly
woodiest
woodland
wood lice
woodpile
woodshed
woodsman
woodsmen
woodwind
woodwork
woodworm
wooliest

woollier
woollies
wooziest
wordiest
wordless
wordplay
workable
workaday
workbook
worked-up
workroom
workshop
wormiest
wormwood
worrying
worthier
worthies
worthily
wrangled
wrangler
wrapping
wrathful
wreathed
wreckage
wrestled
wrestler
wretched
wriggled
wriggler
wringing
wrinkled
writhing

wrongful

xanthous

yachting
yarmulke
yearbook
yearling
yearlong
yearning
yielding
yodeling
yodelled
Yokohama
youngish
yourself
youthful
Yugoslav
yuletide

zaniness
Zanzibar
zeppelin
Zimbabwe
zincking
zippiest
zodiacal
zucchini
zwieback

abandoned
abasement
abatement
abdicated
abdominal
abduction
aberrance
aberrancy
abhorrent
abhorring
abilities
abnegated
abolition
abominate
aborigine
aborively
abridging
abrogated
abscessed
abscissae
abscissas
abseiling
absolving
absorbent
abstainer
abstinent
absurdity
abundance
abusively
abysmally
academies
accession
accessory
accidence
acclimate
acclivity
accompany
according
accordion
accretion
accretive
acetylene
achieving
acidified
acidulate
acidulous
acoustics
acquiesce
acquiring
acquiting
acquittal
acquitted
acrobatic
acropolis
activated
activator
actuality
actualize
actuarial
actuaries
actuating

actuation
acuteness
adaptable
addiction
addictive
addressee
adenoidal
adherence
adiabatic
adiposity
adjacency
adjective
adjoining
adjudging
adjutancy
adlibbing
admirably
admiralty
admission
admitting
admixture
ad nauseam
adoptable
adoration
adoringly
adornment
adpendage
adsorbent
adulating
adulation
adulatory
adulterer
adulthood
ad valorem
advancing
advantage
adventure
adverbial
adversary
adversely
adversity
advertent
advertise
advisable
advisably
advisedly
advocated
aerialist
aerospace
aesthetic
affecting
affection
affective
affidavit
affiliate
affluence
aforesaid
Afrikaans
aftercare
afterglow
afterlife

aftermath
aftermost
afternoon
afterward
aggravate
aggregate
aggressor
aggrieved
agitating
agitation
agonizing
agreeable
agreeably
agreement
agronomic
aimlessly
air-cooled
airworthy
alabaster
albatross
alchemist
alcoholic
alertness
algebraic
Algonquin
algorithm
alienable
alienated
alighting
alignment
alimental
aliphatic
alkalized
all-around
allegedly
allegoric
allergies
allergist
alleviate
alligator
allocated
allopathy
allotment
allotting
allowable
allowance
allowedly
alma mater
aloneness
alongside
aloofness
alterable
altercate
alternate
altimeter
aluminous
amassment
amazement
amazingly
Amazonian
ambergris

ambiguity
ambiguous
ambitious
ambrosial
ambulance
ambulated
ambuscade
amendable
amendment
Americana
americium
amid-ships
amino acid
amnesties
amorously
amorphous
amortized
ampersand
amphibian
ampleness
amplified
amplifier
amplitude
amputated
Amsterdam
amusement
amusingly
analgesia
analgesic
analogies
analogize
analogous
analyzing
anarchism
anarchist
anatomies
anatomist
anatomize
ancestral
anchorage
anchorite
anchorman
anchormen
anchovies
ancillary
andantino
androgyny
anecdotal
angiogram
Anglicism
Anglicize
anglophil
angostura
angriness
anguished
anhydride
anhydrous
animalism
animality
animalize
animating

animation
animistic
animosity
ankyloses
ankylosis
Annapolis
annotated
annotator
announced
announcer
annoyance
annuitant
annulling
annulment
anomalies
anomalism
anomalous
anonymity
anonymous
antarctic
anteceded
antenatal
anthology
antidotal
antipasto
antipathy
antiquary
antiquate
antiquing
antiquity
antiserum
antitoxic
antitoxin
antitrust
anxieties
anxiously
anybodies
apartheid
apartment
apathetic
apocrypha
apodictic
apologies
apologist
apologize
apostolic
appalling
Appaloosa
apparatus
appeasing
appellant
appellate
appendant
appertain
appetizer
applecart
applejack
appliance
applicant
appointee
apportion

appraisal
appraised
appraiser
apprehend
apprising
approving
aquaplane
aqua vitae
arabesque
arbitrary
arbitrate
arboretum
archangel
archducal
archenemy
archetype
archfiend
architect
archivist
Argentina
Argentine
armadillo
armistice
arranging
arrearage
arriviste
arrogance
arrogated
arrowhead
arrowroot
arthritic
arthritis
arthropod
Arthurian
artichoke
articular
artillery
artlessly
ascendant
ascendent
ascension
ascertain
ascribing
ashamedly
Ashkenazi
asininity
asparagus
aspersing
aspersion
aspirated
aspirator
assailant
assembled
assembler
assertion
assertive
assiduity
assiduous
assistant
associate
assonance

assuaging
assuasive
assurance
assuredly
asthmatic
astounded
astraddle
astrakhan
astrodome
astrolabe
astrology
astronaut
astronomy
astucious
asymmetry
atavistic
atheistic
athletics
atomizing
atonality
atonement
atrocious
atrophied
atrophies
attainder
attendant
attention
attentive
attenuate
attorneys
attribute
attrition
aubergine
audacious
au naturel
auricular
austerely
austerity
Australia
authentic
authoress
authority
authorize
autocracy
autograph
automated
automatic
automaton
autonomic
autopilot
autopsies
autos-da-fé
auxiliary
available
availably
avalanche
averaging
avertable
avocation
avoidable
avoidance

avuncular
awakening
awareness
awestruck
awfulness
awkwardly
axiomatic
ayatollah

bacchanal
backboard
backcloth
backdated
backfield
backfired
backpedal
backslide
backspace
backstage
backtrack
backwards
backwater
backwoods
bacterial
bacterium
badminton
bagatelle
bailiwick
baksheesh
balalaika
balancing
balconies
balefully
ballerina
ballistic
balloting
ballpoint
bamboozle
bandaging
banderole
bandicoot
bandoleer
bandolier
bandstand
bandwagon
bannister
banqueted
banquette
baptismal
baptizing
barbarian
barbarism
barbarity
barbarous
barbecued
barcarole
Barcelona
barefaced
barkeeper
barnstorm

barograph
barometer
baronetcy
barracuda
barreling
barricade
barrister
bartender
bashfully
basically
basketful
bas-relief
bastardly
battalion
beachhead
beardless
beatified
beatitude
beau geste
beau monde
beauteous
beautiful
beaux-arts
bedazzled
bedeviled
bedfellow
bedimming
bedridden
bedspread
beefeater
beefsteak
beekeeper
Beelzebub
Bee-tho-ven
befalling
befitting
befogging
befuddled
begetting
beginning
begrudged
beguiling
beheading
beholding
belatedly
beleaguer
believing
belittled
bellicose
belltower
bellyache
benchmark
beneficed
benefited
benighted
benignant
benignity
bereaving
berkelium
beryllium
beseeched

besetting
besieging
bestially
bestirred
betrothal
betrothed
bicameral
bicycling
bicyclist
bifurcate
bilateral
bilharzia
bilingual
billboard
billeting
billiards
billionth
billy goat
bimonthly
binderies
binocular
biography
biologist
bionomics
biorhythm
bipartite
birthmark
birthrate
bisection
bishopric
bitchiest
bivalence
blackball
blackbird
blackeyed
Blackfeet
Blackfoot
blackhead
blackjack
blacklist
blackmail
blackness
blameless
blandness
blanketed
blankness
blaspheme
blasphemy
blatantly
bleakness
blindfold
blindness
blockaded
blockhead
blondness
bloodbath
bloodiest
bloodless
bloodshed
bloodshot
bloodying

blotchier
blow-dried
blow-dries
blowdryer
blowflies
blowtorch
blueberry
bluegrass
blueprint
bluntness
boardroom
boardwalk
boathouse
boatswain
bodyguard
Bolshevik
bolsterer
bombastic
bombazine
bombproof
bombshell
bombsight
bone china
bon voyage
book-maker
bookplate
bookshelf
bootblack
bossiness
botanical
botchiest
bottleful
boulevard
boundless
bounteous
bountiful
bourgeois
bowlegged
bowstring
boyfriend
bracketed
brainiest
brainless
brainwash
brassiere
bratwurst
braveness
braveries
Brazilian
breadline
breakable
breakaway
breakdown
break-even
breakfast
breakneck
breast-fed
breathing
brevetted
breweries
briberies

bric-a-brac
brickwork
brickyard
briefcase
briefness
brigadier
brilliant
brimstone
briquette
briskness
bristlier
bristling
Britannia
broaching
broadcast
broadness
broadside
brocading
brochette
brokerage
bronchial
broodiest
brotherly
brushwood
brushwork
brusquely
brutality
brutalize
bubbliest
buccaneer
Bucharest
buckboard
bucketful
bucktooth
buckwheat
budgetary
buffaloed
buffaloes
Bulgarian
bulkiness
bulldozed
bulldozer
bullfight
bullfinch
bumblebee
bumpiness
bumptious
burlesque
burliness
bushwhack
buttercup
butterfly
byproduct
bystander
Byzantine

caballero
caballing
cablegram
cabriolet

cacophony
caesarean
cafeteria
calaboose
calcified
calcimine
calculate
calibrate
calloused
callously
calorific
calumnies
Calvinism
Calvinist
Cambodian
Camembert
campanile
campanili
canceling
cancerous
candidacy
candidate
Candlemas
canneries
canniness
cannonade
canonical
canopying
cantabile
cantalope
cantaloup
Cantonese
canvasser
capacious
capacitor
capillary
capitally
capriccio
Capricorn
caprioled
capsizing
captaincy
captivate
captivity
capturing
carbonate
carbonize
carbuncle
carcinoma
cardboard
cardsharp
carefully
caretaker
Caribbean
carnality
carnation
carnelian
carnivore
carousing
carpenter
carpentry

carpetbag
carpeting
carrousel
cartelize
Cartesian
cartilage
cartridge
cartwheel
cascading
casserole
cassowary
castigate
castrated
casuistic
casuistry
cataclysm
catalepsy
cataloged
catalogue
catalysis
catalytic
catamaran
catarrhal
catchword
catechism
catechist
catechize
caterwaul
catharsis
cathartic
cathedral
catteries
cattiness
cattleman
cattlemen
Caucasian
Caucasoid
caucusing
causality
causation
causeless
cauteries
cauterize
cavalcade
cavernous
ceasefire
ceaseless
celebrant
celebrate
celebrity
celestial
celluloid
cellulose
censorial
censuring
censusing
centenary
centering
centigram
centipede
centrally

centuries
centurion
certainly
certainty
certified
certifier
certitude
cessation
cha-cha-cha
chaffinch
chagrined
chalkiest
challenge
chameleon
chamomile
champagne
chanciest
changeful
channeled
chanteuse
chaparral
chaperone
charabanc
character
charities
charlatan
charlotte
chatterer
chattiest
chauffeur
cheapness
checkbook
checkered
checklist
checkmate
checkroom
cheekbone
cheekiest
cheerless
cheerless
chemistry
cheongsam
chicanery
chickadee
chickweed
chieftain
Chihuahua
chilblain
childhood
childless
childlike
chilliest
Chinookan
chipboard
chiropody
chirpiest
chiseling
chivalric
chivvying
chockfull
chocolate

choosiest
choppiest
chopstick
chorister
chortling
chorusing
Christian
Christmas
chromatic
chronicle
chrysalis
chubbiest
chuckfull
chuckling
chunkiest
churchman
churchmen
cigarette
circuitry
circulate
cirrhosis
cisalpine
citizenry
civilized
claimable
clammiest
clamorous
clapboard
clarified
classical
classiest
classless
classmate
class-room
cleanness
cleansing
clearance
clearness
clergyman
clergymen
clientele
climactic
clinician
clinquant
clipboard
cloakroom
clockwise
clockwork
cloisonné
cloistral
closeness
closeting
cloudiest
cloudless
cloyingly
clubbable
clubhouse
clumsiest
coagulate
coalesced
coalfield

coalition
coastline
coatdress
coaxingly
cochineal
cockahoop
cockfight
cockiness
cocklebur
cockroach
cockscomb
codifying
coffee-pot
cogitated
cognation
cognition
cognitive
cognizant
coherence
coherency
coincided
Cointreau
collapsed
collating
collation
colleague
collected
collector
collegian
colliding
collimate
collinear
collision
collocate
collusion
collusive
colonnade
colorfast
colorless
Colosseum
colostomy
Columbian
columbine
columbium
columnist
combatant
combating
combative
combining
comforter
comically
Comintern
commander
commingle
commissar
committal
committed
committee
commodity
commodore
commotion

communing
communion
communism
communist
community
communize
commuting
compactly
compactor
companies
companion
comparing
compelled
compendia
competent
competing
compiling
complaint
completed
compliant
complying
component
composing
composite
composure
comprised
computing
concavity
conceding
conceited
conceived
concerned
concerted
concierge
concisely
concision
concluded
concordat
concourse
concreted
concubine
concurred
condensed
condenser
condiment
condition
condoling
condoning
conducing
conducive
conductor
Conestoga
conferred
confessed
confessor
confidant
confident
confiding
confining
confirmed
conflated

confluent
Confucius
confusing
confusion
confuting
congenial
conger eel
Congolese
congruent
congruity
congruous
conjugate
conjuring
connector
conniving
connoting
connubial
conqueror
conscious
conscript
consensus
conserved
consigner
consignor
consoling
consonant
consortia
conspired
conspirer
constable
constancy
constrain
constrict
construct
construed
consulate
consuming
contagion
container
contender
contented
continent
continual
continued
continuum
contralto
contrived
contumacy
contumely
contusing
contusion
conundrum
convector
convening
conversed
converter
convertor
convexity
convinced
convivial
convoking

convolute
convulsed
cooperage
cooperate
copartner
copiously
copulated
copyright
cordially
coriander
corkscrew
cormorant
cornfield
corollary
corporate
corporeal
corpulent
corpuscle
corralled
correctly
correlate
corroding
corrosion
corrosive
corrugate
corruptly
cortisone
coruscate
cosmogony
cosmology
cosmonaut
cosmotron
Costa Rica
co-starred
costuming
cotangent
cotillion
councilor
counseled
counselor
countable
countdown
countless
countries
coup d'état
courteous
courtroom
courtship
courtyard
couturier
coverless
cowardice
crackdown
crackling
craftiest
craftsman
craftsmen
cranberry
crankcase
crankiest
crash-land

crassness
craziness
creakiest
creamiest
credulity
credulous
creepiest
cremating
cremation
crematory
crenelate
crescendo
crestless
cretinism
cretinous
crinklier
crinkling
crinoline
crippling
crispiest
crispness
criterion
criticism
criticize
croakiest
crocheted
crocodile
croissant
crookedly
croquette
cross-over
crosswind
crossword
crotchety
crow's-feet
crow's-foot
crucified
cruciform
crudeness
crudities
cruelness
cruelties
crumblier
crumbling
crummiest
crumpling
crunchier
crustiest
cudgeling
culminate
culs-de-sac
cultivate
culturing
cumbrance
cuneiform
cunningly
curbstone
curiosity
curiously
curliness
currently

curricula
cursorily
curtsying
curvature
custodial
custodian
customary
customize
cutaneous
cutthroat
cyclorama
cyclotron
cylindric
cynically

dachshand
daintiest
Dalai Lama
dalliance
dalmatian
damnaable
damnation
damnedest
dandelion
dandified
dangerous
daredevil
Darwinian
Darwinism
dashboard
dastardly
dauntless
davenport
Davy Jones
deaconess
deadliest
deafening
deaneries
deathblow
deathless
debarment
debarring
debatable
debauched
debauchee
debaucher
debenture
debugging
debutante
decadence
decahedra
Decalogue
decathlon
deceitful
deceiving
decencies
decennial
deception
deceptive
decidedly

deciduous
deciliter
decimated
decimeter
declaring
declining
declivity
décolleté
decompose
decontrol
decorated
decorator
decreased
decreeing
decrement
dedicated
deducible
deduction
deductive
defalcate
defaulter
defeatism
defeatist
defecated
defection
defective
defendant
defensive
deference
deferment
deferring
defiantly
deficient
definable
deflating
deflation
deflector
defoliant
defoliate
deformity
degrading
dehiscent
dehydrate
deionized
deistical
dejection
delegated
delftware
delicious
delighted
delineate
delirious
deliverer
delousing
demagogic
demagogue
demarcate
demimonde
demitasse
democracy
demurring

demystify
denigrate
denounced
densities
dentistry
deodorant
deodorize
deoxidize
departure
dependant
dependent
depicting
depiction
depleting
depletion
deploring
deposable
deposited
depositor
depraving
depravity
deprecate
depredate
depressed
depriving
deputized
deranging
de rigueur
derivable
derogated
derring-do
derringer
Descartes
descended
described
descrying
desecrate
desertion
deserving
desiccate
designate
designing
desirable
desirably
desolated
desperado
desperate
despising
despotism
destinies
destining
destitute
destroyer
desuetude
desultory
detection
detective
detention
detention
detergent
determine

deterrent
deterring
detonated
detonator
detractor
detriment
deuterium
devaluate
devastate
developed
developer
deviating
deviation
devilling
devilment
devisable
devolving
devouring
Dexedrine
dexterity
dexterous
dexterous
diacritic
diagnosed
diagnoses
diagnosis
diagramed
dialectal
dialectic
diametric
diaphragm
diastolic
diathermy
dichotomy
dictating
dictation
dietetics
dietician
different
difficult
diffident
diffusely
diffusing
diffusion
digestion
digestive
digitalis
digitized
dignified
dignitary
dignities
diligence
dilluting
dimension
dimwitted
dinginess
diphthong
diplomacy
direction
directive
directory

dirigible
dirtiness
disabling
disabused
disaffect
disagreed
disappear
disavowal
disbarred
disbelief
disbursed
disburser
discharge
disclosed
discomfit
discourse
discovery
discredit
diseasing
disembark
disembody
disengage
disfigure
disgorged
disgraced
disguised
disgusted
dishonest
disinfect
disliking
dislocate
dislodged
dismantle
dismember
dismissal
disparage
disparate
disparity
dispelled
dispensed
dispenser
dispersal
dispersed
displaced
displease
disposing
disputant
disputing
disregard
disrepair
disrepute
disrobing
disrupter
dissected
dissemble
dissenter
disserved
dissident
dissipate
dissolute
dissonant

dissuaded
distanced
distantly
distemper
distilled
distiller
distingué
distorted
disturbed
disunited
dithyramb
dittanies
divergent
diverging
diversify
diversion
diversity
divisible
divorcing
divulging
Dixieland
dizziness
djellabah
docketing
doctorate
doctrinal
doggiebag
dogmatism
dogmatist
dogmatize
dolefully
domiciled
dominance
dominancy
Dominican
dormitory
doubtless
doughiest
dowdiness
downgrade
downiness
draconian
draftsman
dragonfly
Dramamine
dramatics
dramatist
dramatize
draperies
dreamiest
dressiest
dribbling
drinkable
driveling
drizzlier
drizzling
dromedary
drunkenly
dualistic
dubiously
duffelbag

dumbfound
dumpiness
duplicate
duplicity
duralumin
duskiness
dustiness
dutifully
dwindling
dynamiter
dynamotor
dynasties
dysentery
dyspepsia
dyspeptic
dystrophy

eagerness
eagleeyed
earliness
earnestly
earthwork
earthworm
earwigged
eastbound
easterner
easygoing
eavesdrop
ebullient
eccentric
eclampsia
eclipsing
ecologist
economics
economies
economist
economize
ecosystem
ecstasies
ectomorph
ectoplasm
ecumenism
edelweiss
edibility
Edinburgh
editorial
educating
education
educative
educative
Edwardian
effective
effectual
efficient
effluence
effluvial
effluvium
effulgent
eglantine
egomaniac

egotistic
egregious
egression
eiderdown
eightfold
eightieth
ejaculate
ejectment
elaborate
elastical
electoral
electrify
electrode
elegantly
elegizing
elemental
elevating
elevation
eliminate
ellipsoid
elocution
elongated
elopement
eloquence
elsewhere
elucidate
elusively
emaciated
emanating
emanation
embargoed
embargoes
embarrass
embassies
embattled
embedding
embellish
embezzled
embezzler
embodying
embracing
embrasure
embrocate
embroider
embryonic
emendable
emergence
emergency
eminently
Emmenthal
emollient
emolument
emotional
empathize
emphasize
emphysema
empirical
emplaning
emptiness
emulating
emulation

enactment
enameling
enamelled
encapsule
enchilada
encircled
enclosing
enclosure
encompass
encounter
encourage
endemical
endlessly
endocrine
endomorph
endorphin
endorsing
endoscope
endoscopy
endowment
endurable
endurance
energetic
energized
energizer
enervated
enfeebled
enforcing
engorging
engraving
engrossed
enhancing
enigmatic
enjoyable
enjoyably
enjoyment
enlarging
enlighten
ennobling
en passant
enplaning
enquiries
enquiring
enrapture
enrolling
ensconced
enshrined
ensilaged
enslaving
ensnaring
entangled
enteritis
entertain
enthroned
enthusing
entitling
entourage
entrapped
entrechat
entwining
enumerate

enunciate	etymology	execution
enviously	eucalypti	executive
enzymatic	Eucharist	executrix
epaulette	eulogized	exemplary
ephedrine	euphemism	exemplify
ephemeral	euphemist	exemption
Ephesians	euphemize	exercised
epicenter	euphonium	exerciser
epicurean	evacuated	exfoliate
epicurism	evaluated	exhausted
epidermal	evaluator	exhibited
epidermic	evanesced	exhibitor
epidermis	evangelic	exigently
epileptic	evaporate	existence
Episcopal	evasively	ex officio
episcopal	eventuate	exogamous
epitomize	evergreen	exogenous
eponymous	everybody	exonerate
equalized	evidenced	exorcised
equalizer	evidently	exorcizes
equalling	evincible	exoticism
equalness	evocation	expansion
equerries	evocative	expansive
equipment	evolution	expatiate
equipoise	exactable	expectant
equipping	exactness	expedient
equitable	examining	expedited
equitably	exampling	expediter
equivocal	Excalibur	expelling
eradicate	excavated	expensive
erectable	excavator	expertise
erectness	exceeding	expiating
ergonomic	excellent	expiation
erogenous	excelling	expiatory
eroticism	excelsior	expletive
erroneous	excepting	explicate
errorless	exception	exploding
erstwhile	excessive	exploiter
erudition	exchanged	explosion
escalated	exchequer	explosive
escalator	excisable	expositor
esophagus	excitable	expressly
Esperanto	excitedly	expulsion
espionage	excluding	expulsive
esplanade	exclusion	expunging
espousing	exclusive	expurgate
essential	excoriate	exquisite
establish	excrement	extempore
esthetics	excreting	extension
estimable	excretion	extensive
estimably	excretory	extenuate
estimated	exculpate	extirpate
estimator	excursion	extolling
estivated	excursive	extolment
estranged	excusable	extortion
estuaries	excusably	extortive
eternally	execrable	extractor
ethically	execrably	extradite
Ethiopian	execrated	extremely
ethnology	execrator	extremism
etiquette	executing	extremist

extremity
extricate
extrinsic
extrovert
extruding
extrusion
exuberant
exudation
eye-opener

fabricate
facecloth
facetious
facsimile
factional
factories
factually
faintness
fairyland
faithless
fallacies
Fallopian
falsehood
falseness
falsified
falsities
faltering
fanatical
fanciness
fantasies
fantasize
fantastic
farmstead
farragoes
farseeing
fascicled
fascinate
fascistic
fastening
fatigable
fatiguing
fattiness
fatuities
fatuously
faultiess
faultless
favorable
favorably
fearfully
feathered
featuring
fecundate
fecundity
federally
federated
feistiest
felonious
feminized
feracious
ferocious

ferreting
ferryboat
fertility
fertilize
fervently
festivity
fetidness
fetishism
fetishist
feudalism
feudalize
fictional
fidgeting
fiduciary
field mice
fieldwork
fieriness
fifteenth
figurrate
filigreed
filleting
filminess
filthiest
finagling
finalized
financial
financier
financing
finessing
fingering
fingertip
finicking
firebreak
fireflies
fireguard
firelight
fireplace
firepower
fireproof
firewater
firmament
firstborn
firsthand
first-rate
fisheries
fisherman
fishermen
fishwives
fissuring
fittingly
fittingly
flabbiest
flageolet
flakiness
flamingly
flammable
flashback
flashiest
flatterer
flatulent
flavoring

fledgling
fleetness
flightier
flightily
flimsiest
flinching
flippancy
floatable
floodgate
flophouse
floppiest
floridity
flotation
flouncing
flowering
flowerpot
fluctuate
fluffiest
fluidness
fluoresce
flurrying
flyleaves
flyweight
foaminess
focalized
focussing
fogginess
foliating
foliation
following
foodstuff
fooleries
foolhardy
foolishly
foolproof
footloose
footprint
forbidden
forceable
force-feed
forceless
forcemeat
foreboded
foreclose
forefront
foregoing
foreigner
foreknown
foreshore
foresight
forestall
foretaste
foretoken
forewoman
forewomen
forgather
forgeries
forgetful
forgiving
forgotten
forlornly

formalism
formality
formalize
formation
formative
formatted
formulaic
formulary
formulate
fornicate
forsaking
forsythia
forthwith
fortified
fortitude
fortnight
fortunate
fostering
foundling
foundries
fourscore
fractious
fractured
fragility
fragrance
frailness
frailties
framework
franchise
frangible
franglais
frankness
fraternal
freakiest
freckling
freelance
Freemason
freestyle
freewheel
freeze-dry
freighter
frenchify
Frenchman
Frenchmen
frenzying
frequency
frescoing
freshness
fretfully
fricassee
fricative
frightful
frigidity
frilliest
friskiest
frivolity
frivolous
frizziest
frizzling
frolicked
frostbite

frostiest
frothiest
frugality
fruitcake
fruitiest
fruitless
frustrate
fulfilled
full-blown
fulminate
fulsomely
fumigated
fumigator
fundament
fungicide
funicular
funneling
funnelled
funniness
furiously
furniture
furtively
fusillade
fussiness
fuzziness

gabardine
gaberdine
gainfully
galantine
Galapagos
gallantly
gallantry
galleries
gallicism
gallivant
galloping
gallstone
galvanize
gamboling
gambolled
Garibaldi
garnishee
garniture
garotting
garroting
garrulous
gasholder
gasifying
gasometer
gassiness
gastritis
gathering
gaucherie
gaudiness
gauziness
gawkiness
gazetteer
gearshift
gearwheel

gelignite
geminated
genealogy
generally
generated
generator
generical
geniality
genitalia
genocidal
genteelly
gentility
gentleman
gentlemen
genuflect
genuinely
geography
geologies
geologist
geometric
georgette
geriatric
germanium
germicide
germinate
gestating
gestation
gesturing
ghastlier
gibberish
Gibraltar
giddiness
gigantism
gilt-edged
gimmickry
gladiator
gladiolus
glamorize
glamorous
glandular
glariness
glaringly
glassiest
glassware
gleefully
glimpsing
glissando
gloomiest
glorified
glutenous
glutinous
glycerine
godfather
godliness
godmother
godparent
going-over
goldenrod
goldfinch
goldsmith
gondolier

gonorrhea
goofiness
goose-step
Gorbachov
gossiping
governess
graceless
gradation
gradually
graduated
granaries
grandaddy
grandiose
grand prix
granulate
grapevine
graphical
grappling
grassiest
grassland
gratified
gratitude
gravamina
graveling
gravelled
graveness
graveyard
gravitate
gravities
greasiest
greatcoat
greatness
greediest
greenback
greengage
greenhorn
Greenland
greenness
greenroom
Greenwich
grenadier
grenadine
greyhound
grievance
grimacing
grimalkin
griminess
grittiest
grizzlies
grizzling
groceries
groggiest
grooviest
grosgrain
grossness
grotesque
grouchily
groundhog
grounding
groundnut
groveling

grubbiest
grubstake
gruelling
gruffness
grumbling
grumpiest
guarantee
guarantor
guardedly
guardrail
guardsman
guardsmen
Guatemala
guerrilla
guesswork
guidebook
guideline
guildhall
guileless
guillemot
guiltiest
guiltless
guitarist
gum arabic
gumminess
gunpowder
gunrunner
gushiness
gustatory
gustiness
gymnasium
gymnastic
gyrometer
gyroplane
gyroscope

habitable
habituate
hackneyed
hagiology
hagridden
hailstorm
hairpiece
hairstyle
half-caste
half-lives
halitosis
Halloween
hamburger
hamstring
hamstrung
handiness
handiwork
handlebar
handstand
hangers-on
haphazard
happening
happiness
harangued

harbinger
hardboard
hardihood
hardiness
harlequin
harmfully
harmonica
harmonics
harmonies
harmonium
harmonize
harshness
harvester
hastiness
hatchback
hatefully
haughtier
haughtily
haut monde
haversack
hazardous
headboard
headdress
headfirst
headiness
headlight
headlined
headphone
healthful
healthier
healthily
heartache
heartbeat
heartburn
heartiest
heartless
heartsick
heaviness
heavy-duty
hectogram
hellishly
helpfully
Hemingway
hepatitis
herbalist
herbicide
herbivore
herculean
hereafter
heretical
heritable
hesitance
hesitancy
hesitated
heterodox
heuristic
hexagonal
hibernate
hiccuping
hiccupped
hicupping

hidebound
hideously
hierarchy
high-class
high-flier
high-flown
high-grade
high-level
highlight
high-toned
hijacking
hilarious
hillbilly
Himalayan
hindrance
hindsight
Hiroshima
histamine
historian
histories
hitchhike
hit-or-miss
hoarfrost
hoariness
hobgoblin
hobnobbed
Ho Chi Minh
hoi polloi
hollyhock
Hollywood
holocaust
holograph
Holy Grail
homegrown
homeopath
homestead
homewards
homicidal
homograph
homophone
honesties
honeycomb
honkytonk
honorable
honorably
honorific
hopefully
hopscotch
horoscope
horrified
horseback
horsehair
horseplay
horseshoe
horsewhip
hortatory
hostilely
hostility
hotheaded
Hottentot
hourglass

houseboat
housecoat
household
housemaid
houseroom
housewife
housework
hoydenish
huffiness
humanized
humankind
humdinger
humiliate
humorless
hunchback
hundredth
Hungarian
hungriest
hurricane
hurriedly
husbandry
huskiness
hybridize
hydrangea
hydrating
hydration
hydraulic
hydrofoil
hydroxide
hygienist
hymnaries
hyperbola
hyperbole
hyphenate
hypnotism
hypnotist
hypnotize
hypocrisy
hypocrite
hysterics

Icelander
Icelandic
ice-skated
ichneumon
idealized
identical
idiomatic
idolizing
ignitable
ignoramus
ignorance
illegally
illegible
illegibly
ill-gotten
illiberal
illogical
illumined
imagerial

imageries
imaginary
imagining
imbalance
imbecilic
imbedding
imbroglio
imitating
imitation
imitative
immanence
immanency
immediacy
immediate
immensely
immensity
immerging
immersing
immersion
immigrant
immigrate
imminence
immodesty
immolated
immolator
immorally
immovable
immovably
immunized
immutable
immutably
impaction
impaneled
impartial
impassion
impassive
impatient
impelling
impending
imperfect
imperiled
imperious
impetuous
impieties
impinging
impiously
imploding
imploring
implosion
implosive
impolitic
important
importune
imposture
impotence
impotency
imprecate
imprecise
imprinter
impromptu
improving

improvise
imprudent
impudence
impulsion
impulsive
inability
inamorata
inaneness
inanimate
inaudible
inaudibly
inaugural
incapable
incapably
incarnate
incensing
incentive
inception
incessant
incidence
incipient
inclement
inclining
including
inclusion
inclusive
incognito
incommode
incorrect
increased
increment
incubated
incubator
inculcate
inculpate
incumbent
incurable
incurably
incurious
incurring
incursion
incursive
indecency
indecorum
indelible
indelibly
indemnify
indemnity
indenture
indicated
indicator
indigence
indignant
indignity
indolence
Indonesia
induction
inductive
indulgent
indulging
inebriate

ineffable
ineffably
inelegant
infancies
infantile
infantine
infatuate
infection
infective
inferable
inference
inferring
infertile
infielder
infighter
infirmary
infirmity
inflaming
inflating
inflation
influence
influenza
informant
infringed
infuriate
infusible
ingenious
ingenuity
ingenuous
ingestion
inglenook
ingrowing
inhabited
inhalator
inharmony
inherence
inheritor
inhibiter
initialed
initially
initiated
initiator
injection
injurious
injustice
innermost
innersole
innervate
innkeeper
innocence
innocuous
innovated
innovator
Innsbruck
innuendos
inoculant
inoculate
inorganic
inosphere
inpatient
inputting

inquiries
inquiring
insatiate
inscribed
insensate
insertion
insetting
insidious
insincere
insinuate
insipidly
insistent
insolence
insoluble
insolubly
insolvent
insomniac
inspector
inspiring
installed
instanter
instantly
instating
instigate
instilled
institute
insulated
insulator
insurable
insurance
insurgent
integrant
integrate
integrity
intellect
intendant
intensely
intensify
intension
intensity
intensive
intention
inter alia
interbred
intercede
intercept
interdict
interface
interfere
interject
interlace
interlard
interleaf
interline
interlink
interlock
interlope
interlude
interment
internist
interplay

interpose
interpret
interring
interrupt
intersect
intervene
interview
interwove
intestate
intestine
intimated
intonated
intricacy
intricate
intrigued
intrinsic
introduce
introvert
intruding
intrusion
intrusive
intuiting
intuition
intuitive
inundated
invariant
invective
invention
inventive
inventory
inversion
invidious
inviolate
invisible
invisibly
invoicing
involving
inweaving
inwrought
ipso facto
irascible
ironstone
Iroquoian
irradiate
irregular
irrigated
irritable
irritably
irritated
isinglass
isolating
isolation
isometric
isosceles
Israelite
italicize
itchiness
itemizing
iteration
itinerant
itinerary

itinerate
Ivy League

jackknife
jailbreak
jaundiced
jaywalker
jazziness
jealously
jeeringly
Jefferson
jellyfish
jerkiness
Jerusalem
jessamine
jitterbug
jobholder
jockeying
jockstrap
jocularly
jocundity
joltingly
Jordanian
joss stick
joviality
joyridden
joyriding
jubilance
judgement
judiciary
judicious
juiciness
jumpiness
junketing
Junoesque
justified
juxtapose

Kampuchea
Kandinsky
Kathmandu
keynoting
kibbutzim
kidnaping
kidnapped
kidnapper
kilocycle
kilohertz
kiloliter
kilometer
kindliest
kinematic
kinescope
king-sized
kinswoman
kinswomen
kittenish
kittiwake
kiwifruit

knife-edge
knockdown
knock-knee
knottiest
knowingly
know-it-all
knowledge
knuckling

labelling
laborious
labyrinth
lacerated
lachrymal
lactating
lactation
lagniappe
La Guardia
lallation
lambasted
lambently
laminated
lampblack
lamplight
lampshade
landowner
landscape
landslide
languidly
lankiness
lanthanum
Laplander
larcenous
largeness
larghetto
laryngeal
lassitude
last-ditch
latecomer
laterally
latticing
laudative
laudatory
laughable
laughably
laundress
laundries
lavaliere
lawmaking
lawn mower
lazybones
leafiness
leafleted
leafstalk
leakiness
leasehold
leastways
leastwise
lecherous
lecturing

leeringly	liturgies	Maccabees
legalized	liturgist	macerated
legendary	liveliest	machinate
legionary	Liverpool	machinery
legislate	livestock	machining
leisurely	Ljubljana	machinist
leitmotif	loathsome	macintosh
leitmotiv	localized	macrocosm
lengthier	locksmith	maelstrom
lengthily	lodestone	magically
leniently	lodgement	magicking
Leningrad	loftiness	magnesium
lethargic	logarithm	magnetism
lettering	logically	magnetize
leukocyte	logistics	magnified
levelling	loincloth	magnifier
levelness	lolloping	magnitude
leviathan	loneliest	maharajah
levitated	longevity	mainframe
Leviticus	longingly	mainlined
Lhasa apso	longitude	majesties
liability	long johns	major-domo
libelling	long-lived	majorette
libellous	long-range	makeshift
liberally	look-alike	malachite
liberated	lookers-on	maladroit
liberator	looniness	malformed
liberties	loose-leaf	malicious
libertine	looseness	malignant
libidinal	loquacity	malignity
librarian	lordliest	malleable
libraries	lorgnette	mammalian
licensing	lotteries	mammaries
lifeblood	Louisiana	mammogram
life cycle	lousiness	manacling
lifeguard	love child	Manchuria
lifesaver	loveliest	mandating
lifestyle	lowercase	mandatory
lightness	lowliness	mandoline
lightning	low-minded	man-eating
lightship	loyalties	manganese
light-year	lubricant	manginess
likeliest	lubricate	manhandle
Limburger	lucidness	Manhattan
limelight	luckiness	manicured
limestone	lucrative	manifesto
limitable	lucubrate	manliness
limitless	ludicrous	mannequin
limousine	lullabies	mannerism
limpingly	lumbering	mannishly
lineament	lumpiness	manometer
lionizing	lunchtime	manslayer
liquefied	luridness	many-sided
liquidate	lustiness	marbleize
liquidity	Luxemburg	marcelled
liquidize	luxuriant	Mardi Gras
lithesome	luxuriate	margarine
Lithuania	luxurious	margarita
litigated	lymphatic	marijuana
litigious	lyonnaise	marinaded
litterbug	lyrically	marinated

marketing
marmalade
marquetry
marrowfat
marshaled
marshiest
marsupial
martyrdom
martyring
marveling
marvelled
marvelous
mascaraed
masculine
masochism
masochist
massacred
massaging
massively
masterful
masticate
matchless
maternity
matriarch
matricide
matrimony
Mauritian
Mauritius
mausoleum
maximized
mayflower
mealbolic
mealiness
meanwhile
measliest
measuring
meatiness
mechanics
mechanism
mechanize
medallion
medallist
mediating
mediation
mediatory
medicable
medically
medicated
medicinal
meditated
meditator
megacycle
megadeath
megahertz
megaphone
Melbourne
meliorate
melodious
melodrama
mementoes
memorable

memorably
memoranda
memorized
menagerie
mendacity
mendicant
Mennonite
menopause
menstrual
mentality
mercenary
mercerize
merciless
mercurial
merganser
meritedly
meritless
merriment
merriness
mescaline
mesmerism
mesmerize
messenger
Messianic
messieurs
messieurs
messiness
metalized
metalling
metalloid
metalwork
meteorite
meteoroid
methadone
Methodism
Methodist
methodize
metronome
mezzanine
microbial
microchip
microcopy
microcosm
microfilm
microgram
microwave
micturate
middleman
middlemen
midstream
midsummer
midwifery
mightiest
migrating
migration
migratory
milestone
militancy
militated
milkiness
millennia

milligram
millinery
millionth
millipede
mimicking
mimicries
mincemeat
mincingly
minefield
miniature
minimally
minimized
miniscule
miniskirt
Minnesota
minuscule
minuteman
mirroring
mirthless
misadvise
misbehave
misbelief
mischance
miscreant
misdirect
misemploy
miserable
miserably
misfitted
misgiving
misgovern
misguided
mishandle
misinform
misjudged
mislaying
misleader
mismanage
mismating
misnaming
misplaced
misquoted
misruling
misshaped
misshapen
misstated
mistaking
mistiming
mistiness
mistiness
mistletoe
mitigated
mitigator
mnemonics
mobilized
mobocracy
mockingly
modelling
moderated
moderator
modernism

modernist
modernity
modernize
modifying
modulated
moistener
moldiness
molecular
mollified
mollifier
momentary
momentous
monadical
monarchal
monarchic
monastery
monetized
Mongolian
Mongolism
mongoloid
monitored
monkeying
monograph
monologue
monomania
monoplane
Monsignor
monstrous
Mont Blanc
monthlies
moodiness
moonlight
moonscape
moonshine
moralized
moralizer
morbidity
Mormonism
Morse code
mortality
mortgaged
mortgagee
mortgager
mortgagor
mortician
mortified
mortising
mosquitos
moth-eaten
motivated
motorbike
motorboat
motorcade
motorized
mountable
moustache
mouthwash
moviegoer
muckraked
muckraker
muddiness

mugginess
mulattoes
mullioned
multiplex
multitude
mummified
municipal
murderess
murderous
murkiness
murmuring
Muscovite
mushiness
musically
musketeer
muskiness
muskmelon
Mussolini
mustiness
mutilated
mutilator
mutinying
muttering
mutuality
Mycenaean
mysteries
mysticism
mystified
mythology

naiveness
nakedness
narcissus
narcotism
narcotize
narrating
narration
narrative
nasalized
nastiness
nattiness
naturally
naughtier
naughtily
nauseated
navigable
navigated
navigator
necessary
necessity
necrology
nectarine
needfully
neediness
nefarious
negligent
negotiate
neolithic
neologism
nephritis

neptunium
nerveless
nervously
neuralgia
neurology
neutrally
nevermore
newspaper
newsprint
newsstand
Nicaragua
nicknamed
nicotinic
Nietzsche
niggardly
nightclub
nightfall
nightgown
nightlife
nightmare
nighttime
ninetieth
nitration
nobleness
nocturnal
noiseless
noisiness
nominally
nominated
nonentity
nonmember
nonpareil
nonplused
nonprofit
nonshrink
nonsmoker
nonverbal
normality
normalize
normative
northeast
northerly
northward
northwest
Norwegian
nosebleed
nostalgia
nostalgic
notarized
notedness
notepaper
notifying
notoriety
notorious
nouishing
novelette
novelties
novitiate
nullified
nullifier
numbskull

numerable
numerally
numerated
numerator
numerical
nunneries
nuptially
nursemaid
nurseries
nurturing
nutriment
nutrition
nutritive
nux vomica

obbligato
obedience
obeisance
obeseness
obfuscate
objection
objective
objet d'art
objurgate
obligated
obliquely
obliquity
oblivious
obnoxious
obscenely
obscenity
obscuring
obscurity
observant
observing
obsession
obstetric
obstinacy
obstinate
obtruding
obtrusion
obtrusive
obversely
obviating
obviation
obviously
occluding
occlusion
occlusive
occultism
occultist
occupancy
occupying
occurrent
occurring
octagonal
octahedra
offensive
offertory
officiate

officious
offspring
olfaction
olfactory
ol'igarchy
Oligocene
oligopoly
ombudsman
ombudsmen
ominously
onrushing
onslaught
open house
operating
operation
operative
opportune
opposable
oppressor
optimized
optometry
opulently
Orangeman
Orangemen
orangutan
oratories
orbicular
orchestra
orderlies
ordinance
organized
organizer
orgiastic
orientate
originate
orphanage
orthodoxy
oscillate
ossifying
ostensive
osteopath
ostracism
ostracize
otherness
otherwise
ourselves
outbidded
outermost
outfitter
outgrowth
outlining
outliving
outnumber
out-of-date
outraging
outrigger
outskirts
outspoken
outspread
outvoting
outwardly

outwitted
ovenproof
overboard
overdoing
overdraft
overdrawn
overdrive
overeaten
overexert
overgrown
overheard
overjoyed
overnight
overnight
overpower
overrated
overreach
overreact
oversexed
overshoot
oversight
oversleep
overslept
overstate
overtaken
overthrew
overthrow
overvalue
overwhelm
oviparous
ovulating
ovulation
ownership
oxidation
oxidizing
oxygenate

pacemaker
pachyderm
pacifying
packaging
pageantry
painfully
paintwork
Pakistani
palanquin
palatable
palatably
Paleocene
Paleozoic
Palestine
palisaded
palladium
palliasse
palliated
palmistry
palpating
palpation
palpitate
pancaking

panegyric
panelling
panicking
panoramic
pantaloon
pantheism
pantheist
pantomime
pantyhose
paperback
paperwork
parabolic
parachute
paragraph
paralysis
paralytic
paralyzed
paramedic
parameter
paramount
paranoiac
parasitic
parcelled
parchment
pardoning
paregoric
parentage
parlaying
parleying
parochial
parodying
parqueted
parquetry
parrakeet
parricide
parroting
parsimony
parsonage
partaking
Parthenon
partially
particial
partition
partitive
partridge
pas de deux
passenger
passerine
passersby
passivity
Pasternak
pastiness
pastorate
pasturage
pasturing
patchiest
patchouli
patchouly
patchwork
paternity
pathology

patiently
patriarch
patrician
patricide
patrimony
patriotic
patrolled
patroller
patrolman
patrolmen
patronage
patroness
patronize
patterned
paunchier
pauperism
pauperize
paymaster
peaceable
peaceably
peachiest
peasantry
pebbliest
peccaries
pecuniary
pedagogic
pedagogue
pedalling
pediatric
pedigreed
pedometer
peevishly
Pekingese
penalized
penalties
penciling
pendently
pendulous
penetrate
peninsula
penitence
penknives
penniless
penny-ante
Penobscot
penpusher
pensioner
pensively
pentagram
Pentecost
penthouse
penurious
peppiness
per capita
perceived
perchance
Percheron
percolate
perdition
peregrine
perennial

perfecter
perfectly
perfectly
perforate
performer
perfumery
perfuming
perimeter
perinatal
periphery
periphras
periscope
peristyle
perjuries
perjuring
permanent
permeable
permeably
permeated
permitted
perpetual
perplexed
persecute
persevere
persimmon
personage
personate
personify
personnel
perspired
persuaded
pertinent
pervading
pervasion
pervasive
perverted
peskiness
pessaries
pessimism
pessimist
pesticide
pestilent
petit four
petitness
petrified
petroleum
petrology
petticoat
petulance
petulancy
phalanger
phalanges
phenomena
philander
philately
philippic
philology
phlebitis
Phnom Penh
phonetics
phoniness

phonology
phosphate
photocopy
photostat
phrenetic
phylogeny
physician
physicist
physicked
picaninny
pickaback
picketing
picnicked
picnicker
pictorial
picturing
piecemeal
piecemeal
piecework
piggeries
piggyback
pigheaded
pikestaff
pilferage
pillaging
pilloried
pillories
pilotless
pineapple
pinioning
pintsized
piousness
pip-squeak
piratical
pirouette
pistachio
pistoling
pitchfork
piteously
pithiness
pitifully
pituitary
pityingly
pivotally
pizzicato
placating
placation
placative
placatory
placement
placental
placidity
plainness
plainsong
plaintiff
plaintive
planetary
planetoid
plantable
plastered
plasterer

plasterer
platitude
plausible
plausibly
playfully
playhouse
pleadable
pleasured
plenitude
plenteous
plentiful
plowshare
pluckiest
plumb line
plummeted
plummiest
plumpness
plunderer
pluralism
pluralist
plurality
pluralize
plusfours
plushiest
plutocrat
plutonium
pneumatic
pneumonia
pocketful
pocketing
poetaster
pogo stick
poignancy
poinciana
pointedly
pointless
poisoning
poisonous
polarized
polemical
polevault
policeman
policemen
politburo
political
pollinate
pollutant
polluting
pollution
polonaise
polyandry
polyanthi
polyester
polygonal
polygraph
Polynesia
pommeling
pommelled
pompadour
pomposity
pompously

ponderous
poppycock
popularly
populated
porcelain
porcupine
portaging
portfolio
porticoes
portioned
portliest
portrayal
portrayer
possessed
possessor
postdated
posterior
posterity
posthaste
postilion
postnasal
postnatal
postponed
postulant
postulate
posturing
potassium
potboiler
potentate
potential
potpourri
potteries
powerboat
powerless
practical
practiced
pragmatic
prankster
prattling
prayerful
precancel
precedent
preceding
preceptor
precipice
precisely
precision
precluded
precocity
precursor
predatory
predicate
preemptor
prefacing
prefatory
preferred
prefigure
preflight
pregnancy
prejudged
prejudice

preluding
premature
premising
preoccupy
preordain
preparing
prepaying
prerecord
presaging
preschool
prescient
prescript
preseason
preselect
presently
presently
preserved
preserver
president
presiding
presidium
pressured
presswork
presuming
pretended
pretender
prettiest
prevalent
prevision
priceless
prickling
priestess
primaries
primarily
primitive
princedom
principal
principle
printable
prismatic
privateer
privately
privation
privatize
privilege
probating
probation
probative
probatory
proboscis
procedure
proconsul
procreant
procreate
procuring
prodigies
producing
profaning
profanity
professed
professor

proffered
profiling
profiteer
profiting
profusely
profusion
prognoses
prognosis
programed
programer
projector
Prokofiev
prolixity
promenade
prominent
promising
promoting
promotion
promotive
proneness
pronounce
propagate
propelled
propeller
prophetic
proponent
proposing
propriety
prorating
proration
prosecute
proselyte
prospered
prostrate
protector
protester
prototype
protozoan
Provençal
provender
provident
providing
provision
provisory
provoking
proximate
proximity
prurience
pruriency
psalmbook
pseudonym
psoriasis
psychical
psychoses
psychosis
psychotic
ptarmigan
pubescent
publicist
publicity
publicize

publisher
pudginess
puerility
puerperal
puffiness
pugnacity
pulmonary
pulpiness
pulsating
pulsation
pulverize
pummeling
pummelled
punchball
punchiest
punctilio
punctuate
punctured
pungently
puppeteer
purchased
purchaser
purgation
purgative
purgatory
purifying
purloiner
purposely
purposing
pursuance
purulency
pushiness
pussyfoot
putrefied
pyramidal
pyromania
pyrometer

quadrated
quadratic
quadrille
quadruped
quadruple
Quakerism
qualified
qualifier
qualities
quarreled
quarrying
quarterly
quartette
queasiest
queerness
quibbling
quicklime
quickness
quicksand
quickstep
quiescent
quietness

quintette
quintuple
quirkiest
quitclaim
quittance
quivering
quizzical
quotation
quotidian

rabbeting
rabbiting
racehorse
racetrack
racialism
racialist
racketeer
raconteur
radiantly
radiating
radiation
radically
radiogram
radiology
raininess
rainwater
ramifying
rampaging
rampantly
rancidity
rancorous
randomize
ranginess
rapacious
rapidfire
rapidness
rapturous
rarefying
rascality
raspberry
raspingly
ratifying
rationale
rattiness
raucously
raunchier
ravishing
reachable
readiness
ready-made
realistic
realities
realizing
reanimate
rearguard
rearrange
reasoning
reassured
rebelling
rebellion

rebutting
recapping
recapture
receiving
reception
receptive
recession
recessive
recharged
recherché
recipient
reckoning
reclining
reclusion
reclusive
recognize
recollect
recollect
recommend
reconcile
recondite
reconfirm
recording
recreated
recruiter
rectangle
rectified
rectifier
rectitude
rectories
recumbent
recurrent
recurring
redevelop
red-handed
redheaded
red-letter
redolence
redolency
redoubled
reducible
reduction
redundant
reechoing
reediness
reeducate
reenforce
reexamine
refectory
referable
reference
referenda
referring
refinance
refitting
reflating
reflation
reflector
reflexive
reformist
refresher

refulgent
refurbish
refusenik
refutable
regardful
regarding
regencies
registrar
regretful
regretted
regularly
regulated
regulator
rehearsal
rehearsed
rehousing
Reichstag
reimburse
reinforce
reinstate
reiterate
rejection
rejoicing
rejoinder
rekindled
relapsing
releasing
relegated
relevance
relevancy
relieving
religious
reliquary
relocated
reluctant
remainder
remarried
remedying
reminisce
remission
remitting
remodeled
removable
renascent
rendition
renounced
renovated
renovator
reparable
repayable
repayment
repellent
repelling
repentant
repertory
rephrased
replacing
replenish
repletion
replicate
reportage

repossess	retriever	ruination
repotting	retrofire	ruinously
reprehend	retroussé	rummaging
represent	reuniting	runaround
reprieved	revaluate	runners-up
reprimand	revelling	rupturing
reprobate	revelries	ruralized
reproduce	revenging	Ruritania
reproving	reverence	rusticate
reptilian	reversing	rusticity
repudiate	reversion	rustiness
repugnant	revisited	rustproof
repulsing	revocable	ruthenium
repulsion	revolving	
repulsive	revulsion	
reputable	rewinding	sabotaged
reputably	rewriting	saccharin
reputedly	rewritten	sackcloth
requiring	Reykjavik	sacrament
requisite	rhapsodic	sacrifice
rerouting	rheumatic	sacrilege
rerunning	Richelieu	sacristan
reselling	ridiculed	safeguard
resembled	righteous	safflower
resentful	rigmarole	sagacious
reserving	Rio Grande	sagebrush
reservist	riotously	sainthood
reservoir	riposting	saintlier
resetting	riskiness	salacious
resettled	ritualism	salacious
reshuffle	ritualist	saliently
residence	rivalling	salivated
residency	rivalries	saltiness
resilient	riverside	saltpeter
resistant	roadblock	salt-water
resolving	roadhouse	salvaging
resonance	robberies	salvation
resonated	rock-bound	Samaritan
resonator	rocketing	sanatoria
respecter	rockiness	sanctuary
respiring	roguishly	sandiness
restating	romancing	sandpaper
restfully	rookeries	sandpiper
restoring	roominess	sangfroid
restraint	Roosevelt	Sanhedrin
resultant	Roquefort	sanitized
resurface	rosaceous	sapsucker
resurgent	Rotterdam	sarabande
resurrect	rotundity	sarcastic
retaliate	roughcast	sartorial
retardant	rough-hewn	sassafras
retelling	roughneck	sassiness
retention	roughness	satanical
retentive	roughshod	satellite
rethought	roundelay	satiating
reticence	routinize	satiation
reticular	rowdiness	satinwood
retracing	royalties	satirical
retractor	rubberize	satirized
retrieval	ruddiness	satisfied
retrieved	ruffianly	saturable

saturated
saturnine
sauceboat
sauciness
sauteeing
saxophone
scaliness
scaliness
scantiest
scantness
scapegoat
scarecrow
scarified
scavenged
scavenger
scenarist
scheduled
schematic
schmaltzy
scholarly
schooling
scientist
scintilla
sclerosis
scorbutic
scorching
scorecard
scoreless
scoundrel
scourging
scrabbled
scraggier
scragging
scrambled
scrambler
scramming
scrapbook
scrappier
scrapping
scrawnier
screaming
screening
screwball
screwiest
scribbled
scribbler
scrimmage
scrimshaw
scripture
scrivener
scrounged
scrounger
scrubbier
scrubbing
scruffier
scruffily
scrutable
scuffling
sculpture
scurrying
scuttling

seafaring
seaminess
searching
seasoning
seaworthy
sebaceous
secession
secluding
seclusion
seclusive
secondary
secretary
secreting
secretion
secretive
secretory
sectarian
sectional
sectorial
securable
sedentary
seditious
seducible
seduction
seductive
seediness
seemingly
seemliest
segmental
segregate
selection
selective
self-abuse
self-image
selfishly
semantics
semaphore
semblance
semicolon
semifinal
semifluid
semisolid
senescent
seniority
sensation
senseless
sensitive
sensitize
sensorial
sensually
sentenced
sentiment
separable
separably
separated
separator
Sephardic
Sephardim
September
septicity
sepulcher

sequester
sequinned
serenaded
serialize
seriously
sermonize
serrating
serration
servicing
servilely
servility
servitude
seventeen
seventies
severable
severally
severance
sextuplet
sexuality
sforzando
shabbiest
shackling
shadiness
shaggiest
shakiness
shallowly
shambling
shameless
shampooed
Shangri-la
shapeable
shapeless
shapelier
sharecrop
sharkskin
sharpener
sharp-eyed
sharpness
sheathing
sheepfold
sheepskin
sheerness
sheikhdom
shellfish
shiftiest
shiftless
shingling
shininess
Shintoism
shipboard
shippable
shipshape
shipwreck
shirttail
shlemiehl
shlepping
shoddiest
shoemaker
shoreline
shortcake
shortfall

shorthand	sixteenth	snuggling
short-haul	skeptical	soapiness
shorthorn	sketchier	soberness
shortness	sketchily	sobriquet
short-term	skimpiest	socialism
shovelful	skin-dived	socialist
shoveling	skinflint	socialite
shovelled	skinniest	sociality
showcased	skintight	socialize
showiness	skydiving	societies
showpiece	skyjacker	sociology
shredding	skyrocket	soft-pedal
shrinkage	slackness	sogginess
shrinking	slanderer	soi-disant
shriveled	slangiest	solarized
shrubbery	slantways	soldierly
shrugging	slantwise	solemnity
shuffling	slaphappy	solemnize
shuttling	slapstick	solicited
sibilance	slaughter	solicitor
sibylline	slavishly	solidness
sickening	sleaziest	soliloquy
sickliest	sleekness	solitaire
sideboard	sleepiest	something
sideburns	sleepless	sometimes
sidelight	slickness	somewhere
sidelined	sliminess	somnolent
sideswipe	slinkiest	sons-in-law
sidetrack	slipcover	sootiness
sightless	sloganeer	sophistic
signaling	sloppiest	sophistry
signalled	slouchily	Sophocles
signalman	slumberer	sophomore
signalmen	slummiest	soporific
signatory	slushiest	sorceress
signature	smallness	sorcerous
signboard	smarmiest	sorriness
signified	smartness	sorrowful
Signorina	smelliest	sotto voce
Signorine	smokeless	soubrette
silencing	smokiness	souffléed
silicosis	smudgiest	soulfully
silkiness	smuggling	soundable
silliness	smuttiest	soundless
siltation	snakiness	soundness
similarly	snappiest	southeast
simonized	snazziest	southerly
simpleton	sneakiest	southward
simulated	sniffiest	southwest
simulator	sniffling	souwester
simulcast	sniveling	sovereign
sincerely	snivelled	sovietism
sincerity	snobbiest	spaceship
Singapore	snootiest	spackling
singleton	snorkeled	spadework
Sinhalese	snottiest	spaghetti
sinuating	snowbound	spangling
sinuosity	snowfield	spareness
sinusitis	snowflake	sparingly
situating	snowiness	sparkling
situation	snuffling	spasmodic

spatially
speak-easy
spearhead
spearmint
specially
specialty
specified
speckling
spectacle
spectator
speculate
speechify
speediest
speedwell
spelunker
spendable
spermatic
spherical
sphincter
spiciness
spindlier
spindling
spineless
spininess
spinnaker
spiraling
spiralled
spiriting
spiritous
spiritual
splayfoot
spleenful
splenetic
splintery
splitting
splurging
spokesman
spokesmen
spongiest
sponsored
spookiest
spoon-feed
spoonfuls
spoonsful
sportsman
sportsmen
spotlight
spottiest
spreading
sprightly
springbok
springier
springing
sprinkled
sprinkler
spunkiest
squabbled
squashier
squatness
squatting
squeakier

squeamish
squeezing
squiggled
stability
stabilize
stagnancy
stagnated
staidness
stainless
staircase
stairwell
stalemate
staleness
Stalinism
Stalinist
stampeded
stanchion
starboard
starchier
stargazed
starlight
startling
statehood
stateless
statelier
statement
statement
stateroom
statesman
statesmen
stationer
statistic
statuette
status quo
statutory
staunchly
steadfast
steadiest
steadying
steamiest
steamship
steepness
steerable
stenciled
stepchild
sterility
sterilize
sternness
stevedore
stickiest
stiffener
stiffness
stigmatic
stillborn
stillness
stillroom
stimulant
stimulate
stingiest
stippling
stipulate

stir-fried
Stockholm
stockiest
stockpile
stockroom
stodgiest
stoically
stolidity
stonewall
stoneware
stonework
stoniness
stopwatch
storeroom
stormiest
storybook
stoutness
straggled
straggler
strangely
strangest
strangled
strangler
strapless
strapping
stratagem
strategic
streakier
strenuous
stressful
stretcher
striating
striation
stricture
stridency
stringent
stringier
stringing
stripiest
stripling
stripping
Stromboli
strontium
stropping
structure
struggled
struggler
strumming
strutting
stubbiest
stuccoing
stufffier
stuffiest
stumbling
stumpiest
stupefied
stupidity
stuporous
sturdiest
stutterer
Stuttgart

stylishly
stylistic
stylizing
stymieing
suaveness
subaltern
subarctic
subatomic
subchaser
subdivide
sub judice
subjugate
subleased
sublimate
sublimely
sublimest
sublimity
submarine
submerged
submersed
submitted
subnormal
subregion
subscribe
subsidies
subsiding
subsidize
substance
substrata
subsuming
subsystem
subtropic
subverter
successor
succotash
succulent
suffering
sufficing
suffocate
suffusing
suffusion
suffusive
sugarcoat
sulfurous
sulkiness
sultanate
summaries
summarily
summarize
summation
summing-up
sumptuary
sumptuous
sunbathed
sunbather
sunbonnet
sunburned
sunflower
sunniness
sunstroke
suntanned

superfine
supernova
supersede
superstar
supervene
supervise
suppliant
supplying
supporter
supposing
suppurate
supremacy
supremely
surcharge
surcingle
surfacing
surfboard
surgeries
surliness
surmising
surprisal
surprised
surrender
surrogate
surveying
surviving
suspender
suspicion
sustainer
swaddling
swampiest
swarthier
Swaziland
sweatsuit
sweetener
sweetmeat
sweetness
swiftness
swindling
swingable
swiveling
swivelled
swordsman
swordsmen
sycophant
syllabify
syllogism
sylph-like
symbiosis
symbiotic
symbolism
symbolist
symbolize
symmetric
symphonic
symposium
synagogal
synagogue
syncopate
syncretic
syndicate

synergism
syntactic
syntheses
synthesis
synthetic
syringing

tabularly
tabulated
tabulator
tacitness
tackiness
tactfully
tactician
tactility
tailgated
tailoring
talkative
tangerine
tantalize
tarantula
tardiness
targeting
tarpaulin
tartarous
tasseling
tasselled
tasteless
tastiness
tattooing
tattooist
tautology
tawdriest
tawniness
taxexempt
taxidermy
teachable
teakettle
tearfully
teaseling
technical
technique
tediously
telegraph
telemeter
telemetry
teleology
telepathy
telephone
telephoto
telescope
televised
tellurium
temperate
temporary
temporize
temptable
temptress
tenacious
tenancies

tenderize
Tennessee
tenseness
tensility
tensional
tentacled
tentative
tenuously
tepidness
termagant
terminate
terracing
terrarium
terrified
territory
terrorism
terrorist
terrorize
terseness
testament
testatrix
testified
testimony
testiness
tête-à-tête
thankless
thatching
theocracy
theologic
theoretic
theorized
theorizer
theosophy
therapist
therefore
thereupon
thermally
thesaurus
thickener
thicketed
thickness
thingummy
thirstier
thirstily
thirtieth
thorniest
thralldom
thrashing
threefold
threesome
threshold
thriftier
thriftily
thrilling
throatier
throatily
throbbing
throttled
throwaway
throwback
thrumming

thrusting
thumbnail
thumbtack
tidewater
tightness
tightrope
timepiece
timeshare
timetable
timidness
timpanist
tinderbox
tinniness
tinseling
Tipperary
tipsiness
titillate
tittering
toadstool
tolerable
tolerably
tolerance
tolerated
tollbooth
tollhouse
tomboyish
tombstone
tonsorial
tonsuring
toolmaker
toothache
toothiest
toothless
toothpick
toothsome
top-secret
tormentor
tornadoes
torpedoed
torpedoes
torpidity
torridity
torsional
torturing
totalling
tottering
touchable
touchdown
touchiest
touch-type
toughness
tournedos
towelling
tow-headed
townsfolk
traceable
traceably
tracksuit
tractable
tractably
trademark

tradesman
tradesmen
tradition
traducing
tragedian
tragedies
trainable
traipsing
trammeled
trampling
transcend
transform
transfuse
transient
translate
transmute
transonic
transpire
transport
transpose
transship
Transvaal
trapezium
trapezoid
trappings
trashiest
traumatic
traveling
travelled
traveller
traversal
traversed
treachery
treadmill
treasured
treasurer
treatable
treatment
trembling
tremorous
tremulous
trenchant
trendiest
trepanned
tribalism
tribesman
tribesmen
tributary
trickiest
trickling
trickster
tricuspid
triennial
triennium
trifocals
trilogies
trimester
trisector
triteness
triturate
triumphal

trivially
triweekly
troubling
trouncing
trousseau
truancies
truckling
truckload
truculent
trumpeted
trumpeter
truncated
truncheon
trundling
trustiest
tsetse fly
tubbiness
tuck-point
tularemia
tumescent
tunneling
tunnelled
turbanned
turbidity
turboprop
turbulent
turgidity
turnabout
turnstile
turntable
turpitude
turquoise
tuti-fruti
twentieth
twiddling
twinkling
two-fisted
tympanist
typewrite
typically
typifying
tyrannies
tyrannize
tyrannous

Ukrainian
ulcerated
ultimatum
ululation
umbilical
umpteenth
unabashed
unadorned
unadvised
unaligned
unalloyed
unaltered
unanimity
unanimous
unashamed

unbarring
unbeknown
unbending
unbinding
unbounded
unbridled
unbuckled
uncannier
uncannily
uncapping
unceasing
uncertain
unchanged
uncharted
unchecked
uncivilly
unclaimed
uncleanly
unclothed
uncolored
unconcern
uncounted
uncouthly
uncovered
uncrowned
undamaged
undaunted
undecided
undefined
undercoat
underdone
underfoot
undergoes
undergone
underhand
underlain
underline
underling
undermine
undermost
underpaid
underpass
underplay
underrate
undersell
underside
undersold
undertake
undertone
undertook
underused
underwear
underwent
undiluted
undoubted
undressed
undulated
unearthly
uneasiest
uneatable
unequaled

unequally
unethical
unfailing
unfeeling
unfeigned
unfitness
unfitting
unfocused
unfounded
unfrocked
unguarded
unhappier
unhappily
unhealthy
unheedful
unheeding
unhelpful
unhinging
unhurried
uniformed
uniformly
unimpeded
unionized
Unitarian
univalent
universal
unknowing
unlearned
unlearned
unlimited
unlovable
unluckily
unmarried
unmatched
unmeaning
unmindful
unmusical
unnatural
unnerving
unnoticed
unplugged
unplumbed
unpopular
unraveled
unreality
unrefined
unrelated
unreserve
unrivaled
unruffled
unsaddled
unsalable
unscathed
unselfish
unsettled
unsheathe
unsightly
unskilled
unsmiling
unsnapped
unsparing

unspoiled
unspotted
unstopped
unstudied
unsullied
untangled
untenable
untidiest
untouched
untrained
untreated
untutored
unusually
unvarying
unwelcome
unwilling
unwinding
unwitting
unworldly
unwrapped
unwritten
unzipping
up-and-down
upcountry
upgrading
upholding
upholster
uppermost
upraising
upsetting
upstaging
urbanized
urinating
urination
Ursa Major
Ursa Minor
usability
uselessly
usherette
utilities
utilizing
utterable
utterance
uttermost

vacancies
vaccinate
vacillate
vagarious
vagueness
vainglory
valencies
valentine
valiantly
validated
validness
valuation
valueless
valveless
vandalism

vandalize
vapidness
vaporized
vaporizer
variation
variegate
varieties
variously
varsities
varyingly
vasectomy
vasomotor
vassalage
vastitude
vectorial
vegetable
vegetated
vehemence
vehemency
vehicular
velveteen
veneering
venerable
venerably
venerator
vengeance
veniality
ventilate
ventricle
venturing
venturous
veracious
verbalize
verbosity
verdigris
verdurous
verifying
veritable
veritably
vermiform
vermifuge
vermilion
verminous
versatile
versified
versional
vertebrae
vertebral
vestibule
vestigial
vexatious
viability
vibrating
vibration
vibratory
vicarious
vice versa
viciously
victimize
Victorian
victories

videotape
viewpoint
vigilance
vigilante
vilifying
vindicate
violating
violation
violently
violinist
virginity
virtually
virulence
virulency
viscidity
viscosity
visionary
visualize
vitalized
vitiating
vitiation
vitrified
vitriolic
vivacious
vividness
vivifying
vocalized
voiceless
voice-over
vol-au-vent
volcanoes
volleying
volte-face
voluntary
volunteer
voodooism
voodooist
voracious
vouchsafe
vox populi
voyeurism
vulcanize
vulgarism
vulgarity
vulgarize
vulturous

wackiness
waggishly
Wagnerian
waistband
waistcoat
waistline
wakefully
walkabout
wallabies
wallboard
walloping
wallpaper
warehouse

warmonger
washbasin
washcloth
wasteland
watchword
waterfall
waterfowl
Watergate
waterless
water lily
waterline
water main
watermark
watershed
waterside
wayfaring
waylaying
weak-kneed
wealthier
weariness
wearisome
webfooted
Wedgewood
Wednesday
weediness
weightier
weirdness
welcoming
well-being
well-built
well-known
well-meant
well-timed
westbound
Westerner
westwards
whackiest
whaleboat
whalebone
wheedling
wheelbase
wheeziest
wherefore
whereupon
wherewith
whetstone
whichever
whimsical
whinnying
whirligig

whirlpool
whirlwind
whistling
whitebait
Whitehall
whiteness
whitening
whitewash
whittling
whodunnit
wholeness
wholesale
wholesome
whosoever
wide-angle
wide-awake
widowhood
wiggliest
wigwagged
willfully
willingly
willpower
Wimbledon
windblown
windbreak
windiness
windstorm
winterize
Wisconsin
wisecrack
wishfully
wistfully
withdrawn
withstand
withstood
witticism
wittiness
wittingly
woebegone
wolfhound
wolverine
womanhood
womanizer
womankind
womenfolk
wonderful
woodchuck
woodcraft
wood louse
woolliest

wooziness
wordiness
workbench
workforce
workhorse
workhouse
worktable
worldlier
worldwide
worm-eaten
worriedly
worrisome
worrywart
worshiped
worshiper
worthiest
worthless
wrangling
wreathing
wrestling
wriggling
wrinkling
wrist band
wrongdoer

xenophobe
xylograph
xylophone

yachtsman
yachtsmen
yardstick
year-round
yellowish
yesterday
yodelling
Yom Kippur
youngling
youngster
ytterbium

zealously
Zechariah
Zephaniah
zestfully
zigzagged
zirconium
zoologist
zucchetto

abbreviate
abdicating
abdication
aberration
abhorrence
abjectness
abjuration
able-bodied
abnegating
abnegation
abnormally
abominable
abominably
abominated
aboriginal
aboveboard
abridgment
abrogating
abrogation
abruptness
abscission
absolutely
absolution
absolutism
absorbable
absorbency
absorption
absorptive
abstemious
abstention
abstinence
abstracted
abstractly
absurdness
abundantly
academical
accelerant
accelerate
accentuate
acceptable
acceptably
acceptance
accessible
accessibly
accidental
acclimaing
acclimated
accomplice
accomplish
accordance
accountant
accounting
accredited
accumulate
accurately
accusation
accusative
accusatory
accusingly
accustomed
acephalous

achievable
achromatic
acidifying
acoustical
acquainted
acquiesced
acquiesing
acrobatics
acrophobia
actionable
actionably
activating
activation
activeness
activities
adamantine
adaptation
additional
adequately
adjacently
adjectival
adjudicate
adjunctive
adjuration
adjustable
adjustment
administer
admiration
admiringly
admirrable
admissible
admittance
admittedly
admonition
admonitory
adolescent
adrenaline
adroitness
adsorption
adulterant
adulterate
adulteress
adulterous
advantaged
adventurer
advertence
advertised
advertiser
advisement
advocating
advocation
aerobatics
aerologist
aesthetics
affability
affectedly
affiliated
affinities
affliction
aficionado
afterbirth

aftershave
aftertaste
afterwards
aggrandize
aggravated
aggregated
aggression
aggressive
aggrieving
agronomist
aide-de-camp
airdropped
albuminous
alcoholism
algebraist
Algonquian
alienating
alienation
alimentary
alkalinity
alkalizing
alkaloidal
allegation
allegiance
allegories
allegretto
alleviated
alliterate
allocating
allocation
allopathic
allottable
allurement
alluringly
allusively
alpenstock
alphabetic
altarpiece
alteration
alterative
alternated
alternator
altogether
altruistic
amalgamate
amanuenses
amanuensis
amateurish
amateurism
ambassador
ambivalent
ambulating
ambulatory
ambushment
ameliorate
amenorrhea
amercement
amerciable
Amerindian
amiability
ammunition

amortizing
amphibious
amplifying
amputating
amputation
Anabaptist
analogical
anarchical
anatomical
anatomized
ancestress
ancestries
anemometer
anesthesia
anesthetic
anglophobe
Anglo-Saxon
angularity
angulation
animadvert
annalistic
annexation
annihilate
anno Domini
annotating
annotation
announcing
annunciate
anointment
answerable
antagonism
antagonist
antagonize
Antarctica
antebellum
antecedent
anteceding
antepenult
anthracite
anthropoid
antibiotic
antibodies
Antichrist
anticipate
anticlimax
antifreeze
antiheroes
antimatter
antipodean
antiquated
antisepsis
antiseptic
antisocial
antistatic
antitheses
antithesis
aphoristic
apiculture
apocalypse
apolitical
apologetic

apologized
apoplectic
apostasies
apostatize
apostolate
apostrophe
apothecary
apotheoses
apotheosis
apparently
apparition
appealable
appearance
appendices
appendixes
appetizing
applesauce
applicable
applicator
appointive
apposition
appositive
appraising
appreciate
apprentice
aquamarine
arbitrated
arbitrator
archbishop
archdeacon
archeology
archetypal
aristocrat
arithmetic
Armageddon
aromatical
arrogantly
arrogation
articulate
artificial
Art Nouveau
arty-crafty
asbestosis
ascendance
ascendancy
ascendence
ascendency
asceticism
ascribable
ascription
asexuality
Ashkenazic
Ashkenazim
asphyxiate
aspidistra
aspirating
aspiration
assailable
assemblage
assemblies
assembling

assessable
assessment
asseverate
assignable
assignably
assignment
assimilate
assistance
associated
assortment
assumption
astigmatic
astounding
astringent
astrologer
astrologic
astronomer
astronomic
astuteness
asymmetric
Athabaskan
Athapaskan
atmosphere
atrocities
atrophying
attachment
attainable
attainment
attendance
attenuated
attirement
attraction
attractive
attributed
auctioneer
audibility
audiophile
auditorium
aureomycin
auspicious
Australian
authorized
authorship
autocratic
automating
automation
automatism
automobile
automotive
autonomies
autonomous
avantgarde
avaricious

babysitter
backdating
backfiring
backgammon
background
backhanded

backslider
backspaced
backstairs
backstitch
backstroke
balderdash
ballistics
balustrade
bamboozled
bandleader
bandmaster
Bangladesh
banishment
bankruptcy
banqueting
baptistery
barbecuing
barbershop
bareheaded
bar mitzvah
barometric
barracouta
barrenness
barricaded
baset hound
basketball
basketwork
bassoonist
bastardize
battlement
battleship
bayberries
bayoneting
bayonetted
beatifying
Beaujolais
beautician
beautified
bedazzling
bedchamber
bedclothes
beddraggle
bedeviling
bedwetting
beekeeping
beforehand
befuddling
begrudging
behavioral
behindhand
believable
belittling
belladonna
belongings
benefactor
beneficent
beneficial
beneficing
benefiting
benevolent
benignancy

Benzedrine
beseeching
bespeaking
bestiality
bestirring
bestridden
bestriding
best-seller
betterment
bewitching
biannually
biblically
bichloride
biennially
bifurcated
bigamously
big-hearted
bilberries
billet-doux
biochemist
bioecology
biogenesis
biographer
biographic
biological
biometrics
biophysics
bipartisan
birthplace
birthright
birthstone
bitchiness
bitterness
bituminous
bivalvular
bivouacked
biweeklies
blackberry
blackboard
blackguard
blacksmith
blackthorn
blancmange
blanketing
blasphemed
blasphemer
bleariness
blissfully
blitzkrieg
blockading
blockhouse
bloodhound
blotchiest
bluebottle
bluecollar
blundering
blusterous
boastfully
boastingly
bobby socks
boisterous

bollweevil
Bolshevism
Bolshevist
bombardier
bookbinder
bookkeeper
bookmobile
bookseller
bootlegged
bootlegger
borderland
borderline
bothersome
Botticelli
bottleneck
bottomless
bottommost
boundaries
bowdlerize
bracketing
Brahmanism
brainchild
brainpower
brainstorm
brawniness
breadboard
breadfruit
breakwater
breastbone
breast-feed
breathless
breeziness
brevetting
breviaries
bricklayer
bridegroom
bridesmaid
bridgehead
bridgework
brigantine
brightness
brilliance
brilliancy
bristliest
broadcloth
broadsword
broken-down
bronchitic
bronchitis
broomstick
browbeaten
brutalized
budgerigar
buffoonery
bulldozing
bullheaded
burdensome
bureaucrat
burglaries
burglarize
burlesqued

bush-babies
bushmaster
busybodies
buttermilk
butterwort
buttonhole

cadaverous
cafe au lait
calamities
calamitous
calcifying
calculable
calculated
calculator
calibrated
California
camelopard
camouflage
campaigner
candelabra
candescent
cannonball
canonizing
cantaloupe
canteloupe
cantilever
cantonment
capability
capacitate
capacities
capitalism
capitalist
capitalize
capitation
capitulate
capricious
caprioling
captivated
caramelize
carbonated
carbonized
carburetor
carcinogen
cardiogram
cardiology
carelessly
caricature
caryatides
caseworker
castigated
castrating
castration
casualness
casualties
catafalque
cataleptic
cataloging
catalogued
catalyzing

catechized
categories
categorize
catnapping
cauterized
cautionary
cautiously
celebrator
cellophane
cemeteries
censorious
censorship
censurable
centennial
centerfold
centesimal
centigrade
centiliter
centimeter
centralize
centrifuge
cerebellum
ceremonial
ceremonies
certifying
chagrining
chairwoman
challenged
challenger
chancellor
chandelier
changeable
changeless
changeling
channeling
chaperoned
chargeable
charioteer
charitable
charitably
charmingly
chartreuse
chasteness
chastising
chatterbox
chattiness
Chaucerian
chauvinism
chauvinist
cheapskate
checkpoint
cheekiness
cheerfully
cheeriness
cheesecake
chemically
chickenpox
chiffonier
childbirth
childishly
chilliness

chimpanzee
chinchilla
chiromancy
chivalrous
chlorinate
chloroform
choiceness
choppiness
chopsticks
Christlike
Christmasy
chromatics
chromosome
chronicled
chronicler
chronology
chubbiness
churchgoer
churchyard
cicatrices
cinerarium
circuitous
circulated
circumcise
circumflex
circumfuse
circumvent
Cistercian
citric acid
citronella
civilities
civilizing
clamminess
clangorous
clarifying
claspknife
classicism
classicist
classified
clavichord
clerestory
cleverness
climatical
clinically
clodhopper
cloistered
clothespin
cloudburst
cloudiness
clumsiness
Clydesdale
coagulated
coalescent
coalescing
coarseness
coastguard
coatimundi
cockatrice
cogitating
cogitative
cognizance

coherently
coincident
coinciding
collapsing
collarbone
collateral
collection
collective
collegiate
collieries
colloquial
colonizing
coloration
coloratura
colorblind
Colossians
combustion
combustive
comedienne
comeliness
comestible
commandant
commandeer
commandoes
commencing
commentary
commentate
commercial
commingled
commissary
commission
commitment
committing
commodious
commonalty
commonweal
communiqué
commutable
comparable
comparably
comparison
compassion
compatible
compatibly
compatriot
compelling
compendium
compensate
competence
competency
competitor
complacent
complected
complement
completely
completing
completion
complexion
complexity
compliance
compliancy

complicate
complicity
compliment
compositor
comprehend
compressor
comprising
compromise
compulsion
compulsive
compulsory
conceiving
concentric
conception
conceptual
concertina
concession
conciliate
concluding
conclusion
conclusive
concoction
concordant
concreting
concretion
concurrent
concurring
concussion
concussive
condensing
condescend
condolence
conduction
conductive
confection
conference
conferring
confession
confidante
confidence
confiscate
conflating
conflation
confluence
conformist
conformity
confounded
confusedly
congenital
congestion
congestive
congregate
congruence
congruency
coniferous
conjecture
conjointly
conjugally
conjugated
connection
connective

conniption
connivance
conscience
consecrate
consequent
conserving
consistent
consistory
consolable
consortium
conspiracy
conspiring
constantly
constipate
constitute
constraint
construing
consulship
consultant
consumable
consummate
contagious
contention
contestant
contextual
contexture
contiguity
contiguous
continence
continency
contingent
continuing
continuity
continuous
contortion
contraband
contrabass
contracted
contractor
contradict
contrarily
contravene
contribute
contritely
contrition
contriving
controlled
controller
controvert
convalesce
convection
convenient
convention
convergent
converging
conversant
conversely
conversing
conversion
conveyable
conveyance

conviction
convincing
convoluted
convulsing
convulsion
convulsive
cooperated
coordinate
Copenhagen
Copernican
copulating
copulation
copulative
copywriter
coquettish
cordiality
Corinthian
cornerback
cornflakes
cornflower
corn starch
cornucopia
coronaries
coronation
corpulence
corralling
correction
corrective
correlated
correspond
corrigenda
corrigible
corrugated
corruption
cos lettuce
cosmically
co-starring
cottontail
cottonwood
couchgrass
councilman
councilmen
counseling
counteract
counterspy
countryman
countrymen
courageous
courtesies
courthouse
covetously
cragginess
crankiness
crankshaft
creameries
creaminess
creatively
creativity
credential
creditable
creditably

creepiness
crematoria
crenelated
cretaceous
criminally
crinkliest
crisscross
critically
criticized
crocheting
crossbones
crossbreed
cruciality
crucifying
crumbliest
crustacean
cryogenics
cryptogram
cuddlesome
culminated
cultivated
cultivator
cumbersome
cummerbund
cumulation
cumulative
curability
currencies
curricular
curriculum
cursedness
curvaceous
cussedness
customized
cuttlefish
cyclopedia
cycloramic
cycloramic
czarevitch

daintiness
dandifying
deactivate
deadliness
deadweight
death's-head
deathwatch
debasement
debauchery
debilitate
debilities
decadently
decahedron
decampment
decapitate
decathlete
decelerate
decimalize
decimating
decimation

decisively
declassify
declension
declinable
decomposed
decompress
decorating
decoration
decorative
decorously
decreasing
decrepitly
dedicating
dedication
dedicatory
deductible
deeprooted
deepseated
deescalate
defacement
defamation
defamatory
defecating
defecation
defensible
deficiency
defilement
definitely
definition
definitive
deflection
deflective
defoliated
defrayment
degeneracy
degenerate
degradable
dehiscence
dehumanize
dehumidify
dehydrated
deionizing
dejectedly
delectable
delectably
delegating
delegation
deliberate
delicacies
delicately
delightful
delineated
delineator
delinquent
deliquesce
deliveries
delphinium
delusively
demobilize
democratic
demography

demolition
demoniacal
demonology
demoralize
demureness
denazified
denigrated
denotation
dénouement
denouncing
dentifrice
deodorized
Deo volente
deoxidized
dependable
dependably
dependence
dependency
depilatory
deplorable
deplorably
deployment
depolarize
depopulate
deportment
depositing
deposition
depository
deprecated
depreciate
depredated
depressant
depression
depressive
deputation
deputizing
derailment
derisively
derivation
derivative
dermatitis
dernier cri
derogating
derogation
derogatory
desalinate
descendant
descendent
descending
describing
desecrated
deservedly
deshabille
desiccated
desiderata
designated
designedly
desolating
desolation
despairing
despicable

despicably
despondent
detachable
detachment
detainment
detectable
determined
determiner
deterrence
detestable
detonating
detonation
detraction
devaluated
devastated
developing
devilishly
deviltries
devolution
devotement
devotional
devoutness
diabolical
diagnosing
diagnostic
diagonally
diagraming
diaphanous
dichotomic
Dickensian
Dictaphone
dictionary
didactical
difference
difficulty
diffidence
digestible
digitizing
dignifying
digression
digressive
dilapidate
dilatation
dilatorily
dilettante
dilettanti
diligently
dillydally
diminuendo
diminution
diminutive
diphtheria
diplomatic
dipsomania
directness
disability
disabusing
disappoint
disapprove
disarrange
disastrous

disbarment
disbarring
disbelieve
disbursing
discerning
discharged
discharger
discipline
disclaimer
disclosing
disclosure
discomfort
discommode
discompose
disconcert
disconnect
discontent
discordant
discourage
discoursed
discoverer
discreetly
discrepant
discretion
discursive
discussion
disdainful
disembowel
disenchant
disengaged
disfigured
disgorging
disgracing
disgruntle
disguising
disgusting
dishabille
disharmony
dishearten
disheveled
dishonesty
disincline
disinherit
disjointed
dislikable
dislodging
disloyally
disloyalty
dismantled
dismissive
disordered
disorderly
disparaged
dispassion
dispatcher
dispelling
dispensary
dispensing
dispersing
dispersion
dispirited

displacing
disposable
dispossess
disproving
disputable
disqualify
disrespect
disruption
disruptive
dissatisfy
dissection
dissembled
dissension
dissenting
dissertate
disservice
disserving
dissidence
dissimilar
dissipated
dissociate
dissoluble
dissolving
dissonance
dissuading
dissuasion
distancing
distension
distention
distillate
distillery
distilling
distinctly
distortion
distraught
distribute
disuniting
divagation
divergence
divination
divinities
divisional
divulgence
doggedness
dogmatical
dogmatized
domiciling
dominating
domination
donkeywork
doubletime
doubtfully
downgraded
downstream
drawbridge
dreadfully
dreariness
drizzliest
droopingly
drosophila
drowsiness

drupaceous
dumbwaiter
dunderhead
duodecimal
duplicated
duplicator
durability
Düsseldorf
Dutchwoman
Dutchwomen
dystrophic

earthbound
earthiness
earthquake
earwigging
easterlies
easternize
Eastertide
ebullience
ebullition
ecological
economical
ecstatical
ecumenical
eczematous
effacement
effectuate
effeminacy
effeminate
effervesce
efficacies
efficiency
effloresce
effortless
effrontery
effulgence
effusively
egocentric
Egyptology
eighteenth
Eisenhower
ejaculated
elaborated
elasticity
elderberry
electorate
electrical
electronic
elementary
eliminated
elliptical
elongating
elongation
eloquently
El Salvador
elucidated
emaciation
emancipate
emasculate

embalmment
embankment
embargoing
embarkment
embattling
embezzling
emblematic
embodiment
embossment
embouchure
embroidery
embryology
emendation
emigrating
emigration
emissaries
empathetic
empathized
emphasized
empiricism
empiricist
employable
employment
emulsified
emulsifier
enamelling
enamelware
encampment
enchanting
encircling
encouraged
encyclical
endearment
endogamous
endogenous
energizing
enervating
enervation
enfeebling
engagement
engagingly
Englishman
Englishmen
engrossing
engulfment
enjoinment
enlistment
enormities
enormously
enraptured
enrichment
enrollment
ensconcing
enshrining
ensilaging
entailment
entangling
enterprise
enthralled
enthroning
enthusiasm

enthusiast
enticement
enticingly
entireness
entombment
entomology
entrapment
entrapping
enumerated
enumerator
enunciated
enveloping
envisaging
epiglottis
episcopacy
episcopate
episodical
epistolary
Epsom salts
equability
equalities
equalizing
equanimity
equational
equatorial
equestrian
equilibria
equivalent
equivocate
eradicable
eradicated
eradicator
eremitical
ergonomics
ergonomist
ergosterol
ericaceous
erotically
erysipelas
escalating
escalation
escapology
escarpment
escritoire
escutcheon
esoterical
espadrille
especially
estimating
estimation
estivating
estivation
estranging
eternities
ethereally
ethnically
eucalyptus
eulogistic
eulogizing
euphemized
euphonical

euphonious
eurythmics
eurythmies
euthanasia
evacuating
evacuation
evaluating
evaluation
evanescent
evanescing
evangelism
evangelist
evangelize
evaporated
evaporator
evenhanded
eventfully
eventually
eventuated
everything
everywhere
evidencing
evidential
evilminded
eviscerate
evolvement
exacerbate
exactingly
exactitude
exaggerate
exaltation
exasperate
ex cathedra
excavating
excavation
excellence
excellency
Excellency
excerption
exchanging
excitation
excitement
excitingly
excludable
excoriated
excrescent
excruciate
exculpated
excusatory
execrating
execration
execrative
exercising
exfoliated
exhalation
exhausting
exhaustion
exhaustive
exhibiting
exhibition
exhilarate

exhumation
exigencies
exonerated
exorbitant
exorcising
exorcizing
exotically
expandable
expansible
expatiated
expatriate
expectable
expectably
expectancy
expedience
expediency
expediting
expedition
expendable
experience
experiment
expertness
expiration
expiratory
explicable
explicated
explicitly
exploitive
exportable
exposition
expository
expression
expressive
expressway
expurgated
extendable
extendible
extensible
extenuated
externally
extinction
extinguish
extirpated
extraction
extractive
extradited
extramural
extraneous
extricated
exuberance
exultantly
exultation
exultingly
exurbanite
eyeglasses
eyewitness

fabricated
fabricator
fabulously

face-saving
facilitate
facilities
factitious
Fahrenheit
fairground
fairminded
faithfully
fallacious
falsifying
familiarly
fanaticism
fanaticize
fancifully
fantasized
farfetched
farsighted
fascinated
fastidious
fatalistic
fatalities
fatherhood
fatherland
fatherless
fathomable
fathomless
favoritism
fearlessly
Februaries
fecundated
federalism
federalist
federalize
federating
felicitate
felicities
felicitous
fellowship
femininity
feministic
feminizing
fertilized
fertilizer
fervidness
fetchingly
feverishly
fiberglass
fibrositis
fickleness
fictitious
field mouse
fierceness
figuration
figurative
figurehead
figureless
filamented
filibuster
filterable
filthiness
filtration

finalities
finalizing
fingernail
finiteness
fisticuffs
fitfulness
five-and-ten
flabbiness
flagellant
flagellate
flagitious
flagrantly
flamboyant
flamingoes
flashiness
flashlight
flatfooted
flatteries
flatulence
flatulency
flavorless
fleabitten
fleeciness
fleetingly
fleshiness
fleshliest
fleur-de-lis
flickering
flightiest
flightless
flimsiness
flintiness
flippantly
flirtation
floatation
flocculent
floodlight
floorboard
floppiness
Florentine
florescent
floridness
flouridate
fluctuated
fluffiness
fluidounce
fluoresced
fluttering
fly-by-night
focalizing
foliaceous
folksiness
follicular
footbridge
footcandle
footlights
forbearing
forbidding
forcefully
foreboding
forecasted

forecaster
forecastle
foreclosed
foredoomed
forefather
forefinger
foregather
foreground
forehanded
foreordain
forerunner
foreseeing
foreshadow
foreteller
forfeiture
forgetting
forgivable
forgivably
formalized
formatting
formidable
formidably
formulated
formulator
fornicated
fornicator
forthright
fortifying
fortissimo
fortuitous
fossilized
foundation
fourposter
fourteenth
foxtrotted
fractional
fracturing
fragmental
fragrantly
franchised
Franciscan
frangipani
fraternity
fraternize
fratricide
fraudulent
freakishly
freebooter
freelanced
freeloader
freemartin
freespoken
freightage
frenziedly
frequently
freshwater
fricasseed
frictional
friendless
friendlier
friendship

frigidness
fripperies
friskiness
frizziness
frolicking
frolicsome
frostiness
frothiness
frozenness
fruit flies
fruitfully
frustrated
fuddy-duddy
fulfilling
full-length
fulminated
fumigating
fumigation
functional
fund-raiser
fungicidal
funnelling
fusibility
fusilladed
fussbudget
futilities
futuristic
futurities

gadolinium
gainsaying
galvanized
gambolling
gangrenous
gargantuan
garishness
garnisheed
gastronomy
Gatling gun
gaucheness
gelatinize
gelatinous
geminately
geminating
gemination
gemologist
generalist
generality
generalize
generating
generation
generative
generosity
generously
geneticist
gentlefolk
gentleness
geocentric
geochemist
geographer

geographic
geological
geometries
geophysics
geopolitic
geothermal
geriatrics
geriatrist
germicidal
germinated
gesundheit
Gethsemane
ghastliest
ghostliest
ghostwrite
ghostwrote
ghoulishly
gingivitis
girlfriend
glaciation
glamorized
glassiness
Glaswegian
gloominess
glorifying
gloriously
glossaries
glossiness
Gloucester
gluttonous
gnosticism
goalkeeper
God-fearing
goggle-eyed
goings-over
golddigger
goody-goody
gooseberry
gorgeously
gorgonzola
governable
government
gracefully
graciously
graduating
graduation
graininess
grammarian
grandchild
granulated
grapefruit
graphology
gratefully
gratifying
gratuities
gratuitous
gravelling
gravestone
gravitated
greasiness
greediness

greenhouse
gregarious
grievously
grindingly
grindstone
grisliness
grittiness
grogginess
groundless
groundwork
grubbiness
grudgingly
grumpiness
guaranteed
guarantied
guaranties
guardhouse
Guggenheim
guillotine
guiltiness
gunrunning
gutturally
gymnasiums
gynecology

habiliment
habitation
habitually
habituated
halfwitted
hallelujah
handicraft
handmaiden
handpicked
handsomely
handsomest
hanky-panky
haranguing
harassment
hardbitten
hardboiled
hard palate
harmlessly
harmonious
harmonized
hartebeest
hatcheries
hatchet man
hatchet men
haughtiest
hauntingly
haute monde
headhunter
headlining
headmaster
healthiest
heartbreak
heartiness
heartsease
heartthrob

heaven-sent
heavenward
hectically
hectoliter
hectometer
helicopter
helplessly
hematology
hemisphere
hemoblobin
hemophilia
hemorrhage
hemorrhoid
henceforth
heptagonal
herbaceous
hereditary
heretofore
heroically
hesitantly
hesitating
hesitation
heterodoxy
hibernated
hierarchal
hierarchic
hieroglyph
high-flying
high-handed
high-minded
high-octane
highwayman
highwaymen
hinterland
hippodrome
historical
histrionic
hit-and-miss
hitchhiked
hitchhiker
hoarseness
hobnobbing
hocus-pocus
hodgepodge
hoity-toity
hollowness
homecoming
homeliness
homeopathy
homgenized
homiletics
homogenize
homogenous
homologous
homophobia
homophobic
homosexual
honorarium
hootenanny
hopelessly
horizontal

hornblende
horologist
horrendous
horridness
horrifying
horseflies
horse opera
horsepower
hospitable
hospitably
hot-blooded
housebound
houseproud
house-train
housewives
Hovercraft
hullabaloo
humaneness
humanistic
humanities
humanizing
humbleness
humidified
humidifier
humiliated
humorously
hungriness
hurdy-gurdy
hurly-burly
hybridized
hydraulics
hydrolysis
hydrometer
hydropathy
hydroplane
hygrometer
hymeneally
hyperbolic
hyphenated
hypnotized
hypodermic
hypotenuse
hypotheses
hypothesis
hysteresis
hysterical

icebreaker
ice-skating
iconoclasm
iconoclast
idealistic
idealizing
idées fixes
identified
identities
ideologies
ideologist
idolatries
idolatrous

ignes-fatui
ignobility
ignominies
ignorantly
ill-advised
illegality
ill-favored
illiteracy
illiterate
illuminate
illumining
illustrate
imaginable
imaginably
imbecility
immaculacy
immaculate
immanently
immaterial
immaturely
immaturity
immemorial
immergence
immigrated
immigrator
immobility
immobilize
immoderate
immodestly
immolating
immolation
immorality
immortally
immunities
immunizing
immunology
impairment
impalement
impalpable
impaneling
impassable
impassably
impassible
impatience
impeccable
impeccably
impediment
impenitent
imperative
imperially
imperiling
imperilled
impersonal
impervious
implacable
implacably
implicated
implicitly
impolitely
importable
importance

importuned
imposingly
imposition
impossible
impossibly
impotently
impoundage
impoverish
imprecated
impregnate
impresario
impression
impressive
imprimatur
improbable
improbably
improperly
improvable
improvised
imprudence
impudently
impureness
impurities
imputation
in absentia
inaccuracy
inaccurate
inactivate
inactively
inactivity
inadequacy
inadequate
inaptitude
inasmuch as
inaugurate
inbreeding
incapacity
incarnated
incautious
incendiary
incestuous
incidental
incinerate
incitation
incitement
incivility
inclemency
incoherent
incomplete
inconstant
increasing
incredible
incredibly
incubating
incubation
inculcated
inculpated
incumbency
indecently
indecision
indecisive

indecorous
indefinite
indelicacy
indelicate
indicating
indication
indicative
indictable
indictment
indigenous
indirectly
indiscreet
indiscrete
indisposed
indistinct
individual
Indonesian
inducement
inductance
indulgence
industrial
industries
inebriated
inefficacy
ineligible
ineptitude
inequality
inequities
inevitable
inevitably
inexorable
inexorably
inexpiable
inexpiably
in extremis
infallible
infallibly
infanthood
infantries
infarction
infatuated
infectious
infelicity
infidelity
infighting
infiltrate
infinitely
infinities
infinitive
inflatable
inflection
inflective
inflexible
inflexibly
infliction
influenced
informally
infraction
infrasonic
infrequent
infringing

infuriated
inglorious
ingratiate
ingredient
inhabitant
inhalation
inharmonic
inherently
inhibition
inhibitive
inhibitory
inhumanity
inhumation
inimitable
inimitably
iniquities
iniquitous
initialing
initialled
initiating
initiation
initiative
injunction
in memoriam
innervated
innocently
innovating
innovation
innovative
innovatory
innuendoes
innumerous
inoculated
inoperable
inordinate
inquietude
inquisitor
insanitary
insanities
insatiable
insatiably
inscribing
insecurely
insecurity
inseminate
insensible
insentient
insinuated
insinuator
insipidity
insistence
insobriety
insociable
insociably
insolently
insolvable
insolvency
insouciant
inspection
installing
instalment

instigated
instigator
instilling
instituted
instructor
instrument
insularity
insulating
insulation
insurgence
insurgency
intangible
intangibly
integrated
interbreed
interceded
interested
interfaith
interfered
interferon
interlaced
interlayer
interleave
interloped
interloper
interlunar
intermarry
intermezzi
intermezzo
internally
internment
interposed
interregna
interspace
interstate
interstice
intertidal
intertwine
interurban
intervened
interweave
interwoven
intestinal
intimacies
intimately
intimately
intimating
intimation
intimidate
intolerant
intonating
intonation
intoxicant
intoxicate
intramural
intrastate
intrepidly
intriguing
introduced
introspect
inundating

inundation
invalidate
invalidism
invalidity
invaluable
invaluably
invariable
invariably
investment
inveterate
invigorate
invincible
invincibly
inviolable
inviolably
invitation
invitingly
invocation
involution
ionization
iridescent
Irishwoman
Irishwomen
ironhanded
ironically
irradiated
irrational
irrelevant
irresolute
irreverent
irrigating
irrigation
irritating
irritation
isothermal
Italianate
italicized

jackanapes
jackhammer
jack-knifed
jack-knives
jack rabbit
janitorial
jardiniere
jauntiness
jawbreaker
jealousies
jeopardize
jerry-build
jerry-built
Jesuitical
jeu d'esprit
Jewishness
Jim Crow-ism
jingoistic
jinrikisha
jocularity
journalese
journalism

journalist
journeyman
journeymen
jubilation
judicially
juggernaut
justifying
juvenility
juxtaposed

kettledrum
kidnapping
kindliness
kinematics
kingfisher
kingliness
knickknack
knighthood
knock-kneed
kookaburra
Krugerrand
Kublai Khan
Ku Klux Klan

laboratory
lacerating
laceration
lachrymose
lackluster
lacustrine
ladyfinger
lady-killer
lambasting
lambrequin
lamentable
lamentably
laminating
lamination
lanceolate
landholder
landladies
landlocked
landlubber
landowning
landscaped
landscaped
landscaper
languorous
large-scale
laryngitis
lascivious
laughingly
Laundromat
lavatories
lavishness
law-abiding
lawbreaker
lawfulness
lawrencium

leadership
leafleting
leafletted
left-handed
legalistic
legalities
legalizing
legibility
legislated
legislator
legitimacy
legitimate
legitimize
leguminous
lengthiest
lengthwise
leprechaun
lesbianism
letter bomb
letterhead
letterhead
levitating
levitation
liberalism
liberality
liberalize
liberating
liberation
libidinous
librettist
licentiate
licentious
lieutenant
lighthouse
likelihood
limitation
limitative
limpidness
linebacker
linguistic
lipreading
liquefying
liquidated
liquidator
liquidized
liquidness
lissomness
listlessly
literalism
literality
literature
lithograph
Lithuanian
litigating
litigation
liturgical
livelihood
liveliness
liverwurst
lobotomies
localities

localizing
locomotion
locomotive
loganberry
loggerhead
logistical
logrolling
loneliness
long-winded
loquacious
lordliness
Los Angeles
lotus-eater
lovability
loveliness
lovemaking
lovingness
lower-class
low-tension
lubricated
lubricator
lubricious
lugubrious
lumberjack
luminaries
luminosity
lusciously
lusterless
luxuriance
luxuriated

macadamize
macerating
maceration
machinated
mackintosh
Madagascar
magistracy
magistrate
Magna Carta
magnetized
Magnificat
magnifying
magnum opus
maidenhair
maidenhead
maiden name
mainlining
mainspring
mainstream
majestical
major-domos
majorities
makeweight
maladapted
Malagasies
malapropos
malcontent
malefactor
maleficent

malevolent
malfeasant
malignancy
malingerer
malodorous
manageable
manageably
management
manageress
managerial
manhandled
maniacally
manicuring
manicurist
manifestly
manipulate
manservant
manuscript
Mao Tsetung
maraschino
marcelling
marginally
marguerite
mariculate
marinading
marinating
Mariolatry
marionette
marketable
marrowbone
Marseilles
marshaling
marshalled
marshiness
marvelling
marvellous
masquerade
massacring
mastectomy
mastermind
masturbate
matchmaker
materially
maternally
matriarchy
maturating
maturation
Mauritania
maximizing
mayonnaise
mayorality
meadowlark
meagerness
meaningful
measurable
measurably
mechanical
mechanized
meddlesome
medicament
medicating

medication
mediocrity
meditating
meditation
meditative
meerschaum
melancholy
Melanesian
Melba toast
meliorable
meliorated
meliorator
memberless
membership
membranous
memorandum
memorially
memorially
memorizing
menacingly
mendacious
meningitis
menopausal
menstruate
mensurable
mercantile
mercerized
mercifully
merrymaker
mesmerized
metabolism
metabolize
metalizing
metallurgy
metaphoric
metaphysic
metastasis
metatarsal
metatarsus
metathesis
methodical
Methuselah
meticulous
metrically
metronomic
metropolis
mettlesome
Mickey Finn
microfiche
micrometer
microphone
microscope
microscopy
micturated
middle-aged
middlebrow
midsection
midshipman
Midwestern
mightiness
militarily

militarism
militarist
militarize
militating
militiaman
militiamen
millennial
millennium
milliliter
millimeter
millwright
mimeograph
mineralize
mineralogy
minestrone
minimizing
ministrant
ministries
minorities
miraculous
mirthfully
misapplied
misbehaved
miscarried
miscarrige
miscellany
misconduct
misdealing
misfitting
misfortune
misguiding
mishandled
mishearing
misjudging
misleading
mismanaged
misogynist
misogynous
misplacing
misprision
misquoting
misreading
misshaping
missionary
misspelled
misstating
mistakable
mistakenly
mitigating
mitigation
mitigative
mitigatory
Mitterrand
mizzenmast
mobilizing
moderately
moderating
moderation
modernized
modifiable
Modigliani

modishness
modulating
modulation
modulatory
moisturize
mollifying
monarchies
monarchism
monarchist
monastical
monaurally
monetarily
monetarism
monetarist
monetizing
monitorial
monitoring
monochrome
monoecious
monogamist
monogamous
monolithic
monologist
monomaniac
monopolies
monopolize
monotheism
monotheist
monotonous
Monte Carlo
Montessori
Montevideo
Montmartre
Montserrat
monumental
moralistic
moralities
moralizing
moratorium
morbidness
morganatic
moroseness
morphology
mortgaging
mortifying
mortuaries
mosquitoes
motherhood
motherland
motherless
mother-to-be
motionless
motivating
motivation
motor court
motorcycle
motorizing
mountebank
mournfully
mouthiness
mouthpiece

movability
Mozambique
mozzarella
muckraking
mulberries
mulishness
multilevel
multiplied
multiplier
mumbo jumbo
mummifying
munificent
Murphy's law
Mussorgsky
mutability
mutational
mutilating
mutilation
mycologist
mysterious
mystically
mystifying
mythically
mythologic

namby-pamby
nanosecond
Napoleonic
narcissism
narcissist
narcotized
narrowness
nasalizing
nasturtium
natatorial
natatorium
nationally
nationhood
nationwide
nativeness
nativities
naturalism
naturalist
naturalize
naughtiest
nauseating
nautically
nautiluses
navigating
navigation
Neapolitan
nebulosity
necromancy
necropolis
needlessly
needlework
ne'er-do-well
negatively
negativism
negativity

neglectful
negligence
negligible
negligibly
negotiable
negotiated
negotiator
neighborly
neoclassic
nethermost
nettlesome
neutralism
neutralist
neutrality
neutralize
newfangled
New Orleans
newscaster
newsletter
newsworthy
New Zealand
nicknaming
nightdress
nightshade
nightshirt
nightstick
nihilistic
nimbleness
nineteenth
nit-picking
noblewoman
noblewomen
nom de plume
nominating
nomination
nominative
nonaligned
nonchalant
nonfiction
nonnuclear
nonpayment
nonplusing
nonplussed
nonsmoking
nonstarter
nonsupport
nonviolent
normalized
northbound
northerner
northwards
notability
notarizing
notational
noteworthy
noticeable
noticeably
notifiable
Nova Scotia
novelistic
nucleonics

nullifying
numberless
numerating
numeration
numerology
numismatic
nutcracker
nutritious

obdurately
obediently
obfuscated
obituaries
objectless
objets d'art
objurgated
obligating
obligation
obligatory
obligingly
obliterate
obsequious
observable
observably
observance
obstetrics
obstructor
obtainable
obtainment
obtuseness
occasional
occidental
occupation
ocrurrence
octahedral
octahedron
odiousness
officially
officiated
officiator
offsetting
oftentimes
oleaginous
oligarchic
omnipotent
omniscient
omnivorous
opalescent
openhanded
open-minded
open sesame
ophthalmic
opposition
oppression
oppressive
opprobrium
optimistic
optimizing
optometric
orangeries

oratorical
orchestral
ordainment
ordinarily
ordination
organizing
orientated
originally
originated
originator
ornamental
ornateness
orneriness
orotundity
orthodoxly
orthogonal
orthopedic
oscillated
oscillator
osculation
ostensible
ostensibly
osteopathy
ostracized
outbidding
outer space
outfielder
outgrowing
outlandish
outpouring
outputting
outrageous
outrunning
outselling
outshining
outwitting
overactive
overcharge
overcoming
overeating
overgrowth
overlapped
overlaying
overmanned
overpriced
overrating
overridden
overriding
overseeing
overshadow
overstated
overtaking
overthrown
overvalued
overweight
overworked
ovipositor
oxygenated

packsaddle

pagination
painkiller
painlessly
palatially
palindrome
palisading
pallbearer
pallbearer
palliating
palliation
palliative
palpitated
paltriness
Panamanian
pancreatic
panhandled
panhandler
pantomimed
pantomimic
paper knife
parachuted
paraleling
paralleled
paralyzing
paranormal
paraphrase
paraplegia
paraplegic
parasitism
paratroops
parcelling
parcelling
pardonable
pardonably
parenthood
parimutuel
parliament
paroxysmal
parqueting
partiality
participle
particular
parturient
passageway
passionate
pasteboard
pasteurize
past master
pathogenic
pathologic
patriarchy
patriotism
patrolling
patronized
patronymic
paunchiest
pawnbroker
peace corps
peacefully
peacemaker
peashooter

peccadillo
peculation
peculiarly
pedestrian
pediatrics
pediatrist
pedicurist
pejorative
penalizing
penetrable
penetrably
penetrated
penicillin
peninsular
penitently
penmanship
pennyworth
penologist
pentagonal
pentameter
Pentateuch
pentathlon
peppercorn
peppermint
perceiving
percentage
percentile
perception
perceptive
perceptual
percipient
percolated
percolator
percussion
percussive
perdurable
peremptory
perfection
perfective
perfidious
perforated
perforator
perilously
perimetric
periodical
peripheral
periscopic
perishable
perishably
peritoneum
periwinkle
perjurious
permafrost
permanence
permanency
permeating
permeation
permeative
permission
permissive
permitting

pernicious
pernickety
peroration
perpetrate
perpetuate
perpetuity
perplexing
perplexity
perquisite
persecuted
persecutor
persevered
persiflage
persistent
personable
personally
personated
personator
perspiring
persuading
persuasion
persuasive
pertinence
perversely
perversion
perversity
pestilence
petiteness
petitioned
petitioner
petrifying
petrolatum
petulantly
phantasies
phantasmal
pharmacies
pharmacist
phenomenal
phenomenon
philatelic
Philippine
Philistine
philosophy
phlebotomy
phlegmatic
Phoenician
phonograph
phonologic
phosphorus
photogenic
photograph
phrenology
phylactery
physically
physicking
physiology
pianissimo
pianoforte
picaresque
picayunish
piccalilli

pickaninny
pickpocket
picnicking
pied-à-terre
piercingly
pigeonhole
pigeon-toed
pilgrimage
pillorying
pincushion
pinfeather
pirouetted
pistillate
pitchblack
pitilessly
Pittsburgh
placidness
plagiarism
plagiarist
plagiarize
plantation
plastering
plasticity
plat du jour
playacting
playground
playwright
pleadingly
pleasantly
pleasantry
pleasingly
pleasuring
plebiscite
pliability
pliantness
pluckiness
plummeting
pluperfect
plushiness
plutocracy
pocketbook
podiatrist
poetically
poignantly
poinsettia
point-blank
polarities
polarizing
polemicist
politeness
politician
politicize
politicoes
pollinated
pollinator
pollyphony
polyanthus
polychrome
polygamist
polygamous
polygynous

polyhedron
polymerize
Polynesian
polynomial
polyphonic
polytheism
polytheist
Pomeranian
pommelling
ponderable
pontifical
popularity
popularize
populating
population
porousness
portcullis
portentous
portioning
portliness
Portuguese
positioned
positively
positivism
positivist
possession
possessive
postdating
posthumous
postillion
postmaster
post mortem
postpartum
postponing
postscript
postulated
postulator
potbellied
pot-bellies
powerfully
powerhouse
practicing
praetorian
pragmatism
pragmatist
preachment
prearrange
precarious
precaution
precedence
preceptive
precession
preciosity
precluding
preclusion
preclusive
precocious
precursory
predecease
predestine
predicable

predicated
prediction
predictive
predispose
preeminent
preemption
preemptive
preferable
preferably
preference
preferment
preferring
prefigured
prehensile
prehistory
prejudging
prejudiced
premarital
premedical
prenatally
prepayment
preplanned
prepossess
presbytery
prescience
prescribed
presentter
preserving
presidency
presignify
press corps
pressuring
pressurize
presumable
presumably
presuppose
pretension
prettified
prettiness
prevailing
prevalence
prevention
preventive
previously
pridefully
priesthood
prima donna
prima facie
primordial
principled
priorities
prissiness
privatized
privileged
procedural
proceeding
procession
proclivity
procreated
procreator
proctorial

procurable
procurance
procurator
procurment
prodigally
prodigious
prodtruded
production
productive
profession
proffering
proficient
profitable
profitably
profitless
profligacy
profligate
profoundly
profundity
progenitor
prognostic
programing
programmed
programmer
projectile
projection
projective
prolocutor
promenaded
promenader
Prometheus
promethium
prominence
promiseful
promissory
promontory
promotable
promptness
promulgate
pronominal
pronounced
propaganda
propagated
propagator
propellant
propelling
propensity
propertied
properties
prophecies
prophesied
prophetess
propitiate
proportion
proprietor
propulsion
propulsive
proscenium
proscribed
proscriber
prosecuted

prosecutor
prospector
prospectus
prospering
prosperity
prosperous
prosthesis
prosthetic
prostitute
prostrated
protecting
protection
protective
pro tempore
Protestant
protoplasm
protractor
protrudent
protrusion
protrusive
provenance
proverbial
providable
providence
provincial
prudential
psephology
psychiatry
psychology
psychopath
pubescence
pubescency
publicized
publicness
Puerto Rico
pugilistic
pugnacious
pulverized
pulverizer
pummelling
punch-drunk
punctually
punctuated
puncturing
punishable
punishment
purchasing
Puritansim
purposeful
purrulence
purulently
purveyance
push-button
putrefying
putrescent
putridness
puzzlement
pyromaniac
Pythagoras

quadrangle
quadrantal
quadratics
quadrating
quadrature
quadrupled
quadruplet
quaintness
qualifying
quandaries
quantified
quantities
quarantine
quarreling
quarrelled
quartering
quaternary
queasiness
Queensland
quenchable
queruulous
questingly
questioned
questioner
quid pro quo
quiescence
quintupled
quintuplet
quirkiness
quizmaster

rabbinical
radicalism
radicalize
radiograph
radioscopy
ragamuffin
raggedness
rakishness
ramshackle
rancidness
randomness
rationally
raunchiest
ravenously
ravishment
reactivate
readership
realizable
reanimated
reappraise
rearmament
rearranged
reasonable
reasonably
reassemble
reassembly
reassuring
rebellious
rebuilding

recappable
recaptured
recentness
receptacle
recharging
recidivism
recidivist
recipience
recipiency
reciprocal
recitation
recitative
recklessly
recognized
recoilless
recompense
reconciled
reconciler
reconsider
recoveries
recreating
recreation
recreation
recreative
rectifying
recumbency
recuperate
recurrence
red-blooded
redecorate
rededicate
redeemable
redemption
redemptive
redemptory
redistrict
redoubling
redundance
redundancy
reelection
reenforced
reentrance
reexamined
refereeing
referenced
referendum
refillable
refinement
refineries
reflection
reflective
refraction
refractive
refractory
refreshing
refulgence
refutation
regardless
regeneracy
regenerate
regimental

regionally
registered
registrant
registries
regression
regressive
regretting
regularity
regularize
regulating
regulation
regulative
regulatory
rehearsing
reimbursed
reinforced
reinstated
reiterated
rejuvenate
rekindling
relational
relatively
relativity
relaxation
relegating
relegation
relentless
relievable
relinquish
relocating
relocation
reluctance
remarkable
remarkably
remarriage
remarrying
remediable
reminisced
remissness
remittance
remodeling
remodelled
remorseful
remoteness
remunerate
renascence
rendezvous
renominate
renouncing
renovating
renovation
reorganize
reparation
repatriate
repeatable
repeatedly
repentance
repertoire
repetition
repetitive
rephrasing

replicated
reportable
reportedly
repository
repression
repressive
reprieving
reproduced
republican
repudiated
repugnance
repugnancy
reputation
requiescat
rescission
researcher
resembling
resentment
resettling
reshuffled
resignedly
resilience
resiliency
resistance
resistible
resolutely
resolution
resonating
respectful
respecting
respective
respirator
respondent
responsive
restaurant
restlessly
restrained
restricted
resumption
resurfaced
resurgence
retaliated
rethinking
retirement
retractile
retraction
retrieving
retrograde
retrogress
retrospect
returnable
revelation
revengeful
reverenced
reverently
reversible
revisiting
revitalize
revivalism
revivalist
revivified

revocation
revocation
revolution
rhapsodies
rhapsodist
rhapsodize
rhetorical
rheumatism
rheumatoid
rhinestone
rhinoceros
rhythmical
riboflavin
ricocheted
ridiculing
ridiculous
rightfully
right-of-way
rigidities
rigorously
ringleader
ringmaster
risibility
riverfront
roadrunner
roadworthy
robustness
rockabilly
rock-ribbed
rollicking
roman à clef
Rothschild
rotisserie
rottweiler
rough-hewed
roughhouse
roughrider
roundabout
round-robin
roustabout
routinized
rubberized
rubberneck
rudimental
ruefulness
ruggedness
ruminating
rumination
ruminative
rusticated
ruthlessly
rye whiskey

sabbatical
sabotaging
saccharine
sacerdotal
Sacramento
sacredness
sacrificed

sacristies
sacroiliac
sacrosanct
saintliest
salability
salamander
saleswoman
saleswomen
salivating
salivation
salmonella
saltcellar
saltshaker
salubrious
salutation
salutatory
sanatorium
sanctified
sanctimony
sandalwood
sandbagged
sand-casted
sanguinary
sanitarily
sanitarium
sanitation
sanitizing
Santa Claus
sapiential
sarcophagi
satirizing
satisfying
saturating
saturation
saturnalia
satyriasis
sauerkraut
savageness
savoriness
scabbiness
scandalize
scandalous
scantiness
scarceness
scarcities
scarifying
scarlatina
scathingly
scavenging
scheduling
schematize
schismatic
scholastic
schoolwork
Schweitzer
scientific
scoffingly
scoreboard
scornfully
Scotswoman
Scotswomen

scrabbling
scraggiest
scrambling
scrappiest
scrawniest
screenplay
scribbling
scrimmaged
scrimmager
scriptural
scrollwork
scrounging
scrubbiest
scruffiest
scrupulous
scrutinize
sculleries
sculptress
sculptural
sculptured
scurrility
scurrilous
scurviness
sea lamprey
seamanship
seamstress
seasonable
seasonally
second-best
secondhand
second-rate
secularism
secularize
secureness
securities
sedateness
seduceable
seducement
seemliness
seersucker
see-through
segmentary
segregated
seismology
self-denial
self-esteem
selflessly
self-rising
self-styled
self-taught
self-willed
semantical
semiannual
semicircle
semiformal
semiliquid
seminaries
semipublic
semiweekly
semiyearly
senatorial

Senegalese
senescence
sensitized
sensitizer
sensualism
sensuality
sensualize
sensuously
sentencing
separately
separating
separation
separatism
separatist
separative
septennial
septically
septicemia
sepulchral
sequential
Serbo-Croat
serenading
serialized
sermonized
sermonizer
serpentine
serviceman
servicemen
settlement
seventieth
severeness
Seychelles
shabbiness
shagginess
shamefaced
shamefully
shampooing
shandygaff
shanghaied
shapeliest
sheepishly
shellacked
shenanigan
shibboleth
shiftiness
shillelagh
shish kebab
shockingly
shockproof
shoddiness
shoestring
shopkeeper
shoplifter
shortbread
shortening
short-lived
short-range
shotgunned
shovelling
showcasing
shrewdness

shrillness
shrinkable
shriveling
shrivelled
Shrovetide
sickliness
sidelining
sidesaddle
sideswiped
sidewinder
sightseeer
signalling
signifying
silhouette
silverfish
silverware
similarity
similitude
simonizing
simpleness
simplicity
simplified
simplistic
simulating
simulation
simulative
sine qua non
sinfulness
Singhalese
singleness
singularly
sisterhood
six-shooter
skateboard
skepticism
sketchbook
sketchiest
skillfully
skimpiness
skin-diving
skyscraper
skywriting
slanderous
slanginess
slatternly
sleaziness
sleepiness
sleepyhead
sleetiness
sleeveless
slenderize
slipperier
slipstream
sloppiness
slothfully
slow-motion
slow-witted
sluggishly
slumberous
slushiness
small-scale

smart aleck
smattering
smeariness
smillingly
smirkingly
smokehouse
smokestack
smoothness
smudginess
smuttiness
snapdragon
sneakiness
sneeringly
snippiness
snivelling
snootiness
snorkeling
snottiness
snowblower
snowcapped
snowmobile
snuffiness
socialized
soddenness
soft-headed
soft-spoken
solarizing
solemnized
solemnness
soliciting
solicitous
solicitude
solidarity
solidified
solidstate
solubility
somberness
somersault
somnolence
somnolency
songstress
soothingly
soothsayer
sophomoric
sordidness
sororities
soubriquet
soundproof
soundtrack
southbound
southerner
spacecraft
sparseness
spatiality
specialism
specialist
specialize
specifying
speciosity
speculated
speculator

speechless
speediness
speleology
spellbound
spermaceti
sphericity
spheroidal
spiffiness
spindliest
spiralling
spirituous
spirochete
spitefully
splashdown
splendidly
split-level
spoilsport
spoliation
sponginess
sponsoring
spookiness
spoonerism
spoonerism
sporangium
sportfully
sportiness
sportingly
sportswear
spotlessly
spottiness
springiest
springtime
sprinkling
spunkiness
squabbling
squareness
squashiest
squeakiest
squiggling
stabilized
stabilizer
stagecoach
staggering
stagnating
stagnation
stalactite
stalagmite
stalemated
stampeding
standpoint
standstill
starchiest
stargazing
starriness
starry-eyed
starvation
starveling
statecraft
stateliest
statically
stationary

stationery
statistics
statuesque
steadiness
stealthier
stealthily
steaminess
steeliness
steelworks
stenciling
stencilled
stentorian
stepfather
stepladder
stepmother
stepparent
stepsister
stereotype
sterilized
sterilizer
stertorous
stewardess
stickiness
stigmatize
stillbirth
stimulated
stinginess
stipulated
stir-frying
stockiness
stockpiled
stodginess
stonemason
storefront
storehouse
stormbound
storminess
strabismus
straddling
stragglier
straggling
straighten
strangling
Strasbourg
strategies
strategist
stratified
Stravinsky
strawberry
streakiest
streamline
streetwise
strengthen
stretchier
strictness
stridently
stridulate
stridulous
strifeless
strikingly
Strindberg

stringency
stringiest
striptease
stronghold
strongness
structural
structured
struggling
strychnine
stubbornly
studiously
stuffiness
stultified
stunningly
stuntwoman
stuntwomen
stupefying
stupendous
stupidness
subculture
subdivided
subentries
subheading
subjection
subjective
subjugated
subleasing
subletting
sublimated
subliminal
submachine
submerging
submersing
submersion
submission
submissive
submitting
suborbital
subpoenaed
subscribed
subscriber
subsection
subsequent
subsidence
subsidiary
subsidized
subspecies
substation
substitute
substratum
subsumable
subterfuge
subtleness
subtleties
subtracter
subtrahend
subvention
subversion
subversive
succeeding
successful

succession
successive
succinctly
succulence
succulency
suddenness
sufferable
sufferably
sufferance
sufficient
suffocated
suffragist
suggestion
suggestive
sullenness
sultriness
summarized
summings-up
sunbathing
sunburning
sunderance
sunglasses
superbness
supercargo
superhuman
superiorly
superpower
superseded
supersonic
supervened
supervised
supervisor
supineness
supplement
suppleness
supplicant
supplicate
supportive
supposable
supposably
supposedly
suppressor
suppurated
surcharged
sure-footed
surgically
surpassing
surplusage
surprising
surrealism
surrealist
surrogated
suspension
suspicious
sustenance
svelteness
swaggering
swampiness
swankiness
swarthiest
swaybacked

sweatiness
sweatshirt
sweetbread
sweetheart
sweltering
swimmingly
swirlingly
switchback
swivelling
swooningly
sycophancy
syllabuses
symbolical
symbolized
symmetries
sympathies
sympathize
symphonies
syncopated
syncopator
syncretism
syndicated
syndicator
synecdoche
synecology
synonymous
synthesist
synthesize
syphilitic
systematic

tabernacle
table d'hote
tabulating
tabulation
tachometer
tactically
tactlessly
tailgating
Talmudical
tambourine
tangential
tanglement
tantalized
tantamount
taperingly
tapestried
tapestries
tarantella
tarantulae
tarantulas
tarmacadam
tasselling
tastefully
tattletale
tauntingly
tawdriness
taxability
taxidermic
taxonomies

taxonomist
tearjerker
technetium
technician
technocrat
technology
teetotaler
teetotally
telecaster
telegraphy
telepathic
telephoned
telephonic
telescoped
telescopic
televising
television
temperable
temperance
temporally
temporized
temporizer
temptation
temptingly
tenability
tenantable
tendencies
tenderfoot
tenderized
tenderizer
tenderloin
tenderness
tenebrious
tentacular
tenurially
terminable
terminally
terminated
terminator
terra-cotta
terra firma
Terramycin
terrifying
terrorized
terrorizer
terrorless
terrorless
tessellate
testicular
testifying
tetraethyl
texturally
thankfully
theatrical
themselves
theocratic
theodolite
theologian
theologies
theorizing
theosophic

thereabout
thereafter
thermostat
thieveries
thimbleful
thirstiest
thirteenth
thorniness
thoroughly
thoughtful
thousandth
threadbare
threescore
thriftiest
thriftless
throatiest
thromboses
thrombosis
throttling
throughout
throughput
throughway
thumbscrew
thunderous
timberline
timekeeper
timeserver
timorously
tincturing
Tintoretto
tirelessly
titillated
tobogganed
toiletries
tolerantly
tolerating
toleration
tolerative
tomfoolery
tonelessly
tongue-lash
tongue-tied
toothbrush
toothiness
toothpaste
topicality
topography
topsy-turvy
torchlight
tormenting
torpedoing
torrential
torridness
tortuously
totemistic
touchiness
touchingly
touch-typed
tourmaline
tournament
tourniquet

toxicology
tractional
trafficked
trafficker
tragically
tragicomic
traitorous
trajectory
trammeling
trammelled
trampoline
tranquilly
transactor
transcribe
transcript
transeptal
transferal
transfixed
transfused
transgress
transience
transistor
transition
transitive
transitory
translated
translator
transmuted
transmuter
transpired
transplant
transposed
transverse
trashiness
traumatize
travelling
travelogue
traversing
travesties
treasonous
treasuries
treasuring
tremendous
trenchancy
trepanning
trespasser
triangular
trichotomy
trickiness
tridentate
trilingual
trillionth
trimestral
trimonthly
tripartite
triphammer
triplicate
trisection
triumphant
triviality
trivialize

troglodyte
trombonist
Trotskyist
Trotskyite
troubadour
trousseaux
truculence
trumpeting
truncating
truncation
trusteeing
trustfully
trustiness
trustingly
truthfully
tubercular
tuberculin
tumbledown
tumbleweed
tumultuous
tunelessly
tunnelling
turbidness
turbulence
turbulency
turgidness
turnaround
turpentine
turtledove
turtleneck
tweediness
typescript
typesetter
typewriter
typicality
typography
tyrannical
tyrannized
tyrannizer

ubiquitary
ulcerating
ulceration
ulteriorly
ultimately
ultrasonic
ultrasound
umbrageous
unabridged
unaffected
un-American
unanswered
unarguable
unarguably
unaspiring
unassailed
unassisted
unassuming
unattached
unattained

unattended
unavailing
unbalanced
unbearable
unbearably
unbeatable
unbecoming
unbeliever
unbleached
unblinking
unblushing
unbuckling
unbuttoned
uncanniest
uncared-for
unchanging
uncommonly
uncritical
uncultured
undeceived
undeniable
undeniably
underarmed
underbelly
underbrush
undercover
undergoing
underlined
underlying
undermined
underneath
underrated
underscore
undershirt
undershoot
undersized
underslung
understand
understate
understood
understudy
undertaken
undertaker
undervalue
underwater
underworld
underwrite
underwrote
undeserved
undetected
undirected
undismayed
undisposed
undisputed
undoubting
undressing
undulating
undulation
undulatory
uneasiness
uneconomic

uneducated
unemployed
unenviable
unequalled
unerringly
unevenness
uneventful
unexampled
unexciting
unexpected
unfairness
unfaithful
unfamiliar
unfettered
unfinished
unflagging
unfocussed
unforeseen
unfriendly
unfruitful
ungenerous
ungraceful
ungracious
ungrateful
ungrudging
unhampered
unhappiest
unheralded
unholiness
unhygienic
uniformity
unilateral
unimpaired
unimproved
unionizing
uniqueness
university
unjustness
unkindness
unknowable
unlawfully
unleavened
unlettered
unlikeness
unluckiest
unmannerly
unmerciful
unmolested
unnumbered
unobserved
unoccupied
unofficial
unorthodox
unpleasant
unplugging
unpolluted
unprepared
unprovoked
unpunished
unraveling
unreadable

unrecorded
unreliable
unrelieved
unremarked
unrequited
unresolved
unrewarded
unrivalled
unruliness
unsaddling
unsanitary
unschooled
unscramble
unscripted
unseeingly
unsettling
unshakable
unshakably
unskillful
unsnapping
unsociable
unsporting
unsteadily
unsticking
unstopping
unstressed
unsuitable
unsuitably
unswerving
untangling
unthinking
untidiness
untiringly
untroubled
untruthful
unwariness
unwavering
unworkable
unworthily
unwrapping
unyielding
upbringing
upholstery
upperclass
uppishness
uproarious
upstanding
urbaneness
urbanizing
urinalysis
usableness
usefulness
usurpation

vaccinated
vacillated
vacillator
validating
validation
valorously

vandalized
vanquisher
vaporizing
vaporously
varicosity
variedness
variegated
varietally
vaudeville
vauntingly
vegetarian
vegetating
vegetation
vegetative
vehemently
velocities
venational
veneration
venialness
venomously
venousness
ventilated
ventilator
veracities
verbalized
verifiable
vermicelli
vermicular
vernacular
Versailles
versifying
vertebrate
vertically
vest-pocket
veterinary
vibraphone
vice-consul
vicinities
victimized
Victoriana
victorious
videotaped
Vietnamese
viewfinder
vigorously
villainies
villainous
vindicated
vindicator
vindictive
virginally
virologist
virtuosity
virtuously
virulently
viscidness
visibility
visitation
visualized
vitalizing
vitreosity

vitrifying
vituperate
viviparous
vocabulary
vocalizing
vocational
vociferate
vociferous
voiceprint
volatility
volleyball
volubility
voluminous
voluptuary
voluptuous
vouchsafed
vulcanized
vulgarized
vulnerable
vulnerably

wainwright
wallflower
wall-to-wall
wanderlust
warranties
Washington
wastefully
wastepaper
watchfully
watchtower
waterborne
watercolor
watercress
waterfront
wateriness
water level
watermelon
waterpower
waterproof
water-skied
waterspout
watertight
waterwheel
waterworks
wavelength
weakliness
weak-minded
wealthiest
weathering
weatherman
weathermen
weightiest
well-earned
well-heeled
Wellington
well-spoken
wellspring
well-turned
well-versed

well-wisher
Welshwoman
Welshwomen
werewolves
westernize
whackiness
whatsoever
wheelchair
wheelhouse
wheeziness
white-faced
wholesaler
wholewheat
whomsoever
whorehouse
wickedness
wickerwork
widespread
wifeliness
wigwagging
wildcatted
wildebeest
wilderness
willy-nilly
windjammer
windowpane
window-shop
windowsill

windshield
windsurfer
wingspread
winterized
wintriness
wire-haired
wiretapped
wiretapper
wishy-washy
witchcraft
witch hazel
withdrawal
womanizing
wonderland
wonderment
woodcutter
woodpecker
woolliness
Wordsworth
workaholic
workingman
workingmen
world-class
worldliest
world-weary
worshipful
worshiping
worshipped

worshipper
worthiness
worthwhile
wraparound
wretchedly
wristwatch
wrongdoing
wrongfully

xenophobia
xenophobic
x-radiation
xylography

yardmaster
yellowbird
yesteryear
yin and yang
yourselves
youthfully
Yugoslavia

Zend-Avesta
zigzagging
zoological

abandonment
abbreviated
abnormality
abolishable
abolishment
abominating
abomination
abortionist
abracadabra
absenteeism
absorbingly
abstraction
absurdities
abusiveness
academician
accelerando
accelerated
accelerator
accentuated
acclamation
acclimatize
acclivities
accommodate
accompanied
accompanist
accordingly
accountable
accountably
accountancy
accrediting
accumulated
achievement
acidulation
acknowledge
acquiescent
acquirement
acquisition
acquisitive
acquittance
acrimonious
actualities
acupressure
acupuncture
ad infinitum
adjacencies
adjournment
adjudicated
adjudicator
adolescence
adulterated
advancement
advantaging
adventuring
adventurous
adverbially
adversaries
adverseness
adversities
advertising
aerobically
aerodynamic

aerological
aeronautics
affectation
affectingly
affiliating
affiliation
affirmation
affirmative
afterburner
aftereffect
agglomerate
agglutinate
aggrandized
aggravating
aggravation
aggregating
aggregation
aggregative
agnosticism
agonizingly
agoraphobia
agoraphobic
agrarianism
agriculture
agronomical
aide-mémoire
aides-de-camp
airdropping
air pressure
airsickness
algebraical
all-American
allegorical
allegrettos
alleviating
alleviation
alleviative
alleviatory
alliterated
alphabetize
altercation
alternately
alternating
alternation
alternative
ambiguities
ambiguously
ambitiously
ambivalence
ameliorable
ameliorated
ameliorator
amenability
Americanism
Americanize
amicability
amorousness
amour propre
amphetamine
anachronism
anachronous

analyzation
anarchistic
anatomizing
ancientness
androgynous
anecdotical
anesthetist
anesthetize
angelically
Anglicanism
anglophobia
annihilated
annihilator
anniversary
annunciator
anomosities
anonymously
antecedence
antechamber
anthologies
anthologist
anticipated
anticyclone
antigravity
antimissile
antipathies
antiquarian
antiquaries
antiquating
antiqueness
antirrhinum
anti-Semitic
antislavery
anxiousness
aphrodisiac
apicultural
apocalyptic
apologetics
apologizing
a posteriori
apostolical
apotheosize
Appalachian
apparatuses
appealingly
appeasement
appellation
appellative
application
applicatory
appointment
appreciable
appreciably
approbation
approbatory
appropriate
approvingly
approximate
appurtenant
aquaculture
arbitrament

arbitrarily
arbitrating
arbitration
archaeology
archdiocese
archduchess
archenemies
archipelago
Argentinian
argumentive
aristocracy
arraignment
arrangement
articulated
articulator
artlessness
asphyxiated
assassinate
assemblyman
assemblymen
assentation
asseverated
assiduously
assignation
assimilable
assimilated
associating
association
associative
assuagement
assuredness
astigmatism
astonishing
astringency
atheistical
athleticism
atmospheric
atrociously
attentively
attenuating
attenuation
attributing
attributive
audaciously
audiovisual
austerities
authorities
authorizing
autocracies
automatical
auxiliaries
avalanching
avoirdupois
awestricken
awkwardness
axiomatical

babysitting
bacchanalia
backpedaled

backslidden
backspacing
bactericide
balletomane
bamboozling
bandy-legged
banteringly
barbarities
barbiturate
baronetcies
barrel-organ
barricading
bashfulness
bathyscaphe
bathysphere
battledress
battlefield
beachcomber
bearbaiting
bearishness
beastliness
beautifully
bedevilment
bedraggling
behaviorism
behaviorist
bellicosity
belligerent
bellyaching
Benedictine
benediction
benedictory
benefaction
beneficence
beneficiary
benevolence
bereavement
best-looking
bewitchment
bibliomania
bibliophile
bicarbonate
bicentenary
bifurcating
bifurcation
bilaterally
biliousness
billets-doux
billionaire
bimetallism
biochemical
biographies
birdbrained
bisexuality
bittersweet
bivouacking
bizarreness
blackmailer
blameworthy
blasphemies
blaspheming

blasphemous
blockbuster
bloodstream
bloodsucker
blueberries
blueblooded
blunderbuss
bodybuilder
bombardment
bookbinding
bookkeeping
bootlegging
bourgeoisie
boutonniere
bowdlerized
boysenberry
braggadocio
breadbasket
breadwinner
breastplate
brilliantly
broadcasted
broadcaster
broadminded
brotherhood
brucellosis
brusqueness
brutalities
brutalizing
brutishness
Buenos Aires
bulletproof
bullfighter
bullterrier
bureaucracy
burglarized
burlesquing
businessman
businessmen
butterflies

cacophonous
calculating
calculation
calibrating
calibration
Californian
californium
calligraphy
callousness
callumniate
calumniated
Calvinistic
camaraderie
camouflaged
camphorated
candelabrum
candescence
candidacies
candlestick

cannibalism
cannibalize
capacitated
capillaries
capillarity
Capitol Hill
capitulated
captivating
captivation
caramelized
caravansary
carbonation
carbonizing
carborating
carborundum
carcinomata
cardiograph
carefulness
caressingly
caricatured
carnivorous
cartography
cassowaries
castellated
castigating
castigation
cataclysmal
cataclysmic
catalepsies
cataloguing
catastrophe
catchphrase
catechizing
categorical
caterpillar
catheterize
Catholicism
catholicity
catholicize
cauliflower
caustically
cauterizing
ceaselessly
celebrating
celebration
celebrities
centenarian
centenaries
centerboard
centerpiece
centralized
centrifugal
centripetal
centrobaric
ceremonious
certainties
certifiable
certificate
chain-smoker
chairperson
challenging

chamberlain
chambermaid
chanticleer
chaotically
chaperoning
charismatic
cheer-leader
cheesecloth
chef d'oeuvre
cheval glass
chiaroscuro
Chippendale
chirography
chiropodist
chitterling
chlorinated
chlorophyll
chock-a-block
cholesterol
choreograph
Christendom
christening
Christmassy
chronically
chronicling
chronologer
chronometer
chrysalides
churishness
circularize
circulating
circulation
circulative
circulatory
circumcised
circumspect
citizenries
citizenship
clairvoyant
clandestine
clarinetist
classically
classifying
cleanliness
clericalism
cliffhanger
climacteric
coagulating
coagulation
coalescence
cobblestone
cock-a-leekie
cockleshell
coeducation
coefficient
coexistence
coincidence
coldblooded
collaborate
collapsible
collectible

collocation
colonialism
colonialist
colostomies
combination
combinative
combustible
comeuppance
comfortable
comfortably
comfortless
commandment
commemorate
commendable
commendably
commentated
commentator
commingling
commiserate
commodities
commonplace
communicant
communicate
communistic
communities
communizing
commutation
compactness
comparative
compartment
compendiums
competently
competition
competitive
compilation
complacence
complacency
complainant
complaisant
complicated
comportment
composition
compressing
compression
compromised
comptroller
compunction
computation
computerize
concavities
concealment
conceivable
conceivably
concentrate
concernment
conciliated
conciseness
concomitant
concordance
concurrence
condemnable

conditional
conditioned
conditioner
condominium
condonation
conductance
conductress
confederacy
confederate
confidently
confinement
confiscated
confiscator
conflicting
confliction
conformable
conformance
confutation
congealment
congenially
congregated
congressman
congressmen
congruently
congruously
conjectural
conjectured
conjugating
conjugation
conjugative
conjunction
conjunctive
conjuration
connoisseur
connotation
connotative
conquerable
consciously
consecrated
consecrator
consecutive
consequence
considerate
considering
consignment
consistence
consistency
consolation
consolatory
consolidate
conspicuous
conspirator
constituent
constrained
constrictor
construable
constructor
consultancy
consumerism
consummated
consumption

consumptive
containment
contaminant
contaminate
contemplate
contentedly
contentious
contentment
contestable
continental
contingency
continually
continuance
contractile
contraction
contractive
contractual
contraption
contretemps
contributed
contributor
contrivance
controlling
controversy
conurbation
convalesced
convenience
convergence
convertible
convincible
convocation
convolutely
convoluting
convolution
cooperating
cooperation
cooperative
coordinated
coordinator
copperplate
cornerstone
corollaries
corporately
corporation
corporatism
corporative
corpuscular
correctable
correctness
correlating
correlation
correlative
corrigendum
corroborate
corrugating
corrugation
corruptible
corruptness
cosignatory
cosmogonist
cosmography

cosmologist
cosmopolite
countenance
counterfeit
counterfoil
countermand
counterpane
counterpart
countersign
countersink
countrified
countryfied
countryside
coup de grace
courteously
courtliness
crackerjack
cranberries
crapshooter
credibility
crematorium
crenelating
crepuscular
crestfallen
criminality
criminology
criticizing
cross-legged
crucifixion
cryptically
cryptograph
crystalline
crystallize
culminating
culmination
culpability
cultivating
cultivation
cunningness
curiosities
curiousness
curtailment
curvilinear
customizing
cut-and-dried
cybernetics
cylindrical

dangerously
daredevilry
Dar es Salaam
darlingness
deactivated
deafeningly
debarkation
debauchment
debilitated
decapitated
deceitfully
decelerated

deceptively
decimalized
declamation
declamatory
declaration
declarative
declaratory
declination
declivities
declivitous
décolletage
decomposing
decrepitude
decrescendo
deerstalker
deescalated
defalcation
defectively
defenseless
defensively
deferential
defoliating
defoliation
deformation
deformities
degenerated
degradation
dehumanized
dehydrating
dehydration
deification
delectation
deleterious
deliberated
deliciously
delightedly
delineating
delineation
delinquency
deliriously
deliverance
demagnetize
demagogical
demagoguery
demarcation
demobilized
democracies
democratize
demographer
demographic
demonstrate
demoralized
demystified
denazifying
denigrating
denigration
denominator
deodorizing
deoxidizing
depopulated
deportation

depravation
deprecating
deprecation
deprecatory
depreciated
depredating
depredation
deprivation
deraignment
derangement
dereliction
dermatology
describable
description
descriptive
desecrating
desecration
desegregate
desensitize
desiccating
desiccation
desideratum
designating
designation
desperadoes
desperately
desperation
despoilment
despondence
despondency
destination
destitution
destruction
destructive
desultorily
deteriorate
determinant
determinate
determining
determinism
detestation
detrimental
Deuteronomy
devaluating
devaluation
devastating
devastation
development
deviousness
dexterously
diacritical
dialectical
dichotomies
dichotómous
dictatorial
didacticism
differently
diffidently
diffuseness
dignitaries
dilapidated

dimensional
diminishing
diplomacies
dipsomaniac
directional
directorate
directorial
directories
disablement
disaffected
disagreeing
disapproval
disapproved
disarmament
disarranged
disassemble
disbandment
disbelieved
disbeliever
discernible
discernibly
discernment
discharging
disciplined
discomfited
discommoded
discomposed
discontinue
discordance
discordancy
discotheque
discoursing
discourtesy
discoveries
discrepancy
disembodied
disencumber
disengaging
disentangle
disfiguring
disgraceful
disgruntled
disgustedly
dishonestly
disillusion
disinclined
disinterest
disinterred
disjunction
dislocating
dislocation
dislodgment
dismantling
Disneyesque
disobedient
disobliging
disorganize
disoriented
disparaging
disparately
disparities

dispensable
dispiriting
displeasing
displeasure
disposition
disputation
disquietude
dissembling
disseminate
dissentient
dissentious
dissertated
dissimilate
dissimulate
dissipating
dissipation
dissociated
dissolution
dissolvable
distasteful
distinction
distinctive
distinguish
distracting
distraction
distressful
distressing
distributed
distributor
distrustful
disturbance
dithyrambic
diversified
diversities
doctrinaire
documentary
dogmatizing
domesticate
domesticity
domineering
dormitories
doublecross
doublefaced
doughtiness
downgrading
downhearted
downtrodden
dragonflies
drastically
dreadnought
dromedaries
droughtiest
drunkenness
duplicating
duplication
duplicities
dynamically
dysfunction

earnestness

earthenware
earthliness
easternized
easternmost
eclecticism
economizing
edification
editorially
educational
effectively
effectually
effectuated
efficacious
efficiently
effloresced
egalitarian
egotistical
einsteinium
ejaculating
ejaculation
ejaculatory
elaborately
elaborating
elaboration
elderliness
electioneer
electrician
electricity
electrified
electrocute
electrolyte
electrolyze
electronics
elephantine
eligibility
eliminating
elimination
Elizabethan
elucidating
elucidation
elusiveness
emancipated
emancipator
emasculated
embarkation
embarrassed
embrocation
embroilment
emergencies
Emmenthaler
emotionally
empathizing
emphasizing
empirically
emplacement
emulsifying
encapsulate
enchantment
enchantress
encouraging
encumbrance

endearingly
endorsement
endoscopies
enforceable
enforcement
enfranchise
engineering
engorgement
engrossment
enhancement
enigmatical
enlargement
ennoblement
enrapturing
enslavement
ensnarement
entablature
entertainer
enthralling
entitlement
entrainment
entreatment
entrustment
enumerating
enumeration
enunciating
enunciation
enviousness
environment
environment
epidiascope
eponymously
equableness
equidistant
equilateral
equilibrate
equilibrium
equinoctial
equivalence
equivocated
eradicating
eradication
erratically
erroneously
eruditeness
erythrocyte
essentially
etherealize
ethnography
ethnologist
etiological
etymologies
etymologist
Eucharistic
eugenically
euphemistic
euphemizing
eurhythmics
evangelical
evangelized
evaporating

evaporation
evasiveness
eventuality
eventuating
everlasting
eviscerated
evocatively
evolutional
exacerbated
exaggerated
examination
exasperated
exceedingly
excellently
exceptional
excessively
exclamation
exclamatory
exclusively
exclusivity
excoriating
excoriation
excremental
excrescense
exculpating
exculpation
exculpatory
excursional
executioner
exemplarily
exemplified
exfoliating
exfoliation
exhaustible
exhilarated
exhortation
exhortative
exhortatory
exhortingly
existential
exonerating
exoneration
exonerative
exorbitance
exoskeleton
expansively
expatiating
expatiation
expatriated
expectation
expectingly
expectorant
expectorate
expeditious
expenditure
expensively
experienced
explainable
explanation
explanatory
explicating

explication
explicative
exploitable
exploration
exploratory
explosively
exponential
exportation
ex post facto
expostulate
expressible
expropriate
expurgating
expurgation
expurgatory
exquisitely
extemporize
extensively
extenuating
extenuation
exterminate
externalize
extirpating
extirpation
extortioner
extraditing
extradition
extrapolate
extravagant
extremities
extricating
extrication
exuberantly

fabricating
fabrication
facetiously
facilitated
fairweather
fallibility
familiarity
familiarize
fanatically
fantasizing
fantastical
farinaceous
farreaching
farthermost
farthingale
fascinating
fascination
fashionable
fashionably
father-in-law
faultlessly
favoredness
fearfulness
feasibility
featureless
fecundating

fecundation
federalized
felicitated
femme fatale
ferociously
Ferris wheel
ferruginous
fertileness
fertilizing
festiveness
festivities
feudalistic
filamentary
filamentous
filet mignon
filigreeing
financially
fin de siècle
fingerboard
fingerprint
firecracker
firefighter
first-string
fissionable
flabbergast
flagellated
flamboyance
flamboyancy
flannelette
flauntingly
fleurs-de-lis
flexibility
flightiness
flimflammed
flirtatious
flocculence
florescence
flourishing
fluctuating
fluctuation
fluorescent
fluorescing
fluoridated
fluoroscope
fomentation
foolishness
forbearance
forbiddance
forecasting
foreclosing
foreclosure
foreknowing
forequarter
foreseeable
foreshorten
forestation
foretelling
forethought
forevermore
forgettable
forgiveness

formalities
formalizing
formfitting
formularies
formulating
formulation
fornicating
fornication
forswearing
forthcoming
fortunately
forwardness
fossilizing
foul-mouthed
fourflusher
fox-trotting
fragmentary
fragmentize
franchising
Francophile
frangipanni
frankfurter
frantically
fraternally
fraternized
fratricidal
fraudulence
freelancing
freemasonry
freethinker
freeze-dried
freeze-frame
french fries
frenchified
Frenchwoman
Frenchwomen
frequencies
friendliest
frightening
frightfully
frivolities
frivolously
frostbiting
frostbitten
frugalities
frustrating
frustration
fulfillment
full-blooded
fullfledged
full-fledged
fulminating
fulmination
functionary
fundamental
fund-raising
furnishings
furtherance
furthermore
furthermost
fusillading

gallantries
gallimaufry
galvanizing
garnishment
garrulously
gastronomic
gefilte fish
gemological
genealogies
genealogist
generalized
genetically
Genghis Khan
gentlemanly
gentlewoman
gentlewomen
genuineness
geochemical
geographies
geomagnetic
geometrical
geophysical
geopolitics
germinating
germination
gerontology
gerrymander
gesticulate
ghastliness
ghostliness
ghostwriter
Gila monster
gingerbread
gladioluses
glamorizing
glasnostian
gleefulness
godchildren
goddaughter
godforsaken
godlessness
good-hearted
good-humored
good-looking
good-natured
Gordian knot
gradualness
grammatical
grandaddies
grandfather
grandiosely
grandmother
grandparent
granularity
granulating
granulation
graphically
grasshopper
gravitating
gravitation
greasepaint

grotesquely
grouchiness
groundsheet
guarantying
guillotined
gullibility
gutta-percha
gyrocompass
gyrostatics

haberdasher
habituation
haggardness
Hagiographa
hagiography
hairbreadth
hairdresser
hair-raising
halfhearted
hallucinate
handicapped
handicapper
handwriting
handwritten
haphazardly
hardhearted
hard-hitting
hard-pressed
harebrained
harmfulness
harmonizing
harpsichord
harum-scarum
hatefulness
haughtiness
healthfully
healthiness
heartbroken
hearthstone
heartlessly
heavy-handed
heavyweight
hedonnistic
heinousness
hellishness
helpfulness
hemophiliac
hemorrhaged
herbivorous
herpetology
hibernating
hibernation
hideousness
hierarchies
high-powered
high-tension
hilariously
hillbillies
hindquarter
Hindusstani

Hippocrates
Hippocratic
hippopotami
histrionics
hitchhiking
homeopathic
homogeneity
homogeneous
Homo sapiens
honeymooner
honeysuckle
hooliganism
hopefulness
hornswoggle
hors d'oeuvre
horseradish
hospitality
hospitalize
hostilities
housebroken
housekeeper
huckleberry
humidifying
humiliating
humiliation
hummingbird
hybridizing
hydrocarbon
hydrogenous
hydrophobia
hydroplaned
hydroponics
hyperactive
hyperbolize
hyphenating
hypnotizing
hypocrisies
hypotension
hypothecate
hypothermia
hypothesize

ichthyology
identically
identifying
ideological
idiotically
idolization
idyllically
ignis fatuus
ignobleness
ignominious
illimitable
illogically
ill-tempered
illuminated
illuminator
illusionist
illustrated
illustrator

illustrious
imaginarily
imagination
imaginative
immediacies
immediately
immenseness
immigrating
immigration
immobilized
immortality
immortalize
impartially
impassioned
impassively
impassivity
impatiently
impeachable
impeachment
impecunious
impedimenta
impenitence
imperfectly
imperialism
imperialist
imperilling
imperilment
imperiously
impermanent
impermeable
impersonate
impertinent
impetuosity
impetuously
impingement
impiousness
implausible
implausibly
implemental
implicating
implication
imploration
impoliticly
importantly
importation
importunate
importuning
importunity
impractical
imprecating
imprecation
imprecision
impregnable
impregnated
impregnator
impresarios
impressible
impressment
impropriety
improvement
improvident

improvising
imprudently
impugnation
impulsively
inadvertent
inadvisable
inalienable
inalienably
inalterable
inattention
inattentive
inaugurated
incantation
incarcerate
incarnating
incarnation
incertitude
incessantly
incinerated
incinerator
inclination
incognizant
incoherence
incompetent
incongruity
incongruous
inconstancy
incontinent
incorporate
incorporeal
incorrectly
increasable
incredulity
incredulous
incremental
incriminate
inculcating
inculcation
inculpating
inculpation
incuriously
indefinable
indefinably
indemnified
indemnities
indentation
indenturing
independent
indifferent
indigestion
indignantly
indignation
indignities
indirection
indivisible
indomitable
indomitably
indubitable
indubitably
indulgently
industrious

inebriating
inebriation
ineffective
ineffectual
inefficient
ineluctable
inequitable
inescapable
inessential
inestimable
inexcusable
inexcusably
inexpensive
infanticide
infantryman
infantrymen
infatuating
infatuation
inferential
inferiority
infertility
infestation
infiltrated
infiltrator
infirmaries
infirmities
inflammable
inflictable
influencing
influential
informality
information
informative
informatory
infrangible
infrangibly
infrequency
infuriating
infuriation
ingeniously
ingenuously
ingratiated
ingratitude
inhabitable
inheritance
initialling
injudicious
innervating
innervation
innocuously
innumerable
innumerably
innutrition
inobservant
inoculating
inoculation
inoffensive
inoperative
inopportune
inquiringly
inquisition

inquisitive
inscription
inscriptive
inscrutable
inscrutably
insecticide
insectivore
inseminated
insensitive
inseparable
inseparably
insidiously
insincerely
insincerity
insinuating
insinuation
insipidness
insistently
insouciance
inspiration
instability
installment
instatement
instigating
instigation
instinctive
instinctual
instituting
institution
instruction
instructive
insultingly
insuperable
integrating
integration
intelligent
intemperate
intenseness
intensified
intensifier
intensities
intensively
intentional
interaction
interactive
intercalate
interceding
interceptor
intercessor
interchange
intercourse
interesting
interfering
interlacing
interloping
interlunary
intermingle
intermitted
internalize
internecine
internuncio

interoffice
interpolate
interposing
interpreter
interracial
interregnum
interrelate
interrogate
intersperse
intertwined
intervening
interviewee
intimidated
intolerable
intolerably
intolerance
intoxicated
intractable
intravenous
intrepidity
intricacies
intricately
introducing
intuitively
intumescent
invalidated
inventoried
inventories
investigate
investiture
invigorated
involuntary
involvement
iridescence
ironhearted
irradiating
irradiation
irradicable
irreducible
irrefutable
irregularly
irrelevance
irrelevancy
irreligious
irremovable
irreparable
irreverence
irrevocable
irrevocably
isometrical
italicizing
itineraries
itineration

jack-knifing
jeopardized
Jesus Christ
joie de vivre
judiciously
justiceless

justifiable
justifiably
juxtaposing

kiddishness
Kilimanjaro
kindhearted
kinematical
kitchenette
kitchenware
kitty-corner
kleptomania
know-nothing
Kuala Lumpur
kwashiorkor

labiodental
laboriously
labor-saving
laconically
lamentation
landscaping
languishing
lapis lazuli
latitudinal
latticework
launderette
lawbreaking
lawlessness
leafletting
leapfrogged
leaseholder
leatherneck
leave-taking
lectureship
legerdemain
legionnaire
legislating
legislation
legislative
legislature
legitimated
legitimized
lengthiness
lese-majesty
lethargical
letterpress
level-headed
liabilities
liberalized
libertarian
libertinism
Liederkranz
lieutenancy
life-or-death
lightfooted
light-headed
light-minded
lightweight

Lilliputian
lily-livered
lingeringly
linguistics
lionhearted
lionization
liquefiable
liquidating
liquidation
liquidizing
lissomeness
listeriosis
lithography
lithography
locum tenens
logarithmic
logicalness
Londonderry
long-playing
long-sighted
loudmouthed
loudspeaker
loutishness
lovableness
low-pressure
low-spirited
lubricating
lubrication
lucubration
ludicrously
luminescent
lustfulness
Lutheranism
luxuriantly
luxuriating
luxuriation
luxuriously

machinating
machination
macrobiotic
macroscopic
maderingly
magisterial
magnanimity
magnanimous
magnetizing
magnificent
maid of honor
maidservant
maintenance
make-believe
maladjusted
malapropism
malediction
maledictory
malefaction
malevolence
malfeasance
malfunction

maliciously
malignantly
malpractice
managership
mandatorily
manhandling
manifestoes
manipulable
manipulated
manipulator
mantelpiece
mantelshelf
manufacture
manumission
marchioness
marketplace
marquisette
marshalling
marshmallow
marvelously
masculinity
masculinize
masochistic
masqueraded
mass-produce
masterpiece
masticating
mastication
matchmaking
materialism
materialist
materialize
mathematics
matriarchal
matriculant
matrilineal
matrimonial
mawkishness
meaningless
measurement
mechanistic
mechanizing
medicinally
medievalism
megalomania
megalopolis
melancholia
melancholic
meliorating
melioration
mellifluent
mellifluous
melodically
memorabilia
memorialize
ménage á tois
mendelevium
Mendelssohn
menservants
menstruated
mensuration

mentalities
mentholated
mentionable
mercenaries
merchandise
merchantman
merchantmen
mercilessly
meritocracy
meritorious
merrymaking
meshuggener
mesmerizing
metabolized
metallurgic
metamorphic
metaphysics
meteorology
methodology
metrication
microgroove
micromicron
microreader
microscopic
microsecond
micturating
micturition
millionaire
millisecond
mineralized
minesweeper
miniaturize
ministerial
mirthlessly
misalliance
misanthrope
misanthropy
misapplying
misbehaving
misbehavior
misbeliever
miscarrying
mischievous
miscibility
misconceive
misconstrue
misdemeanor
mise-en-scène
miserliness
misestimate
misfeasance
misguidance
mishandling
misinformer
misjudgment
mismanaging
Mississippi
misspelling
misspending
mistrustful
mockingbird

modernistic
modernizing
moisturized
moisturizer
molestation
mollybdenum
mollycoddle
momentarily
monarchical
monasterial
monasteries
monasticism
monochromic
monogrammed
monographer
monographic
monologuist
monopolized
monopolizer
monseigneur
monstrosity
monstrously
Mornay sauce
moronically
morphologic
mortalities
mortarboard
mother-in-law
mothers-to-be
motorcycled
mountaineer
mountainous
multiplying
multiracial
Munchhausen
municipally
munificence
murderously
muscle-bound
muscularity
musculature
musicalness
muskellunge
mutableness
mythologist
myxomatosis

naphthalene
narcotizing
nationalism
nationalist
nationality
nationalize
nation-state
naturalized
naturalness
naughtiness
Neanderthal
near-sighted
necessaries

necessarily
necessiites
necessitate
neckerchief
necrologies
necromancer
needlepoint
needlewoman
needlewomen
negligently
negotiating
negotiation
neighboring
ne plus ultra
nervousness
Netherlands
netherworld
neurologist
neutralized
neutralizer
nickelodeon
nightingale
nightmarish
nincomppoop
nitrogenous
nitty-gritty
Nobel prizes
noiselessly
nomadically
nom de guerre
noms de plume
nonchalance
nondescript
nonentities
nonetheless
nonexistent
nonmetallic
nonpartisan
nonplussing
nonresident
nonsensical
non sequitur
nonstandard
nonviolence
normalizing
northeaster
northwardly
Nostradamus
notableness
nothingness
notoriously
nourishment
numerically
numismatics
numismatist
nutritional
nymphomania

obfuscating
obfuscation

objectively
objectivity
objurgating
objurgation
objurgatory
obliterated
obnoxiously
obsceneness
obscenities
obscureness
observation
observatory
observatory
obsessional
obsessively
obsolescent
obstetrical
obstinately
obstruction
obstructive
obtrusively
obviousness
octagonally
odoriferous
offenseless
offensively
offertorial
offertories
officialdom
officiating
officiation
officiously
oligarchies
omnipotence
omnipresent
omniscience
opalescence
open-mouthed
operability
operational
opinionated
opportunely
opportunism
opportunist
opportunity
opprobrious
optometrist
orchestrate
orderliness
organically
organizable
orientating
orientation
originality
originating
origination
originative
ornithology
orthodontic
orthodoxies
orthography

orthopedics
orthopedist
oscillating
oscillation
oscillatory
ostensively
ostentation
osteopathic
ostracizing
outbuilding
outdistance
outmaneuver
outstanding
outstripped
overanxious
overbalance
overbearing
overcharged
overcrowded
overdressed
overflowing
overhanging
overhauling
overhearing
overlapping
overmanning
overrunning
overselling
overstating
overstepped
overvaluing
overweening
overworking
overwrought
oxygenating
oxygenation

pacificator
painstaking
paleography
Paleolithic
paleontolgy
Palestinian
palpability
palpitating
palpitation
pamphleteer
Pan-American
pandemonium
panhandling
pantheistic
pantomiming
pantomimist
paper knives
paperweight
papier-mâche
parachuting
parachutist
paradoxical
parallactic

paramountcy
paraphrased
parasitical
paratrooper
parentheses
parenthesis
parenthetic
parishioner
participant
participate
particulate
partitioned
partnership
parturition
passionless
pasteurized
paternalism
paternalist
paternoster
pathologist
patriarchal
patrimonies
patronizing
patternally
paunchiness
peculiarity
pedagogical
penetrating
penetration
penetrative
penitential
penological
pensionable
pensiveness
pentathlete
Pentecostal
penultimate
pepperiness
perambulate
perceivable
perceivably
perceptible
perceptibly
percipience
percolating
percolation
perennially
perestroika
perfectible
perfectness
perforating
perforation
performable
performance
perfunctory
periodicity
peripatetic
peripheries
peristalsis
peristaltic
peritonitis

permanently
permissible
permissibly
permutation
perpetrated
perpetrator
perpetually
perpetuated
perpetuator
persecuting
persecution
persecutive
persevering
persistence
persistency
persnickety
personality
personalize
personating
personation
personified
perspective
perspicuity
perspicuous
persuadable
pertinacity
pertinently
perturbable
pessimistic
pestiferous
petitionary
petitioning
petits fours
petrography
pettifogged
pettishness
pharyngitis
philanderer
philatelist
Philippians
philologian
philologist
philosopher
philosophic
phonetician
photocopied
photocopier
photocopies
photography
photostated
phraseology
physiognomy
picaninnies
picturesque
pieds-à-terre
pigeonholed
pinch hitter
piquantness
pirouetting
piscatorial
pitchblende

pituitaries
placability
plagiarized
plagiarizer
plainspoken
plaintively
planetarium
plantigrade
plasterwork
plastically
plats du jour
pleasurable
pleasurably
Pleistocene
plenipotent
plentifully
pliableness
pluralistic
pluralities
plutocratic
pocketknife
pointillism
pointillist
pointlessly
policewoman
policewomen
politically
politicized
politicking
pollinating
pollination
poltergeist
polyandrous
polystyrene
polytechnic
pomegranate
ponderously
pontificate
popularized
pornography
portability
portmanteau
portraitist
portraiture
positioning
possibility
postponable
postulating
postulation
potentially
practicable
practicably
practically
pragmatical
prearranged
preassigned
Precambrian
precipitant
precipitate
precipitous
precipitous

preciseness
preconceive
predecessor
predestined
predicament
predicating
predication
predicative
predictable
predictably
predigested
predisposed
predominant
predominate
preeminence
preexistent
prefiguring
pregnancies
prehistoric
prejudgment
prejudicial
prejudicing
preliminary
prematurely
prematurity
premeditate
premiership
premonition
premonitory
preoccupied
preparation
preparatory
preplanning
preposition
prerogative
prescribing
presentable
presentably
preservable
pressurized
pressurizer
prestigious
prestissimo
prestressed
presumption
presumptive
presupposed
pretentious
preterition
prettifying
prevaricate
preventable
prickliness
principally
privatizing
privileging
probability
probational
probationer
problematic
procreating

procreation
procreative
procrustean
prodigality
prodtruding
profanatory
profaneness
professedly
proficiency
profiterole
programming
progression
progressive
prohibition
prohibitive
prohibitory
proletarian
proletariat
proliferate
prolificacy
promenading
prominently
promiscuity
promiscuous
promotional
promptitude
promulgated
pronouncing
proofreader
propagating
propagation
propagative
prophesying
prophylaxis
propinquity
proposition
proppitious
proprietary
proprieties
prosaically
prosaicness
pros and cons
proscribing
prosecuting
prosecution
proselytism
proselytize
prospective
prostituted
prostitutor
prostrating
prostration
protagonist
Proterozoic
protractile
protraction
protractive
protuberant
provisional
provocation
provocative

provokingly
prudishness
psychedelic
psychiatric
psychically
psychodrama
psychogenic
psychologic
psychomotor
psychopathy
pterodactyl
publication
publicizing
pulchritude
pulverizing
punctilious
punctuality
punctuating
punctuation
puncturable
purchasable
purgatorial
puritanical
purportedly
purposeless
pussywillow

quadrennial
quadrillion
quadrupling
qualifiable
qualitative
quantifying
quarantined
quarrelling
quarrelsome
quarterback
quarterdeck
quarterlies
quaveringly
queenliness
Queensberry
querulously
questioning
quickfreeze
quicksilver
quick-witted
quintillion
quintupling
quizzically

Rabelaisian
Rachmaninov
radicalized
radioactive
radiocarbon
radiography
radiologist
raffishness

raison d'être
rapaciously
rapscallion
rapturously
rarefaction
Rastafarian
rationalism
rationalist
rationality
rationalize
rattlebrain
rattlesnake
ravishingly
reactionary
reactivated
readability
realignment
realization
reanimating
reanimation
reapportion
reappraisal
reappraised
rear admiral
rearranging
reassembled
reassurance
recantation
recapturing
recceivable
receptivity
recessional
reciprocate
reciprocity
reclaimable
reclamation
recognition
recognizing
recommender
recommittal
recompensed
reconciling
recondition
reconnoiter
reconstruct
recoverable
recriminate
recruitment
rectangular
rectifiable
rectilinear
recumbently
recuperated
redecorated
rededicated
redirection
redoubtable
redoubtably
redundantly
reduplicate
reeducation

reemphasize
reenforcing
reestablish
reexamining
refectories
referencing
referential
reformation
reformative
reformatory
refrangible
refreshment
refrigerant
refrigerate
regenerated
regionalism
regretfully
regrettable
regrettably
regularized
regurgitate
reimbursing
reincarnate
reinfection
reinforcing
reinstating
reinsurance
reiterating
reiteration
reiterative
rejuvenated
reliability
religiosity
religiously
reliquaries
reluctantly
remembrance
reminiscent
reminiscing
remodelling
remonstrate
remorseless
remunerated
renaissance
reorganized
repatriated
repetitious
replaceable
replacement
replication
reportorial
reproachful
reprobation
reproducing
reprovingly
repudiating
repudiation
repulsively
requirement
requisition
resemblance

resentfully
reservation
reshuffling
residential
resignation
resourceful
respectable
respectably
respiration
respiratory
resplendent
responsible
responsibly
restatement
restitution
restiveness
restoration
restorative
restriction
restrictive
restructure
resurfacing
resuscitate
retaliating
retaliation
retaliatory
retardation
retentivity
retractable
retribution
retributive
retroactive
retrorocket
revaluation
reverberate
reverencing
reverential
revisionism
revisionist
revitalized
revivifying
revoltingly
rhapsodized
rhetorician
Rhode Island
rhombohedra
ricketiness
ricocheting
ricochetted
right-angled
right-handed
rightwinger
rigor mortis
ritualistic
Robespierre
roller skate
rolling mill
romans à clef
romanticism
romanticist
romanticize

Rosicrucian
routinizing
rubberizing
rudimentary
rumormonger
rusticating
rustication

sacrificial
sacrificing
safe-conduct
safe-deposit
safekeeping
sagaciously
Sagittarian
Sagittarius
saintliness
salespeople
salesperson
salientness
salvageable
sal volatile
sanctifying
sanctuaries
sandbagging
sand-casting
sandwich man
sandwich men
San Salvador
sarcophagus
satiability
satirically
satisfiable
Saudi Arabia
sauerbraten
savoir-faire
saxophonist
scaffolding
scandalized
Scandinavia
scaremonger
schematized
scholarship
school board
schoolchild
scintillant
scintillate
scorekeeper
scoundrelly
scoutmaster
scrappiness
scrawniness
screwdriver
scrimmaging
scrimpiness
scruffiness
scrumptious
scrutinizer
sculpturing
scuttlebutt

searchingly
searchlight
seasickness
secondaries
secondarily
second-class
second-guess
secretarial
secretariat
secretaries
secretively
secularized
sedimentary
seditionary
seductively
segregating
segregation
seismograph
selectively
selectivity
self-assured
self-control
self-defense
self-evident
self-imposed
self-induced
selfishness
self-reliant
self-respect
self-service
self-serving
self-starter
self-support
semiclassic
semiinarian
semimonthly
semiprivate
semiskilled
semitrailer
semitropics
sensational
senselessly
sensibility
sensitively
sensitivity
sensitizing
sensualized
sententious
sentimental
sequestered
sequestrate
serendipity
seriousness
sermonizing
serviceable
serviceably
servileness
seventeenth
shallowness
shamelessly
shanghaiing

shapeliness
shareholder
sharp-witted
sheath knife
sheepherder
shellacking
shepherdess
shoplifting
short-change
shortcoming
short-handed
short-winded
shotgunning
showmanship
shrivelling
shrubberies
shuttlecock
sickeningly
sidestepped
sideswiping
Sierra Leone
sightseeing
signatories
significant
silhouetted
silveriness
silversmith
simperingly
simplifying
single-space
single-track
singularity
sinuousness
sister-in-law
sizableness
sketchiness
skulduggery
sleepwalker
slenderness
slightingly
slipperiest
smithereens
Smithsonian
smorgasbord
sociability
socialistic
socializing
sociologist
soft-hearted
soft-pedaled
solar plexus
solemnizing
solidifying
soliloquies
soliloquize
solubleness
solvability
sophistical
sophistries
sorrowfully
sottishness

soundlessly
sovereignty
sparingness
spastically
specialized
specialties
specifiable
specificity
spectacular
speculating
speculation
speculative
speedometer
spendthrift
spermatozoa
spic-and-span
spina bifida
spiritually
splashiness
split-second
spokeswoman
spokeswomen
sponsorship
spontaneity
spontaneous
sportswoman
sportswomen
spread-eagle
sprightlier
springboard
springiness
squalidness
squashiness
squeakingly
squintingly
stabilities
stabilizing
stage-manage
stagestruck
stakeholder
stalemating
standardize
standoffish
starchiness
startlingly
stateliness
statistical
statutorily
steadfastly
stealthiest
steamfitter
steamroller
steelworker
steeplejack
stemwinding
stencilling
stenography
stepbrother
stereoscope
stereotyped
sterilizing

stethoscope
stewardship
stickleback
stigmatized
stimulating
stimulation
stimulative
stipendiary
stipulating
stipulation
stipulatory
stockbroker
stockholder
stockpiling
stocktaking
stomachache
storyteller
straggliest
straightway
strait-laced
strangeness
strangulate
straphanger
stratifying
streamlined
streetlight
strenuosity
strenuously
stressfully
stretchable
stretchiest
strikebound
stringently
stringiness
stroboscope
structuring
studiedness
stultifying
stuntedness
stupidities
stylishness
stylistical
stylization
subassembly
subbasement
subcontract
subdividing
subdivision
subfreezing
subjugating
subjugation
subjunctive
sublimating
sublimation
sublimeness
submarginal
submergence
submergible
submersible
subordinate
subornation

subpoenaing
subscribing
subsequence
subservient
subsidizing
subsistence
substandard
substantial
substantive
substituted
subsumption
subsumptive
subtraction
subtractive
subtropical
suburbanite
succulently
sufficiency
suffocating
suffocation
suffocative
suffragette
suggestible
suitability
sulfonamide
summariness
summarizing
summational
sumptuously
supercharge
superficial
superfluity
superfluous
superimpose
superinduce
superintend
superiority
superlative
supermarket
superscribe
superscript
superseding
supertanker
supervening
supervising
supervision
supervisory
supplicated
supportable
supportably
supposition
suppository
suppression
suppurating
suppuration
supremacist
supremeness
surcharging
surpassable
surrogating
surveillant

susceptible
susceptibly
sustainable
sustainment
swarthiness
sweepstakes
switchblade
switchboard
Switzerland
sycophantic
syllabicate
syllabified
syllogistic
symbolizing
symmetrical
sympathetic
sympathized
sympathizer
symptomatic
synagogical
synchronism
synchronize
synchronous
synchrotron
syncopating
syncopation
syndicating
syndication
syntactical
synthesized
synthesizer
synthetical
systematize

taciturnity
tactfulness
talebearing
talkatively
tam-o'-shanter
tangibility
tantalizing
tapestrying
tarnishable
tastelessly
tautologies
taxidermist
taxonomical
Tchaikovsky
tearfulness
technically
Technicolor
technocracy
technologic
tediousness
teenybopper
teetotalism
teetotalist
teetotaller
telecasting
telegraphic

telekinesis
telepathist
telephoning
teleprinter
telescoping
temperament
temperately
temperature
tempestuous
temporality
temporarily
temporizing
tenableness
tenaciously
tendentious
tenderizing
tensionless
tentatively
tenterhooks
tenuousness
terminating
termination
terminative
terminology
Terpsichore
terrestrial
territorial
territories
terroristic
terrorizing
tessellated
testimonial
testimonies
tetrahedron
thalidomide
thanklessly
theatergoer
thenceforth
theocracies
theological
theorematic
theoretical
theosophist
therapeutic
thereabouts
thermometer
Thermopylae
thick-headed
thingamabob
thingummies
thirstiness
thistle-down
thoughtless
threadiness
three-decker
thriftiness
throatiness
thunderbolt
thunderclap
thunderhead
tick-tack-toe

tiddlywinks
tight-fisted
tight-lipped
time-honored
time-sharing
titillating
titillation
title-tattle
toastmaster
tobacconist
tobogganing
tonsillitis
topdressing
topographer
topological
torchbearer
torturesome
totalizator
touch-typing
tour de force
townspeople
tracheotomy
traditional
traducement
trafficking
tragedienne
tragicomedy
trailblazer
trammelling
tranquilize
transaction
transceiver
transcribed
transcriber
transferred
transfigure
transfixing
transfixion
transformer
transfusing
transfusion
translating
translation
translative
translucent
transmittal
transmitted
transmitter
transmuting
transparent
transpiring
transporter
transposing
traversable
treacheries
treacherous
treasonable
treasonably
treasurable
tremulously
trenchantly

trendsetter
trepanation
trepidation
triangulate
tribulation
tributaries
tributarily
trichinosis
trimestrial
Trinitarian
triplicated
triumphally
triumvirate
trivialized
troposphere
troublesome
truculently
trusteeship
trustworthy
tsetse flies
tutti-frutti
twelve-month
typewriting
typewritten
typicalness
typographer
typographic
tyrannizing

ubiquitous
Ultima Thule
ultramarine
ultramodern
ultraviolet
unaccounted
unadvisedly
unalterable
unambitious
unanimously
unannounced
unappealing
unashamedly
unavailable
unavailably
unavoidable
unavoidably
unawareness
unbeknownst
unbelieving
unbeseeming
unblemished
unbreakable
unbuttoning
uncalled-for
uncanniness
unceasingly
uncertainly
uncertainty
unchristian
uncivilized

uncluttered
uncommitted
unconcerned
unconfirmed
uncongenial
unconnected
unconquered
unconscious
uncontested
unconvinced
uncourteous
uncouthness
undauntedly
undeceiving
undefinable
undemanding
undercharge
underexpose
underground
undergrowth
underhanded
underlining
undermanned
undermining
underpinned
underrating
underscored
undersigned
understated
undertaking
undervalued
underweight
underwriter
undesigning
undesirable
undesirably
undeveloped
undignified
undisclosed
undisguised
undisturbed
undoubtedly
unemotional
unendurable
unequivocal
unessential
unethically
unexplained
unfailingly
unfavorable
unfavorably
unfeelingly
unflappable
unflinching
unforgiving
unfortunate
unfurnished
ungodliness
unguardedly
unhappiness
unhealthier

unhurriedly
unicellular
unification
uniformness
unimportant
unimpressed
uninhabited
uninhibited
uninitiated
uninspiring
universally
unjustified
unknowingly
unlooked-for
unluckiness
unmeaningly
unmitigated
unnaturally
unnecessary
unnervingly
unobtrusive
unorganized
unpalatable
unprintable
unpromising
unprotected
unqualified
unreadiness
unrealistic
unreasoning
unrehearsed
unrelenting
unremitting
unrepentant
unrewarding
unsatisfied
unsaturated
unscheduled
unselfishly
unsmilingly
unsolicited
unsoundness
unspeakable
unspeakably
unspecified
unstoppable
unsupported
unsurpassed
unsuspected
unthinkable
untouchable
untrammeled
unusualness
unutterable
unutterably
unvarnished
unwarranted
unwelcoming
unwholesome
unwillingly
unwittingly

up-and-coming
uprightness
uselessness
utilitarian
utilization

vaccinating
vaccination
vacillating
vacillation
vacuousness
vagabondage
valediction
valedictory
valiantness
valuational
vandalizing
variability
variational
varicolored
variegating
variegation
variousness
vascularity
vasectomies
vendibility
ventilating
ventilation
venturesome
verbalizing
verboseness
vermiculate
versatility
verticality
vertiginous
vestigially
vicariously
vice-admiral
vichyssoise
viciousness
vicissitude
victimizing
videotaping
vigilantism
vinaigrette
vincibility
vindicating
vindication
viniculture
violability
violoncello
viscosities
viscountess
visionaries
visualizing
vitrifiable
vituperated
vivaciously
vivisection
vocaliation

voluntarily
voodooistic
voraciously
vouchsafing
voyeuristic
vulcanizing
vulgarizing

wainscoting
wakefulness
warm-blooded
warm-hearted
waspishness
wastebasket
watercourse
water lilies
waterlogged
waterskiing
wealthiness
weathercock
weathervane
weightiness
well-advised

well-behaved
well-dressed
well-founded
well-groomed
well-meaning
well-thumbed
westernized
westernmost
wheelbarrow
wheelwright
whereabouts
wheresoever
wherewithal
white-collar
wholesaling
whosesoever
wide-ranging
wildcatting
willingness
windsurfing
wintergreen
winterizing
wiretapping
wistfulness

withdrawing
withholding
womanliness
wonderfully
word-perfect
workability
workmanlike
workmanship
worldliness
worldly-wise
worshipping
wrong-headed

xylophonist

yachtswoman
yachtswomen
yellow fever
Yevtushenko
Yugoslavian

Zoroastrian

bbreviating	ambidextrous	asphyxiating
bbreviation	ameliorating	asphyxiation
bolitionism	amelioration	assassinated
bolitionist	ameliorative	assassinator
bsent-minded	amenableness	asseverating
bstractedly	Americanized	asseveration
cademically	amortization	assimilating
ccelerating	amphitheater	assimilation
cceleration	anagrammatic	astonishment
ccentuating	anathematize	astrological
ccentuation	anatomically	astronautics
ccidentally	angstrom unit	astronomical
cclimatized	annihilating	astrophysics
cclimattion	annihilation	asymmetrical
ccommodated	announcement	athletically
ccompanying	annunciating	atmospherics
ccomplished	annunciation	attesttation
ccordionist	antagonistic	attitudinize
ccouchement	antagonizing	attractively
ccumulating	antediluvian	attributable
ccumulation	ante meridiem	attributtion
ccumulative	anthropology	audiovisuals
ccurateness	antiaircraft	augmentation
cknowledged	anticipating	auld lang syne
cquaintance	anticipation	auspiciously
cquiescence	anticipative	authenticate
daptability	anticipatory	authenticity
dhesiveness	anticlerical	availability
djectivally	antimacassar	avariciously
djudicating	antipathetic	
djudication	anti-Semitism	
djudicative	antithetical	bacchanalian
dministrate	apiculturist	bachelorhood
dulterating	apologetical	backbreaking
dulteration	apothecaries	backpedaling
dvantageous	appendectomy	backslapping
dventitious	appendicitis	backwardness
dvisability	apperception	backwoodsman
erodynamics	appoggiatura	backwoodsmen
eronautical	appreciating	bactericidal
estheticism	appreciation	bacteriology
ffectedness	appreciative	ballistician
ffectionate	apprehension	bankruptcies
forethought	apprehensive	bantamweight
fro-American	approachable	bedazzlement
fterthought	appropriated	belligerence
ggrandizing	appurtenance	belligerency
ggressively	archdiocesan	benefactress
greeability	archeologist	beneficially
gricultural	architecture	benevolently
ir-condition	aristocratic	beseechingly
limentation	Aristotelian	bewilderment
lkalization	arithmetical	Bhagavad Gita
lliterating	articulately	bibliography
lliteration	articulating	bibliomaniac
lliterative	articulation	bicentennial
phabetical	artificially	biochemistry
lphanumeric	artilleryman	biographical
lterability	artillerymen	biologically
malgamation	artistically	biosynthesis
mbassadress	artsy-craftsy	blackberries

blandishment
bloodletting
bloodstained
bloodthirsty
bluestocking
blusteringly
boastfulness
bodybuilding
boiling point
boogie-woogie
bouquet garni
bowdlerizing
brainwashing
breakthrough
breaststroke
breathtaking
breechloader
brilliantine
brinkmanship
broadcasting
brontosaurus
brother-in-law
Bunsen burner
bureaucratic
burglarizing
businesslike
butterscotch
buttonholing

cabinetmaker
calisthenics
calligrapher
calumniating
calumniation
camouflaging
cancellation
canonization
cantankerous
capabilities
capacitating
capitalistic
capitulating
capitulation
capriciously
caramelizing
caravanserai
carbohydrate
carbonaceous
carcinogenic
cardiography
carelessness
caricaturing
caricaturist
carpetbagger
carte blanche
cartographer
cartographic
case-hardened
catastrophic
categorizing

catheterized
cause célèbre
cautiousness
centralizing
chairmanship
chaise longue
championship
characterize
charnel house
chastisement
chauvinistic
checkerboard
cheerfulness
cheeseburger
cheeseparing
chefs d'oeuvre
chemotherapy
chesterfield
childbearing
childishness
chirographer
chiropractic
chiropractor
chivalrously
chlorinating
chlorination
choreography
Christianity
Christianize
chronologies
churchliness
churchwarden
cinema verité
circumcising
circumcision
circumfluent
circumscribe
circumstance
civilization
clairvoyance
clearsighted
clerestories
clinker-built
clotheshorse
cockfighting
codification
cohabitation
cohesiveness
coincidental
collaborated
collaborator
collectively
collectivism
collectivist
collectivity
collectivize
colloquially
colonization
commemorated
commencement
commendation

commensurate
commentaries
commentating
commercially
commiserated
commissariat
commissaries
commissioned
commissioner
commonwealth
communicable
communicated
companionway
compensating
compensation
compensative
compensatory
complacently
complaisance
completeness
complexities
complicating
complication
complicities
compos mentis
compressible
compromising
compulsively
concentrated
concentrical
conciliating
conciliation
conciliatory
conclusively
concupiscent
concurrently
condemnation
condemnatory
condensation
conditioning
confectioner
confessional
confidential
confirmation
confirmative
confirmatory
confiscating
confiscation
confiscatory
conformation
congeniality
congenitally
conglomerate
congratulate
congregating
congregation
conjecturing
conning tower
conquistador
conscionable
conscription

consecrating
consecration
consequently
conservation
conservatism
conservative
conservatory
considerable
considerably
consistently
consolidated
conspiracies
constabulary
constipation
constituency
constitution
constriction
constrictive
construction
constructive
consultation
consultative
consummating
consummation
contaminated
contemplated
contemporary
contemptible
contemptibly
contemptuous
conterminous
contiguities
contiguously
continuation
continuously
contrapuntal
contrariness
contrariwise
contravening
contributing
contribution
contributory
contriteness
controllable
convalescent
conveniently
conventional
conversation
conveyancing
convincingly
conviviality
convulsively
coordinating
coordination
correctional
corroborated
cosmetically
cosmographer
cosmopolitan
countenanced
counterclaim

counterpoint
counterpoise
countertenor
countrywoman
countrywomen
courageously
court-martial
covetousness
cowardliness
crème de menth
crenellation
crepe de Chine
crepe suzette
criticizable
cross-country
cross-examine
cumulonimbus
Czechoslovak

deactivating
deactivation
debilitating
debilitation
decapitating
decapitation
decelerating
deceleration
decentralize
decimalizing
decipherable
decisiveness
declassified
decommission
decongestant
decontrolled
decreasingly
deescalating
deescalation
deficiencies
definitively
deflationary
degenerately
degenerating
degeneration
degenerative
dehumanizing
deliberately
deliberating
deliberation
deliberative
delicatessen
delightfully
delimitation
demagnetized
demilitarize
demimondaine
demobilizing
democratized
demoniacally
demonstrable

demonstrably
demonstrated
demonstrator
demoralizing
demystifying
denaturalize
denomination
denunciation
denunciation
deoxygenated
dependencies
depopulating
depopulation
depreciating
depreciation
depreciatory
depressingly
derogatorily
desegregated
desensitized
desirability
despairingly
despoliation
despondently
despotically
dessertspoon
destructible
deteriorated
determinable
determinedly
dethronement
deutsche mark
devil-may-care
diabolically
diagrammatic
dialectician
diastrophism
dictatorship
dictionaries
didactically
differential
difficulties
digitization
dilapidating
dilapidation
dilettantism
dillydallied
directorship
disadvantage
disaffection
disagreeable
disagreeably
disagreement
disallowance
disapproving
disarranging
disassociate
disastrously
disbelieving
disbursement
disciplinary

disciplining
discomfiting
discomfiture
discommoding
discomposing
discomposure
disconcerted
disconnected
disconsolate
discontented
discontinued
discordantly
discouraging
discourteous
discoverable
discriminate
disdainfully
disembodying
disemboweled
disentangled
disestablish
disfranchise
disgruntling
disgustingly
disharmonies
dishonesties
dishonorable
dishonorably
disincentive
disinclining
disinfectant
disinfection
disingenuous
disintegrate
disinterment
disinterring
dismissively
disobedience
disorganized
disorientate
dispensaries
dispensation
dispiritedly
displacement
disputatious
disqualified
disquisition
disreputable
dissatisfied
dissemblance
disseminated
dissertating
dissertation
dissimilated
dissimulated
dissociating
dissociation
distillation
distilleries
distractedly
distributing

distribution
diversifying
diversionary
divertimenti
divertimento
dogmatically
domestically
domesticated
Doppelganger
Douay Version
doubledecker
doubleheader
dramatically
dysmenorrhea

earsplitting
earthshaking
easternizing
eau de cologne
eavesdropped
eavesdropper
Eccelsiastes
eccentricity
ecclesiastic
echolocation
eclectically
economically
ecstatically
editorialize
educationist
effectuating
effeminately
effervescent
effervescing
efflorescent
efflorescing
effronteries
Egyptologist
elderberries
electrically
electrifying
electrocuted
electrolysis
electrolytic
electrolyzed
electroplate
eleemosynary
elementarily
elliptically
elocutionary
elocutionist
emancipating
emancipation
emasculating
emasculation
embarrassing
embattlement
embezzlement
embitterment
emblazonment

emblematical
embroideries
embryologist
emotionalism
emphatically
encephalitis
enchantingly
encirclement
encroachment
encrustation
encyclopedia
encyclopedic
endangerment
enduringness
enfeeblement
enfranchised
Englishwoman
Englishwomen
entanglement
enterprising
entertaining
enthrallment
enthronement
enthusiastic
entomologist
entrenchment
entrepreneur
epicureanism
epidemiology
epigrammatic
Episcopalian
epistemology
equalitarian
equalization
equestrienne
equidistance
equilibrated
equivocating
equivocation
escapologist
esthetically
estrangement
eternization
ethnocentric
ethnological
etymological
evangelistic
evangelizing
evenhandedly
eviscerating
evisceration
evolutionary
evolutionism
evolutionist
exacerbating
exacerbation
exaggerating
exaggeration
exasperating
exasperation
Excellencies

exchangeable
excitability
excruciating
excruciation
excursionary
exemplifying
exhaustively
exhilarating
exhilaration
exhilarative
exorbitantly
expansionism
expansionist
expatriating
expatriation
expectorated
experiencing
experiential
experimental
experimenter
explicitness
exploitation
expostulated
expressively
expropriated
extemporized
exterminated
exterminator
externalized
extinguisher
extortionary
extortionate
extortionist
extraditable
extramarital
extrasensory
extravagance
extravagancy
extravaganza
extroversion

facilitating
factionalism
fainthearted
fait accompli
faithfulness
familiarized
fastidiously
fatherliness
fathers-in-law
fatigability
faultfinding
faute de mieux
fearlessness
fearsomeness
feasibleness
featherbrain
federalizing
feebleminded
felicitating

felicitation
feminineness
feminization
fermentation
feverishness
fiddlesticks
figuratively
flagellating
flagellation
flamboyantly
flatteringly
flimflamming
floodlighted
floriculture
fluorescence
fluoridating
fluoridation
footslogging
forbiddingly
force-feeding
formaldehyde
formlessness
fortuitously
foundational
fractionally
Frankenstein
frankincense
fraternities
fraternizing
fraudulently
freestanding
frenchifying
frenetically
fricasseeing
frictionless
friendliness
frontiersman
frontiersmen
frontispiece
fruitfulness
fuddy-duddies
functionally
functionless

galvanometer
gamesmanship
garnisheeing
gasification
genealogical
generalities
generalizing
generosities
genuflection
geochemistry
geographical
geologically
geomagnetism
geophysicist
geopolitical
geriatrician

gesticulated
ghostwriting
ghostwritten
gingerliness
gladiatorial
glassblowing
globetrotter
glockenspiel
gobbledegook
gobbledygook
good-tempered
goody-goodies
gooseberries
goose-stepped
gorgeousness
governmental
graciousness
gram-negative
gram-positive
graphologist
gratuitously
Great Britain
gregariously
guaranteeing
guardianship
guillotining
gynecologist

habeas corpus
haberdashery
habitability
habitualness
hairspliting
halftimbered
hallucinated
hamstringing
handicapping
handkerchief
handsomeness
happenstance
harbormaster
harmlessness
harmonically
harmoniously
haute couture
haute cuisine
headforemost
headmistress
headquarters
headshrinker
heartrending
heart-to-heart
heartwarming
heavy-hearted
helplessness
hemorrhaging
hereditarily
heritability
hermetically
heterosexual

hieroglyphic
high-pressure
high-spirited
hippopotamus
historically
holy of holies
homelessness
homogenizing
hopelessness
horizontally
horrifically
horrifyingly
hors de combat
horsewhipped
horticulture
hospitalized
housebreaker
housewarming
hubble-bubble
humanitarian
humanization
humorousness
hurdy-gurdies
hydrochloric
hydrodynamic
hydroplaning
hydrotherapy
hygienically
hyperbolized
hypertension
hypnotherapy
hypochondria
hypocritical
hypoglycemia
hypothecated
hypothesized
hypothetical
hysterectomy
hysterically

iconoclastic
idealization
identifiable
identifiably
idiosyncrasy
ignitability
illegalities
illegibility
illegitimacy
illegitimate
illuminating
illumination
illusiveness
illusoriness
illustrating
illustration
illustrative
immaculately
immatureness
immeasurable

immeasurably
immobilizing
immoderately
immoralities
immortalized
immovability
immunization
immutability
impartiality
impenetrable
impenetrably
imperceptive
imperfection
imperishable
impermanence
impermanency
impersonally
impersonated
impersonator
impertinence
imperviously
implantation
implicitness
impoliteness
imponderable
impregnating
impregnation
impressively
imprisonment
improperness
improvidence
inaccessible
inaccessibly
inaccuracies
inactivation
inadequacies
inadequately
inadmissible
inadmissibly
inadvertence
inadvertency
inapplicable
inarticulate
inaugurating
inauguration
inauspicious
incalculable
incalculably
incandescent
incapacitate
incapacities
incarcerated
incendiaries
incidentally
incinerating
incineration
incoherently
incommodious
incomparable
incomparably
incompatible

incompetence
incompetency
incompletely
incompletion
inconclusive
inconsistent
inconsolable
inconsolably
incontinence
incontinency
inconvenient
incorporated
incorrigible
incorrigibly
increasingly
incriminated
incrustation
indebtedness
indefeasible
indefensible
indefensibly
indefinitely
indemnifying
independence
independency
indifference
indigestible
indiscipline
indiscretion
indisputable
indisputably
indissoluble
indistinctly
individually
indoctrinate
Indo-European
ineffability
inefficiency
inequalities
ineradicable
ineradicably
inesttimably
inexperience
inexplicable
inexplicably
inexpressive
inextricable
inextricably
infidelities
infiltrating
infiltration
infiniteness
infinitively
inflammation
inflammatory
inflationary
infrequently
infringement
ingloriously
ingratiating
ingratiation

inhabitation
inhospitable
inobservance
inordinately
insalubrious
insecticidal
inseminating
insemination
insolubility
inspectorate
installation
instillation
instrumental
insufferable
insufferably
insufficient
insurability
insurrection
intellectual
intelligence
intelligible
intelligibly
intemperance
intensifying
interception
intercession
interchanged
interconnect
interdiction
interference
interjection
interjectory
interlocutor
intermediary
intermediate
interminable
interminably
intermingled
intermission
intermittent
intermitting
intermixture
internalized
interpolator
interpretive
interrelated
interrogated
interrogator
interruption
intersection
interspersed
interstellar
interstitial
intertwining
intervention
interweaving
intimateness
intimidating
intimidation
intolerantly
intoxicating

intoxication
intramurally
intransigent
intransitive
intrauterine
intriguingly
introduction
introductory
introversion
intumescence
invalidating
invalidation
inventorying
invertebrate
investigated
investigator
invigorating
invigoration
invisibility
invulnerable
irascibility
Irish whiskey
irrationally
irredeemable
irredeemably
irregularity
irrelevantly
irremediable
irremissible
irresistible
irresistibly
irresolution
irrespective
irresponsive
irreverently
irreversible
irreversibly
irritability
irritatingly
isolationism
isolationist

jack-in-the-box
jack-o'-lantern
jeopardizing
jet-propelled
Johannesburg
journalistic
jurisdiction
jurisprudent
juvenesscent

kaleidoscope
kindergarten
kleptomaniac
knight-errant

laboratories

labyrinthian
labyrinthine
lachrymosely
lady's-slipper
laissez-faire
landlessness
lasciviously
leapfrogging
legalization
legitimately
legitimating
legitimation
legitimizing
lexicography
liberalizing
lickety-split
life-and-death
lighthearted
lingua franca
liquefaction
listlessness
literariness
lithographer
lithographic
Liverpudlian
localization
loganberries
longitudinal
longshoreman
longshoremen
love children
lugubriously
luminescence
luminousness
lusciousness

mademoiselle
magistracies
magnetically
magnetometer
magnificence
magniloquent
maids of honor
maintainable
majestically
malevolently
malformation
malignancies
malleability
malnourished
malnutrition
malocclusion
maltreatment
maneuverable
manipulating
manipulation
manipulative
manipulatory
manslaughter
manufactured

manufacturer
marksmanship
marlinespike
marriageable
Marseillaise
masquerading
mass-produced
mastectomies
masturbation
materialized
mathematical
maître d'hôtel
matriarchies
matriculated
matter-of-fact
maximization
mealy-mouthed
meaningfully
mechanically
mediocrities
meditatively
meetinghouse
megalomaniac
melodramatic
memorialized
memorization
menstruating
menstruation
mercantilism
merchandised
merchandiser
meretricious
merry-go-round
mesmerically
metaboliical
metabolizing
metallurgist
metamorphism
metamorphose
metaphorical
metaphysical
methodically
meticulosity
meticulously
metropolitan
mezzo-soprano
Michelangelo
microbiology
microsurgery
middleweight
militantness
militaristic
mind-boggling
mineralizing
mineralogist
miniaturized
minimization
ministration
miraculously
mirthfulness
misadventure

misanthropic
misapprehend
miscalculate
miscellanies
misconceived
misconstrued
misdirection
misinformant
misinterpret
misleadingly
misplacement
mispronounce
misquotation
misrepresent
missionaries
misstatement
mistakenness
mistreatment
mobilization
moderateness
modification
modus vivendi
moisturizing
monetization
monistically
monkeyshines
monogramming
monometallic
monopolistic
monopolizing
monosyllabic
monosyllable
monotheistic
monotonously
monumentally
moonlighting
moralization
morning-glory
morphologist
motherliness
mothers-in-law
motivational
motorcycling
motorcyclist
motorization
mountainside
mucilaginous
muddleheaded
mulligatawny
multicolored
multifarious
multilateral
multilingual
multipartite
multipliable
multiplicand
multiplicity
municipality
munificently
muriatic acid
musicianship

mysteriously
mythological

narcissistic
narrow-minded
nationalized
naturalistic
naturalizing
nauseousness
navigability
navigational
nebulousness
necessitated
negativeness
neglectfully
neighborhood
neoclassical
nerveracking
neurasthenia
neurological
neurotically
neutralizing
nevertheless
Newfoundland
newspaperman
newspapermen
New Testament
nightclothes
nomenclature
noms de guerre
nonalcoholic
nonalignment
nonchalantly
noncombatant
noncommittal
nonconductor
nonessential
nonexistence
nonflammable
nonresidence
nonresidency
nonscheduled
nonsectarian
nonviolently
North America
northeastern
northernmost
northwestern
notabilities
notarization
notary public
notification
nouveau riche
nutritionist
nymphomaniac

obdurateness
obliterating
obliteration

obliterative
obscurantism
obscurantist
obsequiously
obsolescence
obsoleteness
obstetrician
obstreperous
occasionally
occupational
oceanography
octogenarian
officeholder
off-the-record
old-fashioned
Old Testament
oligarchical
omnipotently
omnipresence
one-upmanship
onomatopoeia
onomatopoeic
oppositeness
oppressively
optimization
orchestrated
ordinariness
organization
orienteering
ornithologic
orthodontics
orthodontist
orthodoxness
orthographic
oscilloscope
ossification
ostentatious
osteoporosis
outdistanced
outrageously
outstripping
overbalanced
overcharging
overcrowding
overemphasis
overestimate
overexertion
overgenerous
overshooting
oversimplify
oversleeping
overstepping
overthrowing
oxyacetylene

pacification
pacificatory
palatability
panchromatic
paradisiacal

paralyzation
paramilitary
paraphrasing
par excellence
parkinsonism
parochialism
parsimonious
participated
participator
particolored
particularly
partisanship
partitioning
passe-partout
passionately
passion fruit
pasteurizing
pathetically
pathological
patriarchies
peacekeeping
peccadilloes
pedantically
pediatrician
penalization
penitentiary
Pennsylvania
penny-pincher
peradventure
perambulated
perceptively
peremptorily
perestroikan
perimetrical
periodically
peripherally
permanencies
permanganate
permeability
perpetrating
perpetration
perpetuating
perpetuation
perplexities
perseverance
persistently
personalized
personifying
perspicacity
perspiration
persuasively
pertinacious
perturbation
perverseness
pestilential
petit larceny
petrifaction
pettifogging
pharmaceutic
pharmacology
pharmacopeia

phenomenally
Philadelphia
philanthropy
philharmonic
Philistinism
philodendron
philological
philosophies
philosophize
phlegmatical
phonetically
phonological
phosphoresce
photocopying
photoengrave
photographer
photographic
photogravure
photostating
phrenologist
phylacteries
physiography
physiologist
pickaninnies
pigeon breast
pigeonholing
pigmentation
pinch-hitting
pitter-patter
plagiaristic
plagiarizing
plasterboard
platitudinal
platonically
plausibility
pleasantries
Plimsoll mark
plutocracies
pocketknives
poet laureate
polarization
policyholder
politicizing
polyethylene
polymorphism
polysyllabic
polysyllable
polytheistic
polyurethane
pontifically
pontificated
Popocatepetl
popularizing
pornographer
pornographic
portentously
portmanteaux
positiveness
posteriority
postgraduate
posthumously

post meridiem
postmistress
postponement
postprandial
potentiality
pound-foolish
powerfulness
practicality
practitioner
pragmatistic
praiseworthy
prearranging
precancerous
precariously
preceptorial
preciousness
precipitated
precipitator
precisionist
precociously
precognition
precognitive
pre-Columbian
preconceived
precondition
predestinate
predetermine
predilection
predisposing
predominance
predominancy
predominated
preeminently
preexistence
prefabricate
preferential
pregnability
premeditated
premenstrual
preoccupying
preoperative
preparedness
preponderant
preponderate
preposterous
prepubescent
prerequisite
Presbyterian
presbyteries
prescription
prescriptive
presentation
presentiment
preservation
preservative
presidencies
presidential
presumptuous
presupposing
prevaricated
preventative

priestliness
priggishness
primogenitor
princeliness
principality
prizefighter
probationary
procedurally
processional
proclamation
proclivities
prodigiously
productively
productivity
professional
professorial
profundities
progesterone
projectively
projectivity
prolematical
proliferated
prolifically
prolificness
prolongation
promontories
promulgating
promulgation
propagandism
propagandist
propagandize
propensities
prophylactic
propitiation
propitiatory
propitiously
proportional
proppitiated
proprietress
proscription
proscriptive
prosecutable
proselytized
prostituting
prostitution
protactinium
protectively
protectorate
protestation
protuberance
proverbially
providential
provincially
provisionary
psephologist
pseudonymous
psychiatrist
psychologist
psychometric
psychopathic
pulverizable

pumpernickel
punctualness
purification
purposefully
putrefaction
pyromaniacal
pyrotechnics

quadrangular
quadraphonic
quadriplegia
quadriplegic
quadrivalent
quadrumanous
quantifiable
quantitative
quarantining
quarterfinal
questionable
questionably
quinquennial
quintessence
quixotically

rabbinically
radicalizing
radiographer
radioisotope
radiotherapy
raisons d'être
rambunctious
ramification
ratification
rationalized
rationalizer
razzle-dazzle
reactivating
reactivation
readableness
readjustment
reappearance
reappraising
reassembling
reassessment
reassumption
reassuringly
rebelliously
recalcitrant
recapitulate
recceptively
receivership
receptionist
recessionary
rechargeable
reciprocally
reciprocated
recklessness
recognizable
recognizably

recognizance
recollection
recompensing
reconcilable
reconcilably
reconstitute
recreational
recriminated
recuperating
recuperation
recuperative
redecorating
redecoration
rededicating
rededication
redeployment
redistribute
redundancies
reduplicated
reemphasized
reenlistment
reflationary
reflectively
refreshingly
refrigerator
regenerating
regeneration
regenerative
registration
regularities
regularizing
regurgitated
rehabilitate
reincarnated
reinvestment
rejuvenating
rejuvenation
relationship
relentlessly
reliableness
reminiscence
remonstrance
remonstrated
remorsefully
remunerating
remuneration
remunerative
rendezvoused
renunciation
reorganizing
repatriating
repatriation
repercussion
repositories
repossession
reprehension
reproduction
reproductive
reputability
resettlement
respectfully

respectively
resplendence
restaurateur
restlessness
restructured
resurrection
resuscitated
resuscitator
retrenchment
reverberated
revitalizing
rhapsodizing
rhetorically
rhododendron
rhombohedron
rhythmically
ribbonucleic
Richter scale
ricochetting
ridiculously
Rio de Janeiro
romantically
romanticized
Rosh Hashanah
ruminatively
ruralization
ruthlessness

sacrilegious
sadistically
salesmanship
sanctionable
San Francisco
sardonically
sarsaparilla
Saskatchewan
satiableness
satisfaction
satisfactory
savoy cabbage
scandalizing
scandalously
Scandinavian
scatterbrain
Scheherazade
schematizing
schismatical
scholastical
scintillated
scornfulness
scratchiness
screenwriter
scriptwriter
scrupulosity
scrupulously
scrutinnized
secessionist
secludedness
sectarianism
secularizing

sedulousness
segmentation
seismography
seismologist
self-absorbed
self-centered
self-composed
self-educated
self-effacing
self-employed
self-interest
selflessness
self-reliance
semiannually
semicircular
semidetached
semifinalist
semiofficial
semiprecious
semitropical
sensibleness
sensualizing
separability
separateness
sequentially
sequestrable
sequestrated
serrializing
severability
shamefacedly
sharecropped
sharecropper
sharpshooter
sharp-tongued
shatterproof
sheath knives
shiftingness
shilly-shally
shipbuilding
short-changed
short-circuit
short-cutting
short-sighted
Shostakovich
shuffleboard
sidestepping
sight-reading
significance
silhouetting
similarities
simple-minded
simplicities
simultaneity
simultaneous
single-handed
single-minded
single-spaced
sisterliness
sisters-in-law
sledgehammer
sleepwalking

slipperiness
slovenliness
snobbishness
sociableness
sociological
soft-pedaling
solarization
solicitation
solicitously
soliloquized
solitariness
solvableness
Solzhenitsyn
somnambulant
somnambulate
somnambulism
somnambulist
son et lumière
sonorousness
sophisticate
southeastern
southernmost
southwestern
spaciousness
specializing
specifically
speciousness
spectroscope
spectroscopy
speleologist
spellbinding
spermatozoic
spermatozoon
spick-and-span
spinsterhood
spiritualism
spiritualist
spirituality
spiritualize
spirituosity
spokesperson
spoon-feeding
sporadically
sportscaster
sportswriter
spotlessness
sprightliest
spuriousness
square-rigged
stage-managed
staggeringly
stammeringly
standardized
star-spangled
Staten Island
statistician
stealthiness
steeplechase
stenographer
stenographic
stepchildren

stepdaughter
stereophonic
stereoscopic
stereotyping
stigmatizing
stout-hearted
Stradivarius
straightaway
straightedge
straitjacket
stranglehold
strangulated
stratosphere
strawberries
streamlining
streetwalker
streptococci
streptomycin
stridulation
stroboscopic
strong-minded
structurally
stubbornness
studiousness
stupefaction
stupendously
stutteringly
subassembler
subcommittee
subconscious
subcontinent
subcutaneous
subjectively
subjectivity
subliminally
submissively
subnormality
subordinated
subscription
subsequently
subservience
subserviency
subsidiaries
substantiate
substantival
substituting
substitution
substructure
subterranean
subversively
successfully
successional
successively
succinctness
sufficiently
suggestively
suitableness
superannuate
supercharged
supercharger
supercilious

superhighway
superimposed
supernatural
superstition
supervention
supplemental
supplicating
supplication
supplicatory
suppressible
surmountable
surprisingly
surrealistic
surroundings
surveillance
suspiciously
swashbuckler
sweepingness
sweet-and-sour
switch-hitter
symbolically
sympathizing
synchronized
synchronizer
synthesizing
systematical
systematized
systematizer
systemically

tabernacular
tactlessness
tangentially
tangibleness
tastefulness
tautological
teachability
teaspoonfuls
teaspoonsful
technicality
technocratic
technologies
technologist
telegraphese
Teleprompter
telescopical
temporalness
tercentenary
tergiversate
terribleness
terrifically
terrifyingly
tessellating
tessellation
testamentary
testosterone
thankfulness
thanksgiving
theatrically
thematically

theocratical
theoretician
theorization
theosophical
therapeutics
therapeutist
thermometric
thermostatic
thick-skinned
thievishness
thin-skinned
thoroughbred
thoroughfare
thoroughness
thoughtfully
threequarter
thundercloud
thunderstorm
ticklishness
timelessness
timorousness
tiresomeness
togetherness
tolerability
tortuousness
totalitarian
toxicologist
tractability
tradespeople
tragicalness
trailblazing
traitorously
trajectories
trampolinist
tranquilized
tranquilizer
tranquillity
tranquillize
tranquilness
transcendent
transcribing
transeptally
transferable
transference
transferring
transfigured
transfusable
transfusible
transgressor
transitional
transitively
transitivity
transitorily
translatable
translucence
translucency
transmigrate
transmission
transmissive
transmitting
transmutable

transmutably
transoceanic
transpacific
transparency
transposable
transsection
transshipped
transversely
transvestism
transvestite
Transylvania
trapshooting
tremendously
triangularly
triangulated
triflingness
trigonometry
triplicating
triplication
triumphantly
trivialities
trivializing
troublemaker
truthfulness
tuberculosis
tumultuously
turbocharged
tu-whit tu-whoo
typification
tyrannically

ubiquitously
ultimateness
ultraliberal
umbrageously
unacceptable
unacceptably
unaccustomed
unacquainted
unaffectedly
unanswerable
unappealable
unappetizing
unassailable
unattainable
unattractive
unauthorized
unbelievable
unbelievably
unchallenged
unchangeable
uncharitable
uncharitably
unclassified
uncommonness
unconformity
unconsidered
uncontrolled
unconvincing
uncritically

uncultivated
undemocratic
undependable
underbellies
underclothes
undercoating
undercurrent
undercutting
undergarment
underpinning
underscoring
understating
understudied
understudies
undervaluing
underwriting
underwritten
undetermined
undigestible
undiplomatic
undiscovered
uneconomical
unemployable
unemployment
uneventfully
unexpectedly
unexpressive
unfaithfully
unfathomable
unflattering
unforgivable
unfrequented
unfriendlier
ungainliness
ungovernable
ungraciously
ungratefully
unhealthiest
unhesitating
unidentified
unilaterally
unimaginable
unimportance
unimpressive
uninterested
unionization
United States
universality
universities
unkindliness
unlawfulness
unlikelihood
unlikeliness
unmercifully
unmistakable
unmistakably
unobtainable
unofficially
unparalleled
unpardonable
unpleasantly

unpopularity
unprejudiced
unprincipled
unproductive
unprofitable
unquestioned
unreasonable
unreasonably
unrecognized
unregenerate
unremarkable
unreservedly
unrestrained
unrestricted
unsatisfying
unscientific
unscrupulous
unseasonable
unseasonably
unseemliness
unsegregated
unstableness
unstructured
unsuccessful
unsurprising
unsuspecting
unsweettened
unthinkingly
untimeliness
untruthfully
unwieldiness
unworthiness
urbanization

vainglorious
valorization
valorousness
valuableness
Van Allen belt
vanquishable
vaporescence
vaporishness
vaporization
variableness
vaudevillian
vegetational
venerability
vengefulness
venomousness
verification
verticalness
veterinarian
vice-consular
victoriously
vilification
villainously
vindictively
virtuousness
vitalization
vituperating
vituperation
vituperative
vivification
vocabularies
vocationally
vociferously
volcanically

voluminously
voluptuously

walkie-talkie
watchfulness
weatherglass
weatherproof
well-balanced
well-disposed
well-grounded
well-informed
well-mannered
welterweight
westernizing
whencesoever
whippoorwill
wholehearted
will-o'-the-wisp
withstanding
Wittgenstein
wooden-headed
woolly-headed
wretchedness

yellowhammer
yellow jacket
youthfulness

zoogeography
zoologically

abnormalities
abortifacient
acceptability
accessibility
accident-prone
acclimatizing
accommodating
accommodation
accommodative
accompaniment
accomplishing
accouterments
accreditation
acculturation
acknowledging
actualization
administrator
admissibility
adventuresome
adventurously
advertisement
aesthetically
affenpinscher
affirmatively
afforestation
agglomerating
agglomeration
agglutinating
agglutination
agglutinative
agriculturist
airworthiness
allegorically
alphabetizing
alternatively
ambassadorial
ambidexterity
ambitiousness
Americanizing
amniocenteses
amniocentesis
amplification
anachronistic
anatomization
anesthetizing
anglicization
Anglo-American
animadversion
anniversaries
anthropologic
anthropometry
antibacterial
antiballistic
anticlimactic
anticlockwise
anticoagulant
antihistamine
antilogarithm
antipersonnel
apathetically
applicability

apportionment
apprehensible
appropriately
appropriating
appropriation
approximately
approximation
archaeologist
archeological
archipelagoes
architectonic
architectural
argumentation
argumentative
aristocracies
arithmetician
artificiality
ascertainable
ascertainment
assassinating
assassination
assertiveness
assiduousness
asthmatically
astonishingly
astronautical
atmospherical
authenticated
authoritarian
authoritative
authorization
autobiography
automatically
axiomatically

baccalaureate
beatification
Beaufort scale
béchamel sauce
behavioristic
belles lettres
belligerently
beneficiaries
better-looking
bewilderingly
bibliographer
bibliographic
bicentenaries
biodegradable
bloodcurdling
bombastically
bougainvillea
boysenberries
brainstorming
breast-feeding
broken-hearted
brotherliness
brothers-in-law
brutalization
bureaucracies

butterfingers

calcification
calculability
camera obscura
cannibalizing
caravansaries
carbon dioxide
carboniferous
carbonization
cartilaginous
catchment area
catechization
categorically
catheterizing
cat-o'-nine-tails
cauterization
cerebrospinal
ceremoniously
certification
characterized
chili con carne
choreographer
choreographic
Christianized
Christmastide
chromatically
chronological
chrysanthemum
cinematograph
circularizing
circumambient
circumference
circumspectly
circumvention
clarification
claustropobic
cocker spaniel
coeducational
collaborating
collaboration
colloquialism
commemorating
commemoration
commemorative
commercialism
commercialize
commiserating
commiseration
communicating
communication
communicative
companionable
companionship
comparability
comparatively
compartmented
compassionate
compatibility
complementary

complimentary
comprehension
comprehensive
computerizing
concatenation
concentrating
concentration
conceptualize
condescending
condescension
conditionally
confectionery
confederacies
confederation
configuration
conflagration
confrontation
conglomerated
congratulated
congressional
congresswoman
congresswomen
congruousness
consanguinity
conscientious
consciousness
consecutively
consequential
conservatoire
considerately
consideration
consistencies
consolidating
consolidation
conspicuously
constellation
consternation
consultancies
contaminating
contamination
contemplating
contemplation
contemplative
contentedness
contingencies
contortionist
contraception
contraceptive
contradiction
contradictory
contrastingly
contravention
contributable
controversial
controversies
convalescence
corps de ballet
Corpus Christi
correspondent
corresponding
corrigibility

corroborating
corroboration
corroborative
corroboratory
cosmetologist
countenancing
counteractive
counterattack
countercharge
counterfeiter
counterweight
courts-martial
craftsmanship
creditability
criminologist
crotchetiness

daguerreotype
Dandie Dinmont
dastardliness
daughter-in-law
decaffeinated
deceitfulness
decentralized
declassifying
decomposition
decompression
decontaminate
decontrolling
defensibility
deferentially
deforestation
deliciousness
delinquencies
demagnetizing
democratizing
demonstrating
demonstration
demonstrative
denationalize
denaturalized
deoxygenating
deoxygenation
dermatologist
descriptively
desegregating
desegregation
desensitizing
destructively
deteriorating
deterioration
determination
deterministic
devastatingly
developmental
diagnostician
diametrically
dictatorially
differentiate
digestibility

dillydallying
disadvantaged
disappearance
discoloration
disconcerting
disconnection
discontinuing
discontinuity
discontinuous
discourtesies
discreditable
discrepancies
discretionary
discriminated
disembarkment
disembodiment
disemboweling
disengagement
disentangling
disfigurement
disfranchised
disgracefully
disheartening
disintegrated
disinterested
dismemberment
disobediently
disorientated
disparagement
disparagingly
dispassionate
dispossession
disproportion
disqualifying
disrespectful
dissatisfying
disseminating
dissemination
dissimilarity
dissimilating
dissimilation
dissimilitude
dissimulating
dissimulation
distastefully
distinctively
distinguished
distressingly
documentation
domesticating
domestication
domesticities
Doppler effect
doublejointed
Down's syndrome
dramatization
dyed-in-the-wool

eavesdropping
eccentrically

educationally
effectiveness
effervescence
efficaciously
efflorescence
egocentricity
elaborateness
electrocuting
electrocution
electrolyzing
electromagnet
electromotive
electroplated
elephantiasis
elysian fields
embarrassment
embellishment
embryological
eminence grise
eminent domain
encapsulating
encapsullated
encouragement
encouragingly
encyclopaedia
encyclopaedic
endocrinology
energetically
enfranchising
enigmatically
enlightenment
entertainment
entomological
environmental
environmental
equilibrating
equilibration
ergonomically
esprit de corps
establishment
Eucharistical
euphemistical
evangelically
everlastingly
exaggeratedly
exceptionable
exceptionally
exclusiveness
excommunicant
excommunicate
exhibitionism
exhibitionist
expansibility
expansiveness
expectorating
expectoration
expeditionary
expeditiously
expendability
explosiveness
exponentially

expostulating
expostulation
expostulatory
expressionism
expressionist
expropriating
expropriation
exquisiteness
extemporizing
exterminating
extermination
externalizing
exterritorial
extraordinary
extrapolation
extravagantly

falsification
familiarizing
fantastically
fascinatingly
favorableness
featherweight
femmes fatales
ferociousness
ferroconcrete
ferromagnetic
fertilization
feudalization
fictionalized
floodlighting
foolhardiness
foreknowledge
forgetfulness
formalization
fortification
fortuneteller
fossilization
fragmentation
franchisement
frequentative
frighteningly
functionalism
functionalist
functionaries
fundamentally
funeral parlor

gamma globulin
Geiger counter
generalissimo
geometrically
gerontologist
gesticulating
gesticulation
gesticulatory
glamorization
glamorousness
globetrotting

glorification
goose-stepping
grammatically
grandchildren
granddaughter
grandiloquent
gratification
gravitational
grief-stricken
grotesqueness
gubernatorial
gynecological

Haile Selassie
hallucinating
hallucination
hallucinatory
hazardousness
heartbreaking
heartlessness
helter-skelter
hemispherical
hermaphrodite
heterogeneity
heterogeneous
high-pressured
hilariousness
homosexuality
horrification
horsewhipping
horticultural
hospitalities
hospitalizing
housebreaking
huckleberries
hundredweight
hybridization
hydraulically
hydrocephalic
hydrocephalus
hydrodynamics
hydroelectric
hyperbolizing
hypercritical
hypochondriac
hyposensitize
hypothecating
hypothecation
hypothesizing

ichthyologist
identicalness
ideologically
idiomatically
idiosyncratic
ignominiously
illegibleness
imaginatively
immateriality

immortalizing
immutableness
impalpability
impartialness
impassability
impassibility
impassiveness
impeccability
imperceptible
imperceptibly
imperfectness
imperialistic
imperiousness
impermanently
impersonating
impersonation
impertinently
imperturbable
imperturbably
impetuousness
implacability
importunities
impossibility
impracticable
impressionism
impressionist
impressionist
improbability
improprieties
improvability
improvidently
improvisation
impulsiveness
inadvertently
inappreciably
inappropriate
incandescence
incapacitated
incarcerating
incarceration
incombustible
incommunicado
incompetently
inconceivable
inconceivably
incongruities
incongruously
inconsiderate
inconsistency
incontestable
inconvenience
incorporating
incorporation
incorruptible
incorruptibly
incredibility
incredulously
incriminating
incrimination
indefatigable
indefatigably

independently
indescribable
indescribably
indeterminacy
indeterminate
indifferently
indiscernible
indispensable
indisposition
individualist
individuality
individualize
indoctrinated
industrialism
industrialist
industrialize
industriously
ineffectively
ineffectually
inefficacious
inefficiently
ineligibility
inevitability
inexhaustible
inexorability
inexperienced
inexpressible
inexpressibly
infallibility
infinitesimal
inflexibility
inflorescence
informational
inhospitality
inopportunity
inquisitively
inquisitorial
insatiability
insectivorous
insensibility
insensitivity
insignificant
insincerities
insociability
inspirational
instabilities
instantaneous
instinctively
institutional
insubordinate
insubstantial
insufficience
insufficiency
insupportable
insusceptible
intangibility
intelligently
intentionally
interbreeding
interchanging
intercultural

interestingly
intergalactic
interlocution
interlocutory
intermarriage
intermediator
intermingling
intermittence
intermittency
internalizing
international
interpersonal
interpolation
interposition
interrelating
interrogating
interrogation
interrogative
interspersing
interspersion
intransigence
intransigency
intravenously
intrinsically
introspection
introspective
invariability
inventiveness
investigating
investigation
investigative
investigåtory
invincibility
inviolability
involuntarily
irrationality
irreclaimable
irrecoverable
irrelevancies
irreplaceable
irrepressible
irrepressibly
irresponsible
irresponsibly
irretrievable
irretrievably
italicization

jitterbugging
jurisprudence
justification
justificatory
juxtaposition

kaleidoscopic
knowledgeable
knowledgeably
knuckleduster

lackadaisical
lady-in-waiting
Latin-American
laughingstock
leisureliness
letter-perfect
letters patent
lexicographer
lexicographic
Liebfraumilch
light-fingered
lithesomeness
locum tenentes
long-suffering
lucrativeness
ludicrousness

Machiavellian
magisterially
magna cum laude
magnanimously
magnification
magnificently
malabsorption
maladaptation
maladjustment
maladminister
maladroitness
malleableness
manageability
manifestation
mantelshelves
manufacturing
marketability
marrons glacés
Massachusetts
mass-producing
materialistic
materializing
maternalistic
mathematician
matriculating
matriculation
measurability
mechanization
Mediterranean
melodiousness
memorializing
ménages à trois
merchandising
mercurochrome
meritocracies
mesmerization
metallurgical
metamorphosed
metamorphoses
metamorphosis
meteorologist
methodologies
methodologist

microanalysis
microcomputer
microorganism
mineralogical
miniaturizing
miscalculated
miscalculator
miscegenation
miscellaneous
mischievously
misconceiving
misconception
misconstruing
misemployment
miserableness
misgovernment
mismanagement
mispronounced
mistrustfully
mistrustingly
misunderstand
misunderstood
modernization
modus operandi
mollification
momentousness
monarchically
monochromatic
monochromical
monocotyledon
monogrammatic
monometallism
mononucleosis
monstrosities
morphological
mortification
mother-of-pearl
mouthwatering
multinational
multitudinous
mummification
mystification

nationalistic
nationalities
nationalizing
navigableness
necessitating
nefariousness
negligibility
negotiability
neoclassicism
nervewracking
niggardliness
nitroglycerin
nonagenarian
nonaggression
nonconformist
nonconformity
nonresistance

nonsensically
normalization
northeasterly
northeastward
northerliness
northwesterly
northwestward
nostalgically
notoriousness
nullification
nutritionally

objectionable
objectionably
objectiveness
observational
observatories
obsessionally
obstinateness
oceanographer
oceanographic
offhandedness
oleomargarine
ophthalmology
opportunistic
opportunities
orchestrating
orchestration
orgiastically
ornamentation
ornithologist
outdistancing
outspokenness
outstandingly
overanxiously
overbalancing
overemphasize
overestimated
overpopulated
overstatement
oystercatcher

painstakingly
panic-stricken
panoramically
paradoxically
parallelogram
paraphernalia
parasitically
parenthetical
Parkinson's law
parliamentary
participating
participation
participative
particularity
particularize
passionflower
paterfamilias

paternalistic
patriotically
patronizingly
peculiarities
pedagogically
penetrability
pepper-and-salt
perambulating
perambulation
perambulatory
peregrination
perfectionism
perfectionist
perfunctorily
perishability
perpendicular
personalities
personalizing
perspicacious
petrification
petrochemical
pharmaceutics
pharmacopoeia
phenobarbital
philanthropic
philosophical
phosphoresced
physiognomies
physiognomist
physiographic
physiological
physiotherapy
picturesquely
platitudinize
platitudinous
plausibleness
pluralization
pneumatically
poets laureate
poliomyelitis
polychromatic
polychromatic
pontificating
possibilities
powerlessness
pragmatically
preadolescent
precautionary
precipitately
precipitating
precipitation
precipitative
preconceiving
preconception
predestinated
predetermined
predeterminer
predicability
predominantly
predominating
predomination

prefabricated
preferability
preliminaries
preliminarily
prematureness
premeditating
premeditation
premeditative
premonitorily
preoccupation
preparatorily
preponderance
preponderancy
preponderated
prepossessing
prepossession
preternatural
prevaricating
prevarication
prime meridian
primogeniture
prisoner of war
privatization
probabilities
probationally
procrastinate
professorship
profitability
prognosticate
progressively
prohibitively
projectionist
proliferating
proliferation
proliferative
promiscuously
pronounceable
pronouncement
pronunciation
propagandized
propagational
prophetically
propittiating
proportionate
proselytizing
prostaglandin
protectionist
protestantism
Protestantism
provincialism
provincialist
provinciality
provincialize
provisionally
provocatively
pseudoscience
psychoanalyst
psychoanalyze
psychobiology
psychodynamic
psychogenesis

psychogenetic
psychological
psychosomatic
psychotherapy
psychotically
ptotectionism
pulverization
punctiliously
puritakically
pusillanimity
pusillanimous

quadrilateral
quadrillionth
quadruplicate
qualification
qualitatively
quarantinable
quartermaster
quasijudicial
questioningly
questionnaire
quicktempered
quintillionth

radioactivity
rapprochement
ratiocination
rationalistic
rationalizing
reactionaries
realistically
rearrangement
reasonability
recalcitrance
recalcitrancy
recapitulated
receptiveness
reciprocating
reciprocation
reciprocative
recommendable
reconcilement
reconnoitered
recriminating
recrimination
recriminative
recriminatory
rectification
redevelopment
redistributed
reduplicating
reduplication
reemphasizing
reenforcement
reexamination
reforestation
refrigerating
refrigeration

refrigeriated
regimentation
regretfulness
regurgitating
regurgitation
rehabilitated
reimbursement
reincarnating
reincarnation
reinforcement
reinstatement
remonstrating
remorselessly
rendezvousing
reprehensible
reproachfully
republicanism
resplendently
restructuring
resuscitating
resuscitation
retroactively
retrogression
retrogressive
retrospection
retrospective
reverberating
reverberation
revolutionary
revolutionist
revolutionize
rhapsodically
righteousness
roller bearing
roller coaster
romanticizing
Rorschach test
rutherfordium

sacrosanctity
sadomasochism
sadomasochist
salaciousness
sanctimonious
sarcastically
scandalmonger
scarification
schematically
schizophrenia
schizophrenic
scholarliness
scholasticism
schoolteacher
scintillating
scintillation
seaworthiness
sedentariness
sedimentation
self-abasement
self-addressed

self-adjusting
self-assertive
self-assurance
selfcollected
self-confessed
self-confident
self-conscious
self-contained
self-criticism
self-deception
self-deceptive
self-defeating
self-evidently
self-governing
self-important
self-indulgent
self-inflicted
self-operating
self-possessed
self-propelled
self-restraint
self-righteous
self-sacrifice
self-satisfied
semiautomatic
semiclassical
semiconductor
semiconscious
semipermanent
semipermeable
sensationally
senselessness
sensibilities
sensitivities
sensitization
sententiously
sentimentally
sequestrating
sequestration
Serbo-Croatian
serialization
serious-minded
sewing machine
Shakespearean
shamelessness
sharecropping
shock absorber
short-changing
short-tempered
sidesplitting
significantly
signification
silver-tongued
single-spacing
singularities
sleeplessness
socialization
socioeconomic
solemnization
soliloquizing
somnambulated

sophisticated
soulsearching
southeasterly
southwesterly
spasmodically
specification
spectacularly
speculatively
spiritualized
splendiferous
spontaneously
sportsmanlike
sportsmanship
sprightliness
square-dancing
squeamishness
stabilization
stage-managing
standardizing
statesmanlike
statesmanship
statistically
steadfastness
steppingstone
sterilization
stigmatically
stipendiaries
strangulating
strangulation
strategically
stratocumulus
stratospheric
streptococcus
strikebreaker
stripcropping
structuralism
structuralist
stylistically
subcontractor
subordinately
subordinating
subordination
subordinative
subserviently
subsidization
substantially
substantiated
substantively
substitutable
subterraneous
subversionary
sufficiencies
sulfanilamide
summa cum laude
summarization
sumptuousness
superabundant
superannuated
supercharging
superficially
superfluously

superimposing
superlatively
supernumerary
superstitious
supplantation
supplementary
suppositories
surreptitious
swashbuckling
sycophantical
syllabication
symbolization
symmetrically
symptomatical
synchronistic
synchronizing
synchronously
synthetically
systematizing

tableau vivant
talkativeness
tantalizingly
tastelessness
taxonomically
teachableness
technicalness
technocracies
technological
temperability
temperamental
temperateness
tempestuously
temporariness
temporization
temporizingly
tenaciousness
tendentiously
tender-hearted
tentativeness
tercentennial
terminologies
terpsichorean
terrestrially
terrorization
thanklessness
theatricalism
theatricality
theologically
theoretically
therapeutical
thermodynamic
thermonuclear
thermoplastic
Thessalonians
thoroughgoing
thoughtlessly
threateningly
thundershower
thunderstruck

timeconsuming
toastmistress
tolerableness
tonsillectomy
topographical
tortoiseshell
toxicological
tracheotomies
track-and-field
tractableness
traditionally
tragicomedies
tranquilizing
tranquillized
tranquillizer
transactional
transatlantic
transcendence
transcription
transcriptive
transfiguring
transformable
transgression
transgressive
transistorize
translational
transliterate
translucently
transmigrated
transmigrator
transmissible
transmittable
transmutation
transparently
transpiration
transportable
transposition
transshipment
transshipping
traumatically
treacherously
tremulousness
triangularity
triangulating
triangulation
trigonometric
troublemaking
trustworthily
typographical

unaccompanied
unaccountable
unaccountably
unadulterated
unadvisedness
unanimousness
unappreciated
unbendingness
unboundedness
unceasingness

unceremonious
uncertainness
uncertainties
uncircumcised
uncleanliness
uncomfortable
uncomfortably
uncomplaining
uncomplicated
uncompromised
unconcernedly
unconditional
unconquerable
unconsciously
unconstrained
uncooperative
uncoordinated
undauntedness
undecidedness
underachiever
undercarriage
underclassman
underclothing
underemployed
underestimate
underfinanced
undergraduate
understanding
understudying
underutilized
undisciplined
unearthliness
unemotionally
unequivocally
unexceptional
unfamiliarity
unfashionable
unfeelingness
unforgettable
unforgettably
unfortunately
unfriendliest
ungrammatical
unhealthiness
unhelpfulness
unilateralism
unilateralist
unimaginative
unimpeachable
unimpeachably
uninhabitable
unintelligent
unintentional
uninteresting
uninterrupted
United Kingdom
United Nations
universalness
unjustifiable
unjustifiably
unmentionable

unnaturalness
unnecessarily
unobtrusively
unprecedented
unpredictable
unpredictably
unpretentious
unqualifiedly
unquestioning
unreliability
unremittingly
unselfishness
unsightliness
unspectacular
unsympathetic
untrustworthy
unwillingness
unworldliness

valedictorian

variationally
vegetarianism
venerableness
ventriloquial
ventriloquism
ventriloquist
ventriloquize
venturousness
veraciousness
verbalization
verifiability
veritableness
vernacularism
versatileness
versification
vicariousness
vice-consulate
vice-president
victimization
videocassette

violoncellist
visualization
vitrification
vulcanization
vulgarization
vulnerability

water moccasin
weather-beaten
well-appointed
well-brought-up
well-connected
well-preserved
well-thought-of
wheeler-dealer
window-shopped
winterization
woolgathering
word processor
worthlessness

abstemiousness
accomplishment
accountability
acknowledgment
administration
administrative
advantageously
affectionately
aforementioned
aggrandizement
aggressiveness
air-conditioned
air conditioner
alphabetically
anagrammatical
angina pectoris
anthropologist
antiperspirant
antiseptically
apologetically
apprenticeship
archaeological
archiepiscopal
arithmetically
arrondissement
articulateness
astrologically
astronomically
astrophysicist
attractiveness
aurora borealis
authenticating
authentication
autobiographer
autobiographic
autocratically
autosuggestion

bacteriologist
barometrically
bearnaise sauce
beautification
bibliographies
bioengineering
biographically
boisterousness
bouquets garnis
breathlessness
Brobdingnagian
butterfingered

capitalization
carbon monoxide
cardiovascular
catherine wheel
centralization
characteristic
characterizing
chromatography

cinematography
circumlocution
circumlocutory
circumnavigate
circumspection
circumstantial
classification
claustrophobia
coincidentally
commensuration
comprehensible
comprehensibly
concessionaire
confidentially
conglomerating
conglomeration
congratulating
congratulation
congratulatory
congregational
conjunctivitis
consanguineous
conservatively
conservatories
conspiratorial
constabularies
constituencies
constitutional
constructively
contagiousness
contemporaries
contemptuously
conventionally
conversational
correspondence
corruptibility
counterbalance
counterculture
countermeasure
Coxsackie virus
crème de la crème
cross-pollinate
cross-reference
Czechoslovakia

daughters-in-law
decentralizing
decimalization
decontaminated
dehumanization
demobilization
democratically
demoralization
denationalized
denaturalizing
denazification
denominational
dermatological
detoxification
diagrammatical

diplomatically
disadvantaging
disappointment
disapprobation
disapprobation
disapprovingly
disarrangement
disciplinarian
discombobulate
disconsolately
discontentedly
discontentment
discontinuance
discouragement
discourteously
discriminately
discriminating
discrimination
discriminatory
discursiveness
disembarkation
disembowelment
disenchantment
disenfranchise
disequilibrium
disfranchising
disgruntlement
disinclination
disinformation
disingenuously
disinheritance
disintegrating
disintegration
disorderliness
disorientation
dispensability
divertissement
doublebreasted
double entendre

eccentricities
ecclesiastical
editorializing
educationalist
egalitarianism
electronically
electroplating
electrotherapy
embarrassingly
emblematically
emulsification
enfant terrible
entertainingly
epidemiologist
ethnographical
ethnologically
etymologically
eustachian tube
evangelicalism
evangelization

evenhandedness
excommunicable
excommunicated
excruciatingly
existentialism
existentialist
experimentally
expressionless
extemporaneous
extinguishable
extinguishment

faits accomplis
farsightedness
fastidiousness
featherbedding
featherbrained
federalization
fictionalizing
fictitiousness
floriculturist
foreordination
fortuitousness
fraternization
fructification
fundamentalism
fundamentalist

generalization
gentrification
geocentrically
geographically
geopolitically
grandiloquence
gregariousness
gyrostabilizer

hallucinogenic
hierarchically
high-pressuring
historicalness
histrionically
horticulturist
hydrotherapist
hypersensitive
hyperventilate
hypothetically
hysterectomies

ichthyological
identification
idiosyncrasies
illegitimacies
illegitimately
immaculateness
immaterialness
impassableness

impassibleness
imperativeness
impermeability
imperviousness
implacableness
implausibility
implementation
impoverishment
impregnability
impressionable
impressionably
impressiveness
improbableness
inalienability
inarticulately
inauspiciously
incapacitating
incapacitation
incommensurate
incommunicable
inconsiderable
incontrollable
inconvenienced
indecipherable
indecisiveness
indestructible
indeterminable
indiscriminate
individualized
indoctrinating
indoctrination
indomitability
indubitability
inflammability
inflectionless
infrangibility
infrastructure
in loco parentis
inscrutability
inseparability
insignificance
insufficiently
insuppressible
insurmountable
intangibleness
intellectually
intelligentsia
interdependent
intermediaries
intermediating
intermediation
intermittently
interpenetrate
interplanetary
interpretation
interpretative
intractability
irreconcilable
irreconcilably
irregularities
irreproachable

irrevocability

jurisdictional

knickerbockers

labor-intensive
latitudinarian
Latter-day Saint
legalistically
legitimization
liberalization
libidinousness
licentiousness
lightheartedly
linguistically
linquae francae
longitudinally
loquaciousness

manageableness
mass-production
mathematically
matriarchalism
matter-of-course
Maundy Thursday
melancholiness
Mephistopheles
mesdemoiselles
metamorphosing
metaphorically
metempsychosis
meteorological
methodological
meticulousness
microbiologist
microprocessor
militarization
mineralization
misapplication
misappropriate
miscalculating
miscalculation
misinformation
misinterpreter
mispronouncing
monopolization
motionlessness
multiple-choice
multiplication
municipalities

naturalization
Nebuchadnezzar
neighborliness
neocolonialism

neutralization
newspaperwoman
newspaperwomen
noblesse oblige
nolo contendere
noncommittally
noncooperation
nonrestrictive
notaries public
noteworthiness
nouveaux riches

obsequiousness
obstructionism
obstructionism
obstructionist
occupationally
open-mindedness
optimistically
organizational
ornithological
ostentatiously
overconfidence
overemphasized
overestimating
overindulgence
overpopulation
oversimplified
over-the-counter
overwhelmingly

paleontologist
Papua New Guinea
parapsychology
participatoroy
passionateness
pasteurization
pâté de fois gras
pathologically
penetrableness
penitentiaries
perceptibility
perceptiveness
peremptoriness
perishableness
permissibility
permissiveness
petit bourgeois
petrochemistry
phantasmagoria
phantasmagoric
pharmaceutical
pharmacologist
pharmacopoeial
philanthropies
philanthropist
phosphorescent
phosphorescing
photoengraving

photosensitive
photosynthesis
physiognomical
pithecanthropi
plea bargaining
pneumoconiosis
politicization
polymerization
popularization
possessiveness
postindustrial
potentialities
practicability
practicalities
preadolescence
prearrangement
precariousness
precociousness
predestinating
predestination
predetermining
predictability
predisposition
prefabricating
prefabrication
preferableness
preferentially
preponderantly
preponderating
preponderation
preposterously
Pre-Rapphaelite
presentability
president-elect
pressurization
presumptuously
presupposition
preventability
prima ballerina
principalities
prisoners of war
procrastinated
procrastinator
prodigiousness
professionally
professorially
profitableness
prognosticated
prognosticator
prohibitionist
propagandistic
propagandizing
proportionable
proportionably
proportionally
proprietorship
prosthodontics
prosthodontist
protectiveness
providentially
provincialized

psychoanalysis
psychoanalytic
psychoanalyzed
psychoneuroses
psychoneurosis
psychoneurotic
public-spirited
pugnaciousness

quantification
quintessential

radio frequency
radiotelephone
radiotherapist
reasonableness
rebelliousness
recapitulating
recapitulation
recommendation
reconciliation
reconfirmation
reconnaissance
reconnoitering
reconstruction
redistributing
redistribution
refractoriness
rehabilitating
rehabilitation
rehabilitative
remarkableness
reorganization
representation
representative
respectability
respectfulness
responsibility
responsiveness
revitalization
revivification
Rimsky-Korsakov
rough-and-tumble

sanctification
satisfactorily
scandalization
scatterbrained
schoolchildren
scientifically
scrupulousness
scrutinizingly
secularization
segregationist
self-abnegation
self-confidence
self-controlled
self-correcting

self-discipline
self-expression
self-government
self-importance
self-indulgence
self-interested
self-possession
self-protection
self-respecting
self-satisfying
self-sufficient
self-supporting
semiconducting
sensationalism
sensationalist
sensualization
sentimentalist
sentimentality
sentimentalize
septuagenarian
serviceability
servomechanism
Shalom aleichem
shilly-shallied
short-circuited
simplification
simplistically
simultaneously
single-breasted
single-handedly
single-mindedly
slatternliness
slaughterhouse
sluggardliness
sociologically
sociopolitical
solidification
somnambulating
somnambulation
sophisticating
sophistication
specialization
spiritlessness
spiritualizing
spring-cleaning
staphylococcus
stigmatization
stratification
stretchability
stultification
stupendousness
subconsciously
subjectiveness
submicroscopic
submissiveness
subsequentness
substantiality
substantiating
substantiation
substantiative
substantivally

substitutional
subversiveness
successfulness
successiveness
suggestibility
suggestiveness
superabundance
superannuating
superannuation
superciliously
supererogatory
superficiality
superintendent
supernaturally
superphosphate
superscription
supersonically
superstructure
susceptibility
suspiciousness
sympathizingly
systematically
systematicness

tablespoonfuls
tablespoonsful
Tasmanian devil
tatterdemalion
tautologically
technicalities
telepathically
tercentenaries
terminological
territoriality
theocratically
theosophically
thermodynamics
thermoelectric
thoughtfulness
to-ing and fro-ing
traditionalism
traditionalist
tranquillizing
transcendental
transformation
transformative
transistorized
transitionally
transitiveness
transitoriness
transliterated
transmigrating
transmigration
transmigratory
transmissivity
transparencies
transplantable
transportation
tremendousness
tridimensional

trivialization
troubleshooter
tumultuousness
two-dimensional

ubiquitousness
ultrareligious
umbrageousness
unacknowledged
unaffectedness
unappreciative
unapproachable
unappropriated
unavailability
unavoidability
unbearableness
unbecomingness
unclassifiable
uncompromising
unconscionable
unconscionably
uncontrollable
uncontrollably
unconventional
unconvincingly
undeniableness
underdeveloped
underestimated
undernourished
underpopulated
undersecretary
understandable
understandably
understatement
undesirability
unexpectedness
unfaithfulness
unfriendliness
ungraciousness
ungratefulness
unhesitatingly
unidentifiable
unintelligible
unintelligibly
unpleasantness
unprofessional
unquestionable
unquestionably
unrecognizable
unrestrainedly
unsatisfactory
unsuccessfully
unsurprisingly

vegetationless
ventriloquized
verifiableness
verisimilitude
vice-chancellor

vice-consulship
vice-presidency
victoriousness
villainousness
vindictiveness
vivisectionist
voluminousness

voluptuousness

water-repellent
water-resistant
weatherability

weightlessness
well-thought-out
westernization
whippersnapper
wholeheartedly
window-shopping
word processing

acclimatization
acknowledgeable
aerodynamically
agriculturalist
air conditioning
Americanization
anorexia nervosa
anthropocentric
anthropological
anthropomorphic
appropriateness
archeologically
architecturally
atherosclerosis
attorney-general
aurora australis
authoritatively
autobiographies

bacteriological

catch-as-catch-can
cerebrovascular
chargé d'affaires
chronologically
cinematographer
circularization
circumscription
circumstantiate
compassionately
complimentarily
computerization
condescendingly
confidentiality
conscientiously
conservationist
conspicuousness
contemplatively
contemporaneous
conventionalism
conventionality
conventionalize
correspondingly
counterclaimant
counterirritant
crystallization
curriculum vitae
Czechoslovakian

decontaminating
decontamination
defenselessness
delirium tremens
demagnetization
dementia praecox
democratization
denationalizing
destructibility

destructiveness
differentiation
disadvantageous
disappointingly
discombobulated
disconcertingly
discontinuation
discontinuities
disenfranchised
disentanglement
disillusionment
disinterestedly
disorganization
dispassionately
disrespectfully
dissatisfaction
dissatisfactory
distinctiveness
distinguishable
diversification
dolichocephalic
Dow-Jones average

electrification
electrodynamics
electromagnetic
emancipationist
eminences grises
endocrinologist
enfranchisement
entente cordiale
entrepreneurial
environmentally
Episcopalianism
etherealization
ethnocentricity
ethnomusicology
euphemistically
exchangeability
excommunicating
excommunication
exemplification
experimentalist
experimentation
extemporization
externalization
extracurricular
extraordinarily

familiarization
fantasticalness
fashionableness
flibbertigibbet

gastroenteritis
governor-general
grandiloquently

hermaphroditism
heterosexuality
Hodgkin's disease
hospitalization
humanitarianism
hyperthyroidism
hyperventilated

illustriousness
impassionedness
impecuniousness
impenetrability
imperishability
impermeableness
imponderability
impossibilities
impregnableness
impressionistic
improbabilities
improvisational
inaccessibility
inappropriately
incalculability
incommensurable
incompatibility
incomprehension
inconsequential
inconsistencies
inconspicuously
inconveniencing
incorrigibility
indefensibility
indemnification
indetermination
indigestibility
indissolubility
individualistic
individualizing
ineffectiveness
inevitabilities
inexplicability
inextricability
infinitesimally
inflammableness
inquisitiveness
insignificantly
instantaneously
instrumentalist
instrumentation
insubordination
insurrectionist
intellectualism
intellectualize
intelligibility
intensification
interchangeable
interchangeably
intercollegiate
interconnection
interdependence

internalization
internationally
interscholastic
invulnerability
irresistibility
irreversibility

jack-of-all-trades
jurisprudential

ladies-in-waiting
lares and penates
lily of the valley

machine-readable
malpractitioner
maneuverability
manic-depressive
masochistically
materialization
memorialization
Ménelre's disease
Mephistophelean
Mephistophelian
microbiological
microelectronic
micromillimeter
microphotograph
microscopically
miniaturization
misapprehension
misappropriated
misconstruction
Molotov cocktail
monochromically
Moog synthesizer

nationalization
noncommissioned
non compos mentis
noncontributory
nonintervention
notwithstanding

obstructiveness
oceanographical
ophthalmologist
overemphasizing
oversimplifying

parenthetically
parliamentarian
parthenogenesis
perfectibiliity
perfunctoriness

personalization
persona non grata
personification
pessimistically
philanthropical
philosophically
phosphorescence
physiotherapist
pithecanthropus
plainclothesman
plainclothesmen
plenipotentiary
polyunsaturated
poverty-stricken
practicableness
presentableness
presitdigitator
pretentiousness
preternaturally
pretitification
procrastinating
procrastination
professionalism
professionalize
prognosticating
prognostication
prognosticative
promiscuousness
proportionality
proportionately
provincializing
psychiiatrcally
psychoanalyzing
psychogenically
psychologically
psychopathology
psychotherapist
pulchritudinous
pusillanimously

questionability

rationalization
reapportionment
reconsideration
reestablishment
retrospectively
revolutionaries
round-shouldered

sanctimoniously
self-consciously
self-explanatory
self-fulfillment
self-improvement
self-liquidating
self-pollination
self-realization

self-sacrificing
self-sufficiency
sentimentalized
serviceableness
shilly-shallying
short-circuiting
spontaneousness
standardization
straightforward
subordinateness
substantialness
substantiveness
superabundantly
superficialness
superfluousness
superimposition
superintendence
superintendency
superlativeness
supernaturalism
superstitiously
supplementation
suppositionally
surealistically
surreptitiously
susceptibleness
syllabification
sympathetically
symptomatically
synchronistical
synchronization
synchronousness
systematization

tableaux vivants
technologically
telegraphically
telephotography
temperamentally
tempestuousness
tendentiousness
therapeutically
thermodynamical
thoughtlessness
topographically
totalitarianism
Toulouse-Lautrec
toxicologically
transcriptional
transfiguration
transfigurement
transistorizing
translatability
transliterating
transliteration
transmeridional
transmutability
transparentness
transplantation
treacherousness

trigonometrical
trinitrotoluene
trustworthiness
typographically

unceremoniously
uncommunicative
uncomplainingly
uncomprehending
unconcernedness
unconditionally
unconnectedness
unconsciousness
undemonstrative

undependability
underachievment
underdeveloping
underemployment
underestimating
underestimation
underhandedness
underprivileged
under-the-counter
undesirableness
undistinguished
unexceptionable
unfavorableness
unfortunateness
unintentionally

unobjectionable
unparliamentary
unprepossessing
unpronounceable
unquestioningly
unrealistically
unreconstructed
unsophisticated
unsubstantiated

ventriloquizing

well-intentioned
Wiener schnitzel

acquaintanceship
anesthesiologist
Anglo-Catholicism
anthropomorphism
archaeologically
aristocratically
arteriosclerosis
attorneys-general
autobiographical

bloodthirstiness

characterization
chromolithograph
circumnavigation
collectivization
compartmentalize
constitutionally
counterclockwise
counterespionage
counteroffensive
countersignature
cross-examination
cross-pollination

decentralization
demilitarization
denaturalization
diabetes mellitus
discombobulating
discombobulation
disenfranchising
disestablishment
disfranchisement
disproportionate
disqualification
district attorney
Doberman pinscher
dramatis personae

electromagnetism
enfants terribles
enthusiastically
environmentalism
environmentalist
Epstein-Barr virus
ethnocentrically
ethnographically
evangelistically
extraterrestrial
extraterritorial

fictionalization

gastroenterology

gastrointestinal
governors-general

Heimlich maneuver
hydroelectricity
hypersensitivity
hyperventilating
hyperventilation

imperceptibility
imponderableness
impracticability
incomprehensible
incontestability
incontrovertible
incontrovertibly
incorrigibleness
incorruptibility
indefatigability
indescribability
indigestibleness
indiscriminately
indiscriminating
indiscrimination
indispensability
inexhaustibility
inexpressibility
inextinguishable
institutionalism
institutionalize
insubstantiality
intercommunicate
intercontinental
internationalism
internationality
internationalize
interpenetration
irresponsibility
irretrievability

jacks-of-all-trades

lanthanide series

melodramatically
meretriciousness
mesembryanthemum
militaristically
misappropriating
misappropriation
mispronunciation
misunderstanding
multifariousness
multimillionaire

narrow-mindedness
neo-impressionism
nonproliferation

obstreperousness
onomatopoeically
overcompensation

parsimoniousness
photographically
pornographically
predetermination
preponderatingly
prestidigitation
presumptuousness
professionalized
pseudoscientific
psychoanalytical
psychometrically
psychopathically
psychopathologic

questionableness

reinterpretation
representational
responsibilities

self-aggrandizing
self-perpetuating
self-preservation
self-satisfaction
semiprofessional
sentimentalities
sentimentalizing
sesquicentennial
shortsightedness
simple-mindedness
simultaneousness
single-mindedness
solicitor general
spiritualization
stenographically
stereophonically
stick-to-itiveness
subconsciousness
superciliousness
superficialities
supernaturalness
susceptibilities

telephotographic
terminologically
thermostatically
three-dimensional

tintinnabulation
to-ings and fro-ings
transcendentally
transcontinental
transmissibility
transmutableness
transportability

ultrafashionable

uncharacteristic
uncharitableness
uncompromisingly
unconstitutional
unconventionally
undependableness
undernourishment
undersecretaries
understanability
undiplomatically

unpredictability
unreasonableness
unrepresentative
unscrupulousness
unsophistication

vaingloriousness
vice-presidencies
vice-presidential

Alzheimer's disease
authoritativeness

circumstantiation
commercialization
comprehensibility
conceptualization
Congregationalism
Congregationalist
conscientiousness
constitutionalism
constitutionality
contradistinction
conversationalist
counterrevolution

denationalization
disinterestedness

electrocardiogram
encephalomyelitis
Euclidean geometry

Gregorian calendar

heterogeneousness

imperialistically

impracticableness
inconsequentially
indestructibility
indispensableness
indistinguishable
industrialization
institutionalized
intercommunicated
interdepartmental
interdisciplinary
internationalized
interrelationship
irreconcilability

lilies of the valley

maladministration
materialistically
meter-kilogram-second
misinterpretation
misrepresentation
misrepresentative
monochromatically
multiple sclerosis
muscular dystrophy

Parkinson's disease
personae non gratae
petite bourgeoisie
pièce de résistance

plenipotentiaries
Postimpressionism
Postimpressionist
professionalizing
psychodynamically
psychopathologist
psychosomatically
psychotherapeutic

rationalistically

self-consciousness
self-determination
self-incrimination
self-righteousness
solicitors general
superconductivity
superstitiousness
surreptitiousness
synchronistically

telecommunication
transcendentalism
trigonometrically

ultraconservative
unceremoniousness
uncomfortableness
uncomprehendingly
unconventionality
undemonstratively

antivivisectionism
antivivisectionist

characteristically
cross-fertilization

disenfranchisement
disproportionately

electrocardiograph

institutionalizing
interchangeability
intercommunicating
intercommunication
internationalizing

propagandistically
psychopathological
psychotherapeutics

self-aggrandizement
sentimentalization

unapproachableness
uncompromisingness
unconscionableness
unconstitutionally
United Arab Emirates

acetylsalicylic acid

counterintelligence

deoxyribonuclic acid

interdenominational

monosodium glutamate

nictitating membrane

uncommunicativeness
unconstitutionality
undemonstrativeness

electroencephalogram   internationalization   uncharacteristically electroencephalograph   psychotherapeutically